THEATRE OF ANGER

Radical Transnational Performance in Contemporary Berlin

GERMAN AND EUROPEAN STUDIES

General Editor: Jennifer L. Jenkins

Theatre of Anger

Radical Transnational Performance in Contemporary Berlin

OLIVIA LANDRY

UNIVERSITY OF TORONTO PRESS
Toronto Buffalo London

Toronto Buffalo London
utorontopress.com

ISBN 978-1-4875-0769-5 (cloth)
ISBN 978-1-4875-3676-3 (EPUB)
ISBN 978-1-4875-3675-6 (PDF)

German and European Studies

Library and Archives Canada Cataloguing in Publication

Title: Theatre of anger : radical transnational performance in contemporary Berlin / Olivia Landry.
Names: Landry, Olivia, author.
Series: German and European studies ; 37.
Description: Series statement: German and European studies series ; 37 | Includes bibliographical references and index.
Identifiers: Canadiana (print) 20200322737 | Canadiana (ebook) 20200322842 | ISBN 9781487507695 (hardcover) | ISBN 9781487536763 (EPUB) | ISBN 9781487536756 (PDF)
Subjects: LCSH: Political plays, German – History and criticism. | LCSH: German drama – 21st century – History and criticism. | LCSH: Anger in literature. | LCSH: Social justice in literature. | LCSH: Anger – Social aspects.
Classification: LCC PT669.5 .L36 2021 | DDC 832/.92093552 – dc23

University of Toronto Press gratefully acknowledges the support of Lehigh University, which provided funds toward the publication of this book.

The German and European Studies series is funded by the DAAD with funds from the German Federal Foreign Office.

Deutscher Akademischer Austauschdienst
German Academic Exchange Service

University of Toronto Press acknowledges the financial assistance to its publishing program of the Canada Council for the Arts and the Ontario Arts Council, an agency of the Government of Ontario.

Canada Council for the Arts
Conseil des Arts du Canada

Funded by the Government of Canada
Financé par le gouvernement du Canada

For Ihsan

Contents

List of Illustrations ix

Acknowledgments xi

Glossary of Plays xiii

Introduction: Theatre of Anger as Theatre of *Desintegration* 3

1 In Defence of Anger: From a History of Social Justice to the Theatre 24

2 *Get Deutsch or Die Tryin'*; or, Confronting a History of Exclusion and Violence 49

3 Staging "Muslim Rage" 73

4 Documentaries of Outrage 103

5 Salzmann's Angry Youths 133

6 "Theatre of the Twenty-First Century": An Interview with Sasha Marianna Salzmann 161

Conclusion: Anger in the Future Sense 177

Notes 187

Bibliography 215

Index 229

Illustrations

2.1 Promotional poster for *Get Deutsch or Die Tryin'* 52
2.2 Racially motivated arson attack in Solingen, 1993 60
2.3 Kanak Attak 1997 *Der Spiegel* cover reproduction, May 27, 1999 65
2.4 A promotional pin with the Ballhaus Naunynstraβe logo 67
3.1 The striking staging of *Schwarze Jungfrauen* post striptease 84
4.1 Performing the chants of the Gezi Park Protest in *Aufstand* 127
5.1 The Angry Chorus in *Zucken* 156
6.1 Some of the walls in the foyer of the Studio Я, June 2018 169

Acknowledgments

It seems like a platitude to say that no one writes a book alone, but it is an ineluctable truth.

This book would not have been possible without Sasha Marianna Salzmann. I am not only immensely grateful for the brilliant plays Sasha has given us, not to mention a recent novel, but also for their amazing generosity. Materials, time, and ideas: my many requests were always indulged with enthusiasm. In the nearly two-hour-long interview, which became the final part of this book, Sasha demonstrates their absolute dedication to their craft as well as their stunning ability to discuss the importance and relevance of their work in a manner that is so engaging. For all of this I am forever in their debt.

As I moved through different conceptualizations of this book and through various stages of writing, I have been lucky to call Claudia Breger and Randall Halle my mentors, colleagues, and friends. Both have offered unflagging support over the years as well as inspiration through their own tireless work to broaden the discipline of German studies beyond national and monocultural boundaries. In this vein, I am also grateful to my colleagues and collaborators working within transnational topics and theatre, who have offered support and insight. Dialogues with Ela Gezen, Priscilla Layne, and Teresa Kovacs have been enormously rewarding. The same can be said for the discussions generated through the seminar "(Post)Migrant Theatre Then and Now" at the German Studies Association 2017 conference.

I finally settled on the focus of this book while spending a year at Stanford University. During that time, I had the wonderful opportunity to teach a graduate seminar on postmigrant theatre. I am indebted to the students in that seminar for all of their wonderful ideas and engagement. At Stanford, as well, I am grateful to my former colleague Matthew W. Smith for allowing me to sit in on his own graduate seminar on German theatre. I learned much from his expertise.

I completed writing this book while at my current academic home, Lehigh University. My colleagues in the Department of Modern Languages and Literatures have been extremely supportive. Indeed, without the wonderful friendship of my colleague and co-conspirator Lindsey Reuben Muñoz, I don't know where I would be. I would like to also acknowledge the generous financial support of a Faculty Research Grant from Lehigh, which allowed me to return to Berlin in the summer of 2018 to put finishing touches on the manuscript.

My editor at the University of Toronto Press, Stephen Shapiro, is outstanding. His conviction of the importance of the project has been incredibly motivating. He saw this book through its many stages with such astuteness and calm. To the two anonymous readers for the press I am also immensely grateful. The remarkable care each took with considering the book and providing such incisive feedback has been invaluable. I also cannot thank Alana Dunn enough for her copyediting, which she performed with marvellous vigilance and astounding speed.

Perhaps, though, I am most grateful to those friends and family who have sustained me over the years with their love and support. Enormous thanks to my mom, Sally Landry, and my sister, Christinia Landry. To my close friends in academia and beyond, Erin Noelliste, Anita Lukic, Christopher Chiasson, Nicole Perry, Britta Füchtenbusch, and Neslihan Inalbars, I am very lucky to know you.

I dedicate this book to my partner Ihsan Ata Topaloğlu. Always a tremendous source of joy, love, and unconditional support, he has also spent many a month in Berlin with me attending plays, discussing them, and reading these chapters. He has indelibly shaped my life and my work. Also, as a Turkish passport holder, he has patiently endured implicit and explicit discrimination at the hands of German immigration authorities. To you, Ihsan, and so many others, I offer this book.

Some material in chapter 4 appears in different form as "Greek Dispossession Staged, or When Street Politics Meets the Theater," *TRANSIT: A Journal of Travel, Migration and Multiculturalism in the German-speaking World* 10:2 (online, 2016). The second part of an earlier version of chapter 5 appears as "Anger as Theatrical Form in Sasha Marianna Salzmann's *Zucken*," in *Postdramatisches Theater als transkulturelles Theater*, eds. Teresa Kovacs and Koku G. Nonoa, (Narr Francke Attempo Verlag 2018): 335–48. I am grateful to *TRANSIT* and Narr Francke Attempo Verlag for permission to republish some of this work here. Many thanks also go to the Bertolt Brecht estate, Max Czollek, Esra Rotthoff, Rainer Henkel, Kanak Attak, Lauren Berlant, Ute Langkafel, and Uwe Heinrich for permission to use their fantastic images or their insightful words as epigraphs throughout this book. Finally, many thanks to Anna Bause at the Gorki for generously providing digital material.

Glossary of Plays

The main plays I analyse in this study are all in German. The titles are also primarily in German, with the exception of two. Throughout, I employ the German-language titles, but I also include the English translation in parentheses when the play is mentioned for the first time in the book and then again in the chapter, in which it is scrutinized.

Plays in order of appearance in the book:

Get Deutsch or Die Tryin' (written by Necati Öziri; directed by Sebastian Nübling; premiere 2017)

Schwarze Jungfrauen (*Black Virgins*; written by Feridun Zaimoğlu and Günter Senkel; directed by Neco Çelik; premiere 2006)

Verrücktes Blut (*Mad Blood*; written by Nurkan Erpulat and Jens Hillje; directed by Nurkan Erpulat; premiere 2010)

Telemachos – Should I Stay or Should I Go? (written and directed by Anestis Azas and Prodromos Tsinikoris and Ensemble; premiere 2013)

Aufstand: Monolog eines wütenden Künstlers (*Rebellion: Monologue of an Angry Artist*; written by Mely Kiyak; directed by András Dömötör; premiere 2014)

Weißbrotmusik (*White Bread Music*; written by Sasha Marianna Salzmann; directed by Nick Hartnagel; premiere 2010)

Zucken (*Twitching*; written by Sasha Marianna Salzmann; directed by Sebastian Nübling; premiere 2017)

THEATRE OF ANGER

Radical Transnational Performance in Contemporary Berlin

Theatre of Anger as Theatre of *Desintegration*

We need a type of theatre that not only facilitates the sensations, insights and motivations permitted by the particular historical field of human relations on which the action happens to take place, but also employs and produces those thoughts and feelings which help transform the field itself.

Bertolt Brecht, "A Short Organum"[1]

Sasha [Marianna Salzmann], with two generations of grief, trauma and anxiety behind us, isn't it time to be angry?

Max Czollek, *Desintegration: A Congress on Contemporary Jewish Positions*

On May 8, 2016, in central Berlin, just off the main boulevard, Unter den Linden, there was a book burning. At nearly four in the morning, a two-day event named *Desintegration: A Congress on Contemporary Jewish Positions* came to a close at the experimental black box Studio Я theatre, attached to the mainstage of the Maxim Gorki Theatre. The congress ended with an incendiary act: the burning of Hitler's *Mein Kampf*. As of 2016, the book may be printed, sold, and purchased for the first time in Germany since the end of the Second World War. The Jewish American musician and performer Daniel Kahn, who is based in Berlin and active at the Maxim Gorki Theatre, did not want this fact to go unremarked. He procured an original edition and invited lingering spectators to tear out pages from the book and fling them into the small bonfire in the garden in front of the theatre canteen. No one was certain if the event had been officially planned or not. It felt rather spontaneous. Yet the historical and geographical resonance of this performance could not be overlooked. Just across the vast boulevard, Unter den Linden, sits the imposing Humboldt University Faculty of Law building in front of which the Nazis had burned over 20,000 books on a fateful night in May nearly a century earlier. While this re-performance of a different kind was a transgressive event that evoked myriad ethical and political questions about whether burning books as an act, even such a book as *Mein Kampf*, could ever be admissible, it speaks to the crux of *Theatre of Anger: Radical Transnational Performance in Contemporary Berlin*.

The title announces the subject of this book: the theatre of anger. Broadly speaking, this is a form of theatre in which minoritized subjects perform anger, and perform in anger, to speak out against social injustice that is the result of racism, anti-Semitism, Islamophobia, sexism, homophobia, and transphobia. The angry plaint of this theatre is directed towards the institutional and the everyday, theatre and society. I invoke the aforementioned 2016 event as an opening to this study because it makes vivid what is for me at the heart of the theatre of anger: an open and aggressive refusal to integrate into an unjust society.[2] In exhortative language and performance, *Desintegration: A Congress on Contemporary Jewish Positions* articulated a position of anger and demonstrated it within the theatre space. This is also brought forth with the congress's provocative slogans, such as "'Go play your theatre alone,' 'We won the war,' 'No more Jews for Germans,' and 'Jud Sauer' ['Jew Sour' in contrast to 'Jud Süss,' the title of the notorious 1941 Nazi propaganda film]."[3] These slogans, much like the performative act of publicly burning *Mein Kampf*, engage with the history of the Holocaust in a refusal to allow non-Jewish Germans to write and perform the narratives of national memory in a manner that suits dominant forms. These slogans are a refusal of forgiveness and reconciliation. They are even a call for revenge. In an email correspondence with playwright Sasha Marianna Salzmann, Max Czollek (who co-organized the event with them) writes: "De-integration also means: No, things won't be all right again. No, I won't light these candles with you. No, our mothers and our fathers did not go to Auschwitz together. No, my biography is not available to you. No, my opinion about Israel has nothing to do with you, damn it. No, you're not going to get off that lightly!"[4] These powerful statements are similarly given voice in Czollek's angry 2018 manifesto, titled *Desintegriert Euch!*. As the co-architect of the 2016 event, and the recurring *Radical Jewish Culture Days*, Czollek has contemplated the possibilities of *Desintegration*, which is affirmative in its angry affectivity. For Czollek, *Desintegration* is a resolute and polemical call for the recognition of radical diversity. He asserts:

> Wenn ich Ihnen, verehrte Leser*innen, "Desintegratiert Euch!" zurufe, dann geht es um mehr als um eine jüdische Emanzipation auf seiner allzu

engen Rollenerwartung. Es geht um die grundlegende Reflexion des Verhältnisses zwischen deutscher Dominanzkultur und ihren Minderheiten. Desintegration bedeutet, die Rollen kritsch zu reflektieren, die jede und jeder in diesem Spiel einnimmt. Das ist dringend notwendige gesellschaftliche Arbeit, denn die Forderung nach Integration und Gedächnistheater reicht tief hinab in das schmutzige Reservoir deutscher Geschichte vor und nach 1945.

When I call out for you, honoured readers, "to de-integrate yourselves!" this goes beyond a Jewish emancipation from its excessively narrow role expectation. It is about the fundamental reflection on the relationship between the German "culture of dominance" (Dominanzkultur) and its minorities. De-integration means critically reflecting on the roles assumed by each group in this game. This societal work is urgently needed because the charge of integration and theatre of memory (Gedächtnistheater) plumbs the depths of the filthy reservoir of German history before and after 1945.[5]

Desintegration (translatable in this context as "de-integration") is by no means a polemic and movement unique to the Jewish community in Germany.[6] Czollek's indictment resonates with other minoritized individuals and communities in Germany and with the labour of the theatre of anger. Like *Desintegration,* anger is critical to this readjustment of perception, since it is against the notion that everyone must adapt or adjust to a dominant culture. Integration is a term fervently advanced in discourses of migration politics in Germany and elsewhere as though it were the panacea for all immigration problems and the sine qua non of becoming a functioning member of a society by way of which differences often become reducible to a grammar of similarity.

The term *Desintegration* has been adopted and applied to the broader project of postmigrant theatre – a topic I consider more closely throughout this book. Postmigrant theatre is an established transnational movement that emerged in the first decade of the 2000s with the intent to carve out a space for new, culturally diverse narratives in German theatre. Now prominently positioned at the Maxim Gorki Theatre, the repertoire and practitioners of postmigrant theatre have achieved significant visibility and influence in the German cultural scene. In 2017 the Maxim Gorki Theatre launched a new season and its third Herbstsalon (Fall Salon) with *Desintegration* as its theme. With this direct adoption of the concept and theme of *Desintegration,* the programming for the season rejected the present conditions of a culture and society, and publicly demanded change at a time when an eddy of politics of hate seemed to take hold. Reflecting on the rise of radical rightwing politics in Germany (and elsewhere) with the success of the political party Alternative for Germany (AfD), the uncovering of the National Socialist Underground (NSU) murder series, and the protest marches of Patriotic Europeans Against the Islamization of the Occident (PEGIDA) all just in the last decade, *Desintegration* says we don't want any part of it. To paraphrase Shermin Langhoff, the founder of postmigrant theatre and the general director of the Maxim Gorki, theatre must support diversity, individual perceptions, and independent forms of expression rather than serve a hegemonic ideology.[7] *Desintegration* is a term applied in theatre and used by practitioners within postmigrant theatre to assert and explore the performance of refusal and anger, and it offers a direct pathway for thinking about the theatre of anger as an extension of and possible alternative to postmigrant theatre. *Theatre of Anger* examines contemporary postmigrant theatre in Germany in different directions and through new affective-political means. That having been said, the theatre of anger does not account for all of postmigrant theatre. This book proposes that there is a strain of postmigrant theatre that performs anger in striking and often diverging ways.

Attaching such a loaded affect as anger to the cultural work of transnational artists and bodies of colour might at first appear to repeat injury, discrimination, and racism. This is by no means the intention of this book, but since such an interpretation might be made, I speak to it at various turns. In its manifestation here, anger is instead a response to injustice and a call for action. It is politics and protest; it is in-yer-face and a refusal to comply; it is collectivity and it is a future. The theatre of anger is all of these things. It combines important cultural and political work with aesthetic rigour in the creation of new forms and a new language of theatre, which has emerged from the fringes (what is called "freies Theater" in German) and has become influential. Framed by the recuperation of discourses and theories of anger as affirmative in philosophy and theory, *Theatre of Anger* offers close and sustained analyses of seven plays produced and performed between 2006 and 2017 in Berlin at five different theatres, including Hebbel am Ufer (HAU), Theater Strahl, Ballhaus Naunynstraβe, Maxim Gorki Theatre, and the Studio Я. The works, in the order they appear in the book, are Necati Öziri's *Get Deutsch or Die Tryin'* (premiere 2017); Feridun Zaimoğlu and Günter Senkel's *Schwarze Jungfrauen* (*Black Virgins*, premiere 2006); Nurkan Erpulat and Jens Hillje's *Verrücktes Blut* (*Mad Blood*, premiere 2010); Anestis Azas and Prodromos Tsinikoris's *Telemachos – Should I Stay or Should I Go?* (premiere 2013); Mely Kiyak's *Aufstand: Monolog eines wütenden Künstlers* (*Rebellion: Monologue of an Angry Artist*, premiere 2014); and Sasha Marianna Salzmann's *Weiβbrotmusik* (*White Bread Music*, premiere 2010) and *Zucken* (*Twitching*, premiere 2017). These plays are linked through an investment in affirmative anger and its important sociopolitical possibilities. Broadly speaking, they are representations of a time when political protest and theatre intersect in uncompromising ways. My investigations of these plays rely heavily, although not exclusively, on live performance and the experiences and meanings produced onstage.

Sketching a Brief History

The theatre of anger developed as a part of postmigrant theatre. The history of the latter may be familiar to some, but a comprehensive study does not yet exist. Thus, what I offer in the following is a broader picture and context from within which we can begin to position the theatre of anger. Langhoff has maintained that theatre was a latecomer to the transnational narratives and positions that for several decades had already been taken up in literature and film in Germany. The first generation of Turkish German authors to develop a postmigrant voice *avant la lettre*, Aras Ören (1939–) and Emine Sevgi Özdamar (1946–), were instrumental in the creation of a nuanced transnational literature. In the spirit of refusal that later became so defining for the theatre of anger, these authors likewise rejected the categorization and labels that sought to marginalize and typecast them based on their social and ethnic backgrounds, such as "Gastarbeiterliteratur" (guest worker literature), "Ausländerliteratur" (foreigner literature), and "Migrantenliteratur" (migrant literature).[8] Others followed their lead and further developed the possibilities of a postmigrant literature. Langhoff cites the work of Ören, Özdamar, and others as important literary precursors to postmigrant theatre. Slightly later in the film world, the bold narratives of Turkish German directors, such as Fatih Akın (1973–), Ayşe Polat (1970–), and Aysun Bademsoy (1960–), have also been of consequence. Yet in theatre, despite the minor efforts of more community-oriented stages, such as the Turkish theatre Tiyatrom in Berlin and others across Germany, there was an absence of sustained transculturally complex spaces.[9] This absence became a possibility for the creation of a new kind of theatre in the mid-2000s that became postmigrant theatre. The concept of "postmigrant," whose meanings and opportunities are complex and myriad (something I will return to), comes from this radical turning point in theatre. Langhoff and her team of playwrights, directors, dramaturgs, and artists shaped not only a new theatre but also a new discourse, which has subsequently shaped other cultural, political, and social contexts in the German space.[10]

It is possible to divide postmigrant theatre in Berlin into three historical phases (and between three theatrical stages), all of which are represented through the plays scrutinized in this book. Postmigrant theatre is thought to have originated as a new kind of theatre and performance movement at the Hebbel am Ufer (HAU), an alternative theatre in Berlin-Kreuzberg, as a direct initiative of Langhoff's 2006 festival *Beyond Belonging – Migration²*,[11] which featured, among other things, the world premiere of the groundbreaking play *Schwarze Jungfrauen*. The festival consisted of a series of films, dramatic readings, musical performances, talks, and plays bearing narratives that sought to not only move beyond but also trouble the threadbare themes of identity and belonging that have conditioned so much transnational cultural work in Germany, such as victimhood, melancholic inbetweenness, homesickness, and so forth.[12] At this time, the focus was on Turkish German histories and narratives. Forming Germany's largest minority community, indeed roughly 5 per cent of Germany's population, Turkish citizens had migrated in vast numbers to West Germany between 1961 and 1973 as contract workers to perform mostly manual labour. Between 1955 and 1973 in West Germany (and until the late 1980s in East Germany), workers were recruited from abroad to help rebuild Germany in the decades after the Second World War. Although these workers, referred to as "Gastarbeiter" (guest workers) in the West and "Vertragsarbeiter" (contract workers) in the East, were only meant to stay in Germany temporarily, many settled. Much of mainstream German society still pushes back against such a reality. Germany has long refused the designation of "country of immigration." *Beyond Belonging – Migration²* addressed this in a manner that was much more aggressive than previously seen in theatre, and only peripherally in film and literature. Following the success of the 2006 festival, Langhoff, who had tirelessly culled the support and funds from government agencies and artists (notably, Fatih Akın), headed the reopening of the small Ballhaus Naunynstraβe theatre in 2008 as a space for transnational performance and theatre. The space had in fact been used since the late 1800s for cultural and recreational events, in particular for dance, hence the name "Ballhaus" ("ballroom" on Naunyn Street).

The appellation "postmigrant" in connection with theatre was first publicly introduced by Langhoff in an interview shortly after the reopening of the Ballhaus Naunynstraβe.[13] However, the term "postmigrant" had previously appeared in the Anglophone academic context in the 1990s.[14] A provocative response to a history of marginalization and treatment as noncitizens, the "post" in postmigrant allows so-called first-, second-, and third-generation migrants to assert a national status that is not underpinned by the transitoriness of being a migrant. As Lizzie Stewart writes, a "self-chosen descriptor to the more sociological categorization of 'people with a background of migration,'" "postmigrant" offers a "potential alternative."[15] There is much to be gained from this label. Yet it is also one that demands interrogation.

Reading the prefix "post" of postmigrant theatre critically calls for nuance and not a description of simply being over and done with migration. Wendy Brown's definition of "post" is instructive in this regard: "[T]he prefix 'post' signifies a formation that is *temporally after but not over* that to which it is affixed. 'Post' indicates a very particular condition of afterness in which what is past is not left behind, but, on the contrary, relentlessly conditions, even dominates a present that nevertheless also breaks in some way with this past."[16] The "post" is thus, as Marianne Hirsch succinctly puts it, "an uneasy oscillation between continuity and rupture."[17] Although read productively by Brown, Hirsch, and others, the condition of "post" can become a kind of entrapment, antithetical to self-positioning and self-determination. Given this, some artists and scholars have indicated the potentially problematic nature of the term "postmigrant," in particular through its broader, slightly later, adaptation in cultural and sociological discourse. Further, "postmigrant" runs the risk of resonating with the whitewashing of the term "postracial" in its possible assertion that discrimination based on race or heritage no longer exists.[18] Examining these plays as theatre of anger rather than as postmigrant theatre indirectly offers a solution to this concern. As I theorize it, the theatre of anger both disrupts and aggressively pushes toward a self-determining future. But I do not propose that anger replaces postmigrant; rather, anger becomes an alternative step that extends the complexity of these plays and this movement.

The intervention of anger here invites a more radical reading of the work of postmigrant theatre. That the plays associated with the latter present something ideationally and formally novel – a break of sorts – is important. For one, postmigrant theatre is distinct from intercultural theatre. As Erika Fischer-Lichte elucidates in her introduction to the 2014 study *The Politics of Interweaving Performance Cultures: Beyond Postcolonialism*, the concept of "intercultural theatre," introduced in the late 1970s and early 1980s, entails the borrowing of one cultural repertoire by another and frequently bears a Western-centric perspective, as typical examples include the performance of classical Western theatre in countries outside of Europe.[19] Postmigrant theatre does not co-opt. The germ of postmigrant theatre is rather straightforward: minoritized Germans and migrants have been systematically shut out of the established German theatre scenes for not being "German enough" to participate in "national" high culture, so they decided to make their own theatre. According to Langhoff, postmigrant theatre was indicative of the struggle practitioners, artists, and performers of colour faced (and still do) in getting their theatre staged, their narratives performed, and their voices heard.[20]

From 2008 to the end of the theatre season in the early summer of 2013, Langhoff and her expanding team of directors, dramaturgs, playwrights, actors, and artists built up the repertoire at the Ballhaus Naunynstraβe, making it one of the busiest, most vibrant, and most innovative independent theatres in the city, despite its limited funding and small scale.[21] Over the course of these five years, the theatre's repertoire, including its manifold guest performances, both accrued and evolved. The initial dramatic explorations of Turkish German experiences continued at the Ballhaus Naunynstraβe into the early 2010s with plays such as the three-part *Die lange Nacht der Generationen* (*The Long Night of the Generations*, premiere 2009), *Lö bal Almanya* (premiere 2010), and most famously *Verrücktes Blut*. In many ways, the popularity and eminence of *Verrücktes Blut*, which was not only invited to the prestigious *Berliner Festspiele – Theatertreffen* in 2011 but whose director, Nurkan Erpulat, was also named best new director, became the pinnacle of the burgeoning postmigrant movement and brought it unprecedented visibility.

By 2013, when Langhoff and her team eventually left the Ballhaus Naunynstraβe, it had developed into a venue for a variety of experimental theatre and performance work. The move from the Ballhaus Naunynstraβe in Berlin-Kreuzberg to the large state venue, the Maxim Gorki Theatre, in central Berlin in the fall of 2013, marked the third stage of development and expansion of postmigrant theatre in the city. The move signalled the transition of postmigrant theatre and, by extension, the theatre of anger from "freies Theater" (translated as "free-scene theatre" or sometimes referred to simply as independent theatre" or "fringe theatre" in English)[22] to "Staatstheater" ("state theatre," which is frequently also a repertory theatre). It transitioned from an experimental place, in which alternatives to traditional modes of representation are pursued, to a place in which these modes are generally upheld. But to propose a complete separation of the two kinds of theatre practice would be inexact.[23] If anything, postmigrant theatre found a more permanent home with a less precarious (albeit still less than other major Berlin theatres) state-funded budget. The explicitly experimental work of the Ballhaus Naunynstraβe continued with new direction, under Wagner Carvalho and Tunçay Kulaoğlu (until 2014), in its old home and in the new space – the Studio Я. Studio Я, with the Russian letter, speaks volumes about the performative project of this experimental theatrical space, in particular about identity politics, assertion, and exploration. The final letter of the Russian alphabet, Я is also the subjective "I." With this newly established theatrical apparatus, the repertoire of postmigrant theatre and, by extension, the theatre of anger has broadened significantly. Entering its sixth year at the Maxim Gorki Theatre, this work has become a formidable arena for all manner of political and cultural theatre and performance. Already twice named "Theatre of the Year" (2014; 2016) by the esteemed German-language journal, *Theater heute*, the Maxim Gorki Theatre and its new transnational direction have certainly left a mark on the theatre landscape in Germany. Yet this brief historical overview is just a gloss and focuses on Berlin. While central in many ways, the theatre work in Berlin cannot stand in for all postmigrant and angry theatrical production nationally. A growing body of literature on the topic of postmigrant theatre demonstrates both the movement's historical longitude and its geographical stretch.

Early scholarship in this direction focused on Turkish German theatre and its inception in cabaret. Historically embodying that space of so-called low culture on the periphery of theatre, the cabaret offered marginalized performers flexibility and a place of expression. The pioneering text in the study of postmigrant theatre is Erol Boran's unpublished dissertation *Eine Geschichte des türkisch-deutschen Theaters und Kabaretts*, (A History of Turkish-German Theatre and Cabaret, 2004). Boran's dissertation was the first book-length study on the Turkish German theater scene and offers a comprehensive prehistory of postmigrant theatre more broadly.[24] But Boran's study also moves from the cabaret to the theatre with the pivotal work of Emine Sevgi Özdamar, who has written six plays, most famous among them *Karagöz in Alamania* (*Black Eye in Germany*, premiere 1986) and *Keloğlan in Alamania* (*Keloğlan in Germany*, premiere 1991). Although her work as a playwright is frequently overshadowed by her prose output, Özdamar is without doubt the first Turkish German playwright and theatre practitioner of significance.[25] As plays that explore and perform Turkish German identity and history through the vectors of political theatre, Özdamar's *Karagöz in Alamania* and *Keloğlan in Alamania* are foundational for postmigrant theatre. Preceding Boran's study, Katrin Sieg's influential book *Ethnic Drag* (2002) also dedicates significant space in its final chapter to the theatre work of Özdamar, with a focus on *Keloğlan in Alamania*, which Sieg describes as a play explicitly about the heterogeneity of identity and culture, what could be called a form of *Desintegration*, or, to borrow Sieg's equally fitting term, "antiassimilationism."[26]

The influence of Bertolt Brecht both in the theory and praxis of earlier Turkish German theatre and later postmigrant theatre has been pivotal. His impact can also be felt throughout these pages. Özdamar emigrated to a divided Berlin in 1976 from western Turkey to work with Benno Besson, (a Swiss theatre director who also went to East Berlin to work in the tradition of Brecht) at the Volksbühne am Rosa-Luxemburg-Platz.

Their collaboration marks the beginning of a cultural exchange that would develop into Turkish German theatre and become crucial for postmigrant theatre and the theatre of anger. In her recent study entitled *Brecht, Turkish Theater, and Turkish-German Literature* (2018), Ela Gezen meticulously explores inter alia the theatre practices of Özdamar in the context of Brechtian traditions. In Gezen's historically driven analysis, Brecht's influence on Turkish German theatre can be viewed through a rich transnational dialogue, which moves circuitously from Germany to Turkey and then back again.[27]

Viewed within this longer chronology, a turn to other Berlin theatres in the 1980s and 1990s reveals a wide spectrum of related cultural work, including the repertoires of the Türkisches Ensemble an der Schaubühne am Lehniner Platz (1979–1984) and the Tiyatrom (since 1984), as well as the ensembles attached to certain cultural associations (Arbeitertheater des Türkenzentrums Schinkenstraße), adult education centres (in the neighbourhoods of Wedding, Kreuzberg, and Neukölln), and cultural institutions and venues such as Künstlerhaus Bethanien, and Theatermanufaktur am Halleschen Ufer. But postmigrant theatre's effect has also been felt outside of the German capital, in cities such as Bochum, Cologne, and Stuttgart. Azadeh Sharifi's extensive study on postmigrant theatre in Cologne, *Theater für alle? Partizipation von Postmigranten am Beispiel der Bühnen der Stadt Köln*, or "Theatre for Everyone? Participation of Postmigrants on the Stages of the City of Cologne" (2011), has further encouraged a glance beyond Berlin to venues such as the Bühne der Kulturen – Arkadaş Theater.[28] But with the possible exception of the Schauspielhaus Bochum, many of these theatres were, as mentioned above, often community-based spaces, whose reach was limited to the very local.[29]

Scholarly efforts have asserted that the aesthetics and forms of postmigrant theatre as a broader movement emerged and took shape in the sway of other significant contemporaneous theatrical traditions spanning from the period of unification to the 2000s, from theatre of performativity and presence to postdramatic theatre. Respectively, Claudia Breger (2012) and Matt Cornish (2017) have productively brought postmigrant theatre into conversation with these concurrent developments in German theatre.[30] Since the early 2010s a prodigious number of articles have been written, mostly on individual plays, to form a significant part of a growing archive of literature on postmigrant theatre. Scholars engaged in this work include Nora Haakh, Priscilla Layne, Onur Suzan Kömürcü Nobrega, Azadeh Sharifi, Katrin Sieg, and Lizzie Stewart, and I draw on this archive throughout this book.[31]

My own writing on postmigrant theatre and my gradual turn to the theatre of anger has coincided with this recent wave of scholarship and is beholden to its influences and the compelling dialogue it provides. Since my first article on Nurkan Erpulat's plays *Verrücktes Blut* (2010) and *Clash* (2011) appeared in 2012, my insights and understanding of postmigrant theatre have developed and deepened.[32] What I maintain is the conviction of postmigrant theatre's singularity and its political force, which I work out here through the lens of anger. A case can certainly be made for a longer tradition of theatre practices in line with postmigrant theatre impulses, in particular beginning with Özdamar; however, I read the theatre of anger (and the historical moment in 2006 with the premiere of *Schwarze Jungfrauen*) as a radical break from what has more broadly been called "migrant theatre" or "Turkish German theatre." This is a break in both content and form and, as I will examine more fully in this book, is made perceptible via a focus on anger. The theatre of anger is thus not simply the theatre of a new generation – the "postgeneration" – it is also a theatre that refuses to partake in those threadbare narratives and representations of previous generations. If the theatre of anger has a notable precedent in the tradition of transnational cultural production and practice in Germany, then it is the politically charged performance and artistic network Kanak Attak of the mid-1990s, which I explore at greater length in chapter 2. Above all, the theatre of anger is political theatre. It responds to social injustice; it prepares its audience with the readiness to act, that is, to do politics; and it even performs politics itself.

A final note might be made about my geographical concentration in this study. I focus my attention on Berlin theatres and performances, with which I have the most experience, a direct experience initiated in 2011. No doubt this study could pursue a greater geographical reach to a number of other cities and theatres throughout Germany.[33] I do not argue that the theatre of anger is a movement unique to Berlin. Indeed, all of the plays I examine have also been performed outside of Berlin. *Verrücktes Blut* and *Zucken* were even co-produced with other theatres in Germany and Switzerland, respectively. But as the city with the largest number of state and independent theatres, Berlin is one of the few urban centres where radical transnational theatre is performed at multiple sites on a regular basis and where I have repeatedly witnessed these performances of righteous anger on the stage.

Methods for New Theatrical Forms

Through close readings of individual plays and an adherence to a rigorous theoretical apparatus, *Theatre of Anger* traces a new mode of theatre that has emerged as part of postmigrant theatre. The theatre of anger is one that engages affective forms and politics. I read this engagement through the insights of theatre and performance theories and traditions, which I map together here in a manner that takes us from the earliest historical influences to the most recent. This mapping of theatrical anger begins with an unlikely object: the statue of the Laocoön and its beautifully raging portrayal, which is, I propose, in a rereading of Gotthold Ephraim Lessing's conceptualization, the Ur-form of bodily anger for art and theatre.[34] While Lessing elides anger and describes the Laocoön instead as the representation of pain (*Schmerz*) in art, I propose a more directed focus on the corporeal mass of the Laocoön, which reveals itself to be very much alive with anger. Indeed, sometimes the body tells another version of the story, and this is the version I pursue here. The enraged morphology of the Laocoön becomes a model for the angry body onstage. But the theatre of anger lingers only briefly with the theatrical forms of the eighteenth century and quickly moves through to later modern theatre forms. It is a theatre movement most firmly positioned within the traditions of the twentieth and twenty-first centuries.

Throughout this book, I draw connections between the theatre of anger and the British "in-yer-face" theatre movement of the 1990s. A term coined by Aleks Sierz (2001), in-yer-face theatre introduced a new dramatic vocabulary and sensibility to the stage that was direct and raw.[35] Most of all, in-yer-face theatre was intensely aggressive and angry. It aimed to shock the audience out of its conceit of cultural, phenomenological, and social apathy. Thinking about the theatre of anger with the experiential thrust of in-yer-face theatre with its emphasis on the visceral, on feeling, and on physical response is compelling. I pair this pursuit with the traditions of Artaudian vitality, sensualism, and rupture as well as Brechtian epic theatre with its appeals to political reflection, meaning, and action. The challenge that this frame poses is not so much that its elements may seem to be at odds, but that despite their political and formal radicalness, all three modes (in-yer-face, Artaudian, Brechtian) are still examples of the theatre of white European males and thus conservative in their own way. This is an issue I take up throughout this book. Indeed, much radical and political European theatre is culturally specific and narrow; it ignores the minoritized subject. Intervening in this tradition of whiteness, the theatre of anger also stretches theatrical categories and theoretical frames further.

To call the theatre of anger Brechtian or post-Brechtian, because it is political theatre after Brecht, requires some qualification. A rather capacious and sinuous term, post-Brechtian is applied indiscriminately to much political theatre that arose after Brecht's death in 1956.[36] But it has been most insightful when it provides a frame for critically engaging with Brecht's concepts of theatre, such as through the feminist recuperations of Janelle G. Reinelt (1996) and Elin Diamond (1988) and the postcolonial applications in the work of Augusto Boal (1985).[37] For as Heiner Müller famously contends, "[t]o use Brecht without criticizing him is to betray him."[38] Important to the present study is Stanton B. Garner Jr.'s argument for a return of the centrality of the phenomenological body in political theatre after Brecht (1994). He observes: "By exploiting the body's centrality in the theatrical medium, contemporary political dramatists have refigured the actor's body as the principal site of theatrical and political intervention, thereby reconfiguring the political field in corporeal terms and establishing a contemporary 'body politic' rooted in the individual's sentient presence."[39] The body that assumed a predominantly analytic role in Brecht's theatre (particularly in his earlier work), as the representational social body and not the phenomenal flesh-and-blood body, in other words, the figure of *Gestus*, is re-embodied in much of post-Brechtian theatre. As a political theatre that is concerned with the embodied subject, for this is a theatre chiefly preoccupied with putting hitherto absent bodies onto the stage and in positions of creative authority, the theatre of anger resonates with this strain of post-Brechtian theatre.

As a variant of post-Brechtian theatre that also brings the complex return of the body into relief and seeks to attack the spectator in a manner not dissimilar to in-yer-face theatre, Hans-Thies Lehmann's postdramatic theatre offers insight at various turns.[40] In Lehmann's rendering, postdramatic theatre "situates itself in a space opened up by the Brechtian inquiries into the presence and consciousness of the process of representation within the represented and the enquiry into a new 'art of spectatorship.'"[41] This "new art of spectatorship" consisted of observation and confrontation from outside instead of involved sympathy. Yet postdramatic theatre relinquishes the Brechtian penchant for fables and greater meaning and thereby abandons the dogmatic and didactic side of the political. It does not part ways with politics altogether; however, it is safe to say that it is also not a straightforward political theatre form. In his reading of postunification theatre in Germany, Matt Cornish presents a convincing argument for the possible intersections of postdramatic and postmigrant theatre. He posits that in its drive to challenge traditional modes of representation, postdramatic theatre holds the capacity to rupture (dominant) structures of national narratives, thereby making space for transnational ones.[42] The link between postdramatic and postmigrant theatre echoes and gives theoretical heft to Hasibe Kalkan Kocabay's observation that retelling German history through postmigrant theatre can be an important emancipatory act for long-marginalized groups, whose histories had been previously produced for them or not at all.[43]

But where a postdramatic approach proves particularly fruitful to an examination of the theatre of anger is through its focalization of performance, energy, and corporeality, three categories to which the theatre of anger frequently returns. Such a methodological trajectory also intuitively prompts kinships with performative theatre, its critical focus on the body, and its heady interactive and transformative predicates in a tradition from Richard Schechner's environmental theatre (1973) to Erika Fischer-Lichte's aesthetics of the performative (2004).[44] Finally, this methodological approach of the theatre of anger coalesces with the theoretical pulses of performance studies, which generates a more interdisciplinary mode. In particular, it speaks to José Esteban Muñoz's work on cultural identity and disidentification as that self-determining act that displaces the prerogative of conventional life and orientation (1999), and André Lepecki's writing on postcolonial movement and dance (2006).[45] This coalescence attests to the felt continuity between theatre and performance in the German context, in contradistinction to the American one, which has routinely insisted on the fault lines between the two.[46] This national distinction has much to do with infrastructure funding. German theatres are less dependent on the market and can thus be more experimental in their productions, which gives rise to new types of theatre and performance modes. An overall momentum towards performance and social event in the theatre, two elements critical to the analysis of the theatre of anger, bring me briefly to the matter of genre.

Theatre of anger is not beholden to one particular style or genre of theatre. It does not, despite what one might think, adhere to the sensationalism of melodrama and its investment in and appeal to overemotionality in its congestion of rage. The theatre of anger manifests itself in dramatic, naturalist, documentary, and postdramatic forms. Its plays often contain elements of comedy, but they are never exclusively comedic. It also finds motivation in the direct theatre modes of global protest movements. Yet one device significant to the theatre of anger is the dramatic monologue, which I dub here the "raging monologue." Confrontation between performer and audience finds its roiling manifestation at the site and moment of the monologue, which addresses itself directly at the audience. For no other technique, short of physically alighting into the house, has the capacity to defy the fabled fourth wall and open up the feedback loop like the dramatic monologue.

The unmediated confrontational scene of theatre as a live event aligns form with content, for anger is always a response that contests, a speech act that challenges. The theatre of anger is a performance of and performative engagement with a philosophical tradition of anger that begins with Aristotle's *Nicomachean Ethics*, in which he positions anger as a reasonable passion, both attributed and justifiable in the face of injustice towards oneself and others.[47] This is a conceptual articulation developed further and expanded on in the late eighteenth century with the emergence of a new discourse of feeling. As Johannes F. Lehmann contends in his comprehensive study on anger, *Im Abgrund der Wut* (2012), anger in the eighteenth century becomes endowed with the qualities of agency, energy, strength, and resistance.[48] But anger as an expression of resistance is most fully taken up and expanded on much later by feminist theorists of colour: by Audre Lorde in essays collected in *Sister Outsider* (1984), bell hooks in *Talking Back* (1989) and *Killing Rage* (1996), and Sara Ahmed in *The Cultural Politics of Emotion* ([2004] 2015), *The Promise of Happiness* (2010), and *Living a Feminist Life* (2017). The insight of these three thinkers, in particular, resonates throughout *Theatre of Anger*. They are my principal interlocutors in this pursuit of anger. In distinct ways, each articulates anger as both an attributed affect that directs us towards a future, in which social justice is possible. While hailing from other theoretical and national contexts, their work nonetheless opens up the possibilities of the plays I examine. More recent feminist reclamations of anger, such as Brittney Cooper's *Eloquent Rage* (2018), Soraya Chemaly's *Rage Becomes Her* (2018), and Rebecca Traister's *Good and Mad: The Revolutionary Power of Women's Anger* (2018), also speak out in righteous anger against the present moment in the United States and elsewhere in the wake of Trumpism and the #MeToo movement. All three similarly draw on the germinal works of Lorde and bell hooks, among others. These important contemporary voices directly and indirectly also inform this book.

My approach to anger thus pushes back against the affect theory convention of reading anger as negative, originally proposed by Silvan S. Tomkins in the second volume of his groundbreaking study, *Affect Imagery Consciousness* (1963). According to Tomkins, anger is an affect that can lead to destructive behaviour.[49] Affirmative anger also disturbs the assumptions of contemporary political philosophy, in particular in the works of Martha C. Nussbaum's (2016), Carolin Emcke (2016), and Pankaj Mishra (2017), which focus on the negative effects of anger as an affect frequently linked to hate, violence, and even terrorism, and that call for an embrace of forgiveness and reconciliation.[50] Not necessarily reading anger against the grain, the present book instead makes way for more productive readings of anger, which also have a history, as an affect that is, as Lorde has succinctly referred to it, "loaded with energy and information."[51]

Bringing anger to bear on theatre regalvanizes theatre's capacity as a medium of confrontation, protest, and resistance. For, to paraphrase Fischer-Lichte, the very possibility of theatrical performance emerges from an encounter, a confrontation, an interaction.[52] Theatre interrupts, just as an encounter interrupts. The theatre of anger returns politics to the stage in a direct way as it pioneers new modes of theatre. If the popularity of postmigrant theatre and its integrality to the Berlin theatre scene suggest that it cannot be that radical, then *Theatre of Anger* proposes a closer look. It is no secret that the Maxim Gorki Theatre has become popular with tourists to Berlin, in particular because it is the only major venue that surtitles all of its productions in English. On the face of it, postmigrant theatre has transformed itself from the early days of the Ballhaus Naunynstraβe and is thriving because of it. But to propose that the movement has simply gone mainstream would be an inexact and unfair assessment. Postmigrant theatre might appear to play by the rules, but it also continues to resist present structures and interrogate their cultural position (from within). A focus on the theatre of anger gets at this element of resistance. In the ethos of *Desintegration*, the theatre of anger refuses to participate in the embedded traditions of a theatre given of a specifically national culture, language, and representation. In this context, it bears noting that the Maxim Gorki Theatre is the most meagerly state-funded theatre in Berlin and is repeatedly the target of right-wing politics. As Sasha Marianna Salzmann reveals in their interview later in this book, one of the first ambitions of the extreme right-wing party Alternative for Germany (AfD), when it entered the federal parliament in 2017, was to cut funding to the Maxim Gorki Theatre.

The theatre of anger's own assault on theatre is indeed angry. It is evocative of, yet distinct from, postdramatic theatre's disintegration of the dramatic structures, as so vividly demonstrated in Oliver Frljić's play *Gorki – Alternative für Deutschland?* (*Gorki – Alternative for Germany?*, premiere 2018), when Igor Pauška's theatrical set, a stage-size replica of the Gorki theatre itself, is aggressively dismantled piece by piece until only a shell of its original structure still stands. This antagonistic and in-yer-face act spoke both to the politics of the present and, as Sierz reminds us, that "the history of outrage is not a simple narrative of progress from repression to liberation. Instead, taboos are broken, reformed, and then are broken yet again. And sometimes it takes the hammer of high art to smash them."[53] To invoke and question Lorde's famous feminist injunction, can we perhaps in fact use the master's tools to dismantle the master's house? Well, we have to start somewhere and there is something to be said about the energizing jerk of the hammer and its performative power.

Overview of the Chapters

Theatre of Anger is derived from a long and committed engagement with transnational theatre practices more broadly. My experience with the plays I examine here has been mostly as spectator, but sometimes as amateur director back in my university setting. Initially, I set out to write a comprehensive study of postmigrant theatre, but this project quickly became too large in scope. With time, I began to notice the affective-political force of some of the plays I was looking at. Anger is hard to miss these days, but it seemed to be working against the status quo in these examples. It was affirming. The anger of these plays drew me in. *Theatre of Anger* is by no means a survey or an anthology of contemporary or postmigrant theatre in Germany. I offer no pretence of totality in the account that I put forth here. Instead, this study highlights a set of seven plays that do something riveting with affirmative forms of anger at a time and in a political climate when this affect is often otherwise perceived as negative and only capable of leading to hate and destruction. In the theatre of anger, minoritized subjects speak out in anger against social injustice in order to shape a world in which we can all flourish.

The study applies a focused analysis of this set of plays that incisively opens them up. It is my intention to show how anger is performed and shapes these performances; how it assumes important theatrical forms and what these forms look like; and finally how theatrical anger speaks to contemporary sociopolitical issues. The book is divided into five chapters, an interview, and a conclusion. With the exception of the first chapter, which provides a comprehensive investigation of anger's discursive and philosophical history, each of the following chapters attend to different aspects of the central topic by way of close analyses of plays associated with the theatre of anger. With individual foci, shaped by a common theme or genre, each chapter offers a slightly different portrait of the theatre of anger and its possibilities. An interview with the playwright Sasha Marianna Salzmann concludes the book with another, altogether much more expert, voice than my own.

A study about the theatre of anger must begin with anger itself. Chapter 1 reads somewhat like a manifesto as it makes its way through a history and philosophy of anger, which begins with Aristotle and leads all the way to the Black Lives Matter movement via Black feminist theory, with particular attention to the resonating voices of Audre Lorde, bell hooks, and Sara Ahmed, and added reference to the literary insights of James Baldwin and Toni Morrison. This chapter traces a simmering tale of anger for justice that runs counter to stoic narratives of reticence and *apatheia*. This account is positioned in defence of anger, insofar as anger is a form of knowing, of energizing, of empowering, and of caring. Anger meets theatre in this chapter by way of a historical form of fury that called eighteenth-century German art and theatre into being: the Laocoön, whose rage is, all told, not as (beautifully) contained as Lessing contended but actually corporeally revealing – and revelling in rage. An encounter of anger and theatre is then traced historically and more globally through the tragedies of the ancient Greeks to the shadow puppet theatre of the Ottoman Empire, finally to British in-yer-face theatre and direct theatre articulated by the Mothers of the Plaza de Mayo and the Saturday Mothers of Istanbul. An investigation of the postmodern practice of the monologue – a theatrical device that marks much of the theatre of anger – from its explosive manifestation in Peter Handke's *Publikumsbeschimpfung* (*Offending the Audience*, premiere 1966) to more contemporary examples concludes this first chapter. We can approach our study of the theatre of anger through a rich and impressive archive of theatre and performance.

But where does the theatre of anger fit into all this? How can we contextualize its culturally and historically specific emergence in the mid-2000s? Indeed, the theatre of anger also does something new. The second chapter begins with Necati Öziri's *Get Deutsch or Die Tryin'*. Perhaps more than any other play considered in this book, this one typifies the theatre of anger. It explores the history of exclusion and violence experienced by a young Turkish man, born to migrants and raised in Germany, haunted by his past and burdened by a present that not only feels static but is full of loss. This narrative, told and performed almost exclusively in monologue, is replete with anger. The play offers radical contextualization and ushers in a turn to the cultural performances of anger that emerged in the tumultuous period of postunification in Germany. The subversively activist and political art and performance of Kanak Attak is a notable precursor to the theatre of anger and one that positions these plays more firmly in a historical trajectory of a broader social justice movement in Germany. The chapter is rounded off with a more in-depth analysis of postmigrant history as a movement from which the theatre of anger emerges.

The following three chapters all contain close analyses of plays grouped in pairs, based on theme or genre. To begin, chapter 3 concentrates on Feridun Zaimoğlu and Günter Senkel's *Schwarze Jungfrauen* and Nurkan Erpulat and Jens Hillje's *Verrücktes Blut*. The most acclaimed among the plays I examine in this book, both offer examples of the theatre of anger's early impulses of Turkish German and Muslim culture in Germany, with an emphasis on the anger and resistance, expressed in blasting verbiage, of so-called second- and third-generation migrant youth. The first is a rather confessional play about (neo-)Muslim women presented exclusively in the format of the dramatic monologue; and the second is a more naturalistic play about disenfranchised (mostly) male Muslim youths at a high school in Berlin. Simply put, these plays respond with anger to invidious narratives of religious radicalism and violence. Revisiting the label "Muslim rage," called into being as a deliberately hateful speech act, is meant to incite reflection. What does it mean that mainstream discourses in the West have long linked young Muslim (especially) men to fantasy figures of the macho, the violent criminal, and the terrorist? Read as a negative affect, anger all too often gets stuck to certain types of bodies; in the case of Muslim males, this is an anger that arises from moral panic and the projection of hateful fantasies. It is an anger thought to lead to hate and violence. *Schwarze Jungfrauen* and *Verrücktes Blut* perform this projected anger and defiantly thrust it back in the faces of those who hurtfully assign it. At the same time, these plays distil radical theatrical forms of anger that flout troublesome stereotypes. Echoing bell hooks: They talk back. They act out against culturally assigned rage.

If the focus of chapter 3 catches the drift of the early 2000s – that deleterious decade marked by widespread Islamophobia in the wake of 9/11 (and still not over) – then chapter 4 speaks to the revolutionary spirit of outrage in the first part of the 2010s at the incendiary moment of Arab Spring, Occupy, Gezi, and so forth. It examines two documentary-style plays, Anestis Azas and Prodromos Tsinikoris's *Telemachos – Should I Stay or Should I Go?* and Mely Kiyak's *Aufstand: Monolog eines wütenden Künstlers*, which track, respectively, the austerity protests in Athens in the summer of 2011 and the anti-government protests in Gezi Park in Istanbul in the summer of 2013. With Stéphane Hessel's boisterous call for anger and outrage against the prevailing conditions of economic injustice as a point of departure, this chapter examines anger and its imbrication with active protest movements as they are presented onstage. This is not a new phenomenon to the theatre, especially not in Germany. From the work of Erwin Piscator in the 1920s to Peter Weiss in the late 1960s, documentary theatre has a long tradition of converging theatre with politics and protest in (West) Germany, a tradition which marked the inception of independent theatre ("freies Theater") in the 1960s, which I also briefly trace in this chapter. What does theatre offer a protest movement? To speak of the dramaturgy of a protest, its theatricality, has become commonplace, but what if, in the spirit of Artaud, the politics of the street returns to the theatre space?[54] Such is the address of this chapter. On offer here, in particular, is anger's capacity to perform politics while unsettling the unspoken agreements and regulating binary structures of theatre.

Although this book is more acutely attentive to performance than to the dramatic text, in the fifth chapter I turn to the work of playwright Sasha Marianna Salzmann. Salzmann's dramatic writing is profoundly open and theatrical, and their active contribution to the theatre scene at the Maxim Gorki Theatre, in particular, thoroughly embeds their dramatic texts in a thick theatrical and performance-based field. Further, they are actively involved in the staging of their plays. In the context of this study, much of Salzmann's dramatic writing could fit into this frame of a theatre of anger, but for the purposes of this book and for the sake of uniformity with previous chapters, I concentrate on two plays that demonstrate the rich expanse of their work: their earliest piece, *Weißbrotmusik*, and their most recent play to be produced, *Zucken*. Both are youth plays inspired by contemporaneous news events about anger and violence, even terrorism. The former is written and has been performed in more naturalist style; the latter is highly experimental. What drives this investigation of their work is an interest in language and form and their convergence through the affective scope of anger. Among other things, this chapter asks what forms the theatre of anger takes. A reading with Lehmann's postdramatic theatre as a theatre of the energetic body is surprising (because how can we speak of postdramatic playwriting?), but illuminating. The corporeal exertion of the "twitch" (central to the latter play) that easily transforms into a violent "spasm" is unleashed by Salzmann's theatre of anger. This is a theatre that confronts, even, to paraphrase Artaud, "lacerates" its audience.[55] The emphasis on the energetic body – unable to remain still – is paired with the urgency of youths and their investment in the future.

Moving towards a conclusion, the chapters are framed by an interview with Salzmann. Salzmann's own confessional indebtedness to the blatant extremism of Sarah Kane's angry plays and the tradition of in-yer-face theatre offers at once an opening and a closing to this book, a dramatic frame that felicitously falls into place. Not only a playwright affiliated with the theatre of anger, Salzmann has also been the in-house author at the Maxim Gorki Theatre. At its inception, they were, furthermore, the artistic director of Studio Я. As someone involved in the production, creativity, and direction of the theatre of anger on a broad scale, Salzmann's voice lends this study depth and insight, as well as some variance. This interview is not meant solely as a means of supporting what has already been said throughout the book's chapters. As much as Salzmann finds merit in my pursuit of the theatre of anger, they also express their own views as they speak candidly and effusively about their development as a playwright and theatremaker. Their own lived anger at the state of things, particularly the stifling structures of racism, anti-Semitism, Islamophobia, and homophobia, which still give shape to German mainstream society, found an outlet in playwriting and, appropriately, in their pursuit of boxing in their youth. On a panel of young theatre practitioners at the Berlin *Theatertreffen*, in 2018, Salzmann declared that *Wut* (rage) is what brought them to theatre.[56] But to propose that the theatre of anger gave them a space to write and develop as an artist would be a lopsided interpretation. Salzmann's influence on the movement, its directions and forms, has been indelible. For me, their work embodies the spirit of the theatre of anger as a true practice of resistance. This interview was further essential to this project because it gets at the experiential and the subjective in a manner that goes beyond my own capacity as a spectator and scholar. By proposing that these plays form a theatre of anger, I implicitly claim that they may come from a place of anger, but the business of assigning affects and emotions bears the detested conceit of superiority. Salzmann is just one voice and cannot speak for all of the theatre practitioners presented in this book, but theirs is an important voice and one that resonates from a place of experience. Ultimately, Salzmann's own words bring this book together, giving it added meaning and substance. The interview moves from Salzmann's early engagement with the theatre of anger as a community and space of inclusion and creativity to the specific role of anger in their work as a motivating force, a politics, and a creative form that has developed through their plays.

My interview with Salzmann took place in June 2018 and coincided with a month-long stay in Berlin to collect impressions of the new – where transnational theatre in the city is now and where it might be going – as a means of putting the finishing touches on this book. In that month, I attended a total of sixteen different plays. I looked for anger. As much as we tend to find what we are looking for, this search was not a challenging task. It was everywhere.

Chapter One

In Defence of Anger: From a History of Social Justice to the Theatre

Anger is better. There is a sense
of being in anger. A reality and
presence. An awareness of worth.
It is a lovely surging.

Toni Morrison, *The Bluest Eye*

Anger is the affect that keeps on shaking. In one way or another, anger sears and seethes in our contemporary world. We have entered what Pankaj Mishra calls the "age of anger" (2017), a new crisis of the present.[1] This is nothing new. Already in 2012, Johannes F. Lehmann introduced his important book on anger, *Im Abgrund der Wut*, with the observation that anger was already "booming" in 2010.[2] If Lehmann's book attempts to make sense of a discursive turn to anger in the 2010s with the publication of Peter Sloterdijk's *Zeit and Zorn* (*Time and Rage*, 2006), Arjun Appadurai's *The Fear of Small Numbers: An Essay on the Geography of Anger* (2006), and *The International Handbook of Anger* (2010), then the present study responds to Mishra's *The Age of Anger* (2017), Martha Nussbaum's *Anger and Forgiveness* (2016), and to some extent, Carolin Emcke's *Gegen den Hass* (*Against Hate*, 2016). The anger that marks this long decade is overwhelmingly read as caused by economic instability, globalization, disenfranchisement, unemployment, and so forth. Yet the ubiquitously roaring presence of anger, frequently attached to disaffected young men the world over, holds to a different conviction of injustice that I will not explore in greater depth here. This is the telos of these later books on anger, which pursue a negative tale of anger that turns on hate. The tale of anger to which this study is oriented, instead, recuperates anger as a tool for social justice and in this way turns on hope for the future. This is a creative hope for (other) worldmaking, a political hope for change.

That said, anger is tricky, and such neat logic of division does not always stay in place. Anger's powerful surging can, after all, sweep us away and misdirect our intentions, cause us to lose sight of our object, cause us to act and speak out of anger alone. It can also fuel terrible and even senseless violence. As a result, anger tout court all too often gets a bad rap. Even with the recent increased interest in the history and form of emotions and affects in academia, anger often occupies either a peripheral or a negative position. For psychologist Silvan S. Tomkins, whose early writing on affects has been instrumental in the development of contemporary affect theories, anger is not only a negative affect that must be minimized for the sake of mental health, but it is also linked to distress and anguish, and ultimately hinders action.[3]

These are claims which feminist thinkers Audre Lorde, bell hooks, and Sara Ahmed have broadly disputed. They have drawn our attention to the problems of negative and biased perceptions of anger. To be called angry so frequently means to be admonished, to be told that something is wrong with you and not that something is wrong with the world, because to paraphrase Ahmed, most anger is read as unattributed.[4] Not the most pleasant of emotions nor one that brings with it the promise of happiness, anger is still dynamic and revelatory. It can be painful, but it also confronts and attends to the pain that is carried around, often quietly repressed, and expertly displaced – if resurgent at all. Lorde writes: "My anger has meant pain to me but it has also meant survival, and before I give it up I'm going to be sure that there is something at least as powerful to replace it on the road to clarity."[5] Another issue with anger is that it often becomes attached to certain types of bodies, even communities. It can be perceived as an obscure symptom and not a direct result of the experience of injustice. It can even be turned against itself as a means of disparaging a person or group. For instance, the angry Black woman is frequently described as a killjoy. Drawing on the insights of Lorde and hooks, Brittney Cooper most recently takes this up in *Eloquent Rage*, in which she writes: "Angry Black women get dismissed all the time. We are told we are irrational, crazy, out of touch, entitled, disruptive, and not team players."[6] Anger is neither an easy emotion, nor an easy solution. It can be unwieldy, and certainly unpopular. Yet anger's power of redress and its capacity to raise critical consciousness, by virtue of its provision of "clarity," as Lorde lucidly words it, open up a threshold to the political, insofar as it proceeds from the recognition that the pain caused by racism, or other forms of injustice, is real and wrong.[7] These thinkers argue instead that anger is attributed, it is a response to something; it is an affirmation. Lorde, hooks, and Ahmed recuperate anger as a powerful tool against social injustice, a source of strength, and a catalyst for change. Writing at the intersection of gender and race, all three thinkers engage anger as speech and the assertion of presence and identity in a place where speech and presence have been denied. *Theatre of Anger* is informed by this important wave of feminist thought and action. It similarly resists a pathologizing approach to anger, which holds the implication that *something is wrong with the person* displaying anger and not that *something is wrong*. This is a critical point to which I return throughout this book.

Consciousness, emancipation, and power can speak in profound moments of anger. Those weighed down by histories of abuse and violence find motivation to move forward and to invoke change in anger. This is an anger provoked by acts of injustice against the freedom and rights of individuals and groups, such as racism, sexism, Islamophobia, anti-Semitism, homophobia, transphobia, and ableism. It is a loud refusal to participate in these hurtful histories and narratives; it is a refusal to "adjust to an unjust world." For Lorde, hooks, and Ahmed, anger speaks out and talks back. But anger can also be a creative force. It can both respond and create something new. Anger can inspire art. Still working in the service of utterance against injustice, anger in art or artistic forms of anger can be recalibrated into aesthetic genres. Such recalibration does not propose the dilution of anger; it does not scupper the impact of anger's heady charge. Instead, anger is engaged as the rivet that fixes politics to art, because angry art is always political. But that is not the extent of angry art. There is much more at stake here. Drawing on philosophy as well as aesthetic and theatrical traditions, the theatre of anger is, as this book seeks to establish, not merely concerned with bringing politics to the stage. Its project is much more ambitious.

By way of limning the work of anger in theatre in a manner that will inform subsequent readings of the plays, which form the theatre of anger, this chapter begins by following the history of anger across philosophical and political traditions. Recuperating anger as an affirmative and empowering emotion and manifestation of ethics and politics throughout history is at the crux of this chapter. For anger born of the experience of injustice and raised as a means of pursuing self-assertion and worth has a longer, albeit fluctuating, history in Western discourse. Applications of this emotion in art, and in particular theatre, through a broader historical lens follow with equal significance. Considered here with radical revision, Gotthold Ephraim Lessing's project of formalizing and aestheticizing the body in theatre through the statue of the Laocoön offers a charged signifier. In my revision, subdued rage (hitherto perceived as the more noble "pain" of the Laocoön) acquires exteriority through the body's morphology. This reading sets up an important precedence for thinking about theatre beyond the scope of standard (and acceptable) theatrical emotions, such as pity and fear. (Re)thinking anger with theatre and the theatrical in broad strokes, this chapter takes us to continental Europe, the United Kingdom, the United States, Turkey, and Argentina. An examination of the dramatic monologue completes this chapter. Dramatic monologue provides a tangible link, a saturated performative moment where theatre and anger come together in a verbal delivery of confrontation. The raging monologue lets loose the possibilities of a formal, expressive manifestation of anger in theatre. While not a device dominant in all the plays reflected on in *Theatre of Anger*, its presence is nonetheless significant.

A Philosophical History of Anger

Anger's ethical capacity as a responsive measure against injustice has a long history in Western philosophy and politics. As early as Aristotle's *Nicomachean Ethics*, anger was cautiously perceived as a necessary passion that had its proper time and place. He writes that "[t]here is praise for someone who gets angry at the right things and with the right people, as well as in the right way, at the right time, and for the right length of time."[8] In Aristotle's account, anger is a passion experienced, not by angry people (what he calls the "irascible man"), but by "good-tempered" people. While this might appear paradoxical at first, as Philip Fisher points out, such is informative to Aristotle's overall equitable approach to the passions, more generally, by way of which a call for the exercise of moderation and correctness is always sound pedagogy.[9] Yet that one should be driven to anger in a legitimate context is not only acceptable and justifiable for Aristotle, it is furthermore expected. For the person who does not respond in anger to an injustice committed fails to feel pain and is a fool.[10] If anger is thus a justified state, it is because it is always in the form of a response; it never initiates social exchange. In Aristotle's account: "This is why actions done from spirit are rightly thought to be unpremeditated, because the first principle is not in the person who acts from spirit, but in the one who made him angry."[11] Insofar as it appears to serve justice in an unequivocal cause-and-effect sequence, anger's drama bears an impersonal quality. Put a different way, anger is not simply effected by individual will. What is at stake for Aristotle is not the state of the emotional subject, apparently writhing with rage. Rather, his preference to engage the social character of anger as both an external force and a site of justice is of central concern.

The notion that anger has an important social quality may in some respects portend a wide turn to the Lockean social contract, but this is not the direction I wish to take. Instead, as Fisher astutely remarks, Aristotle's interest in the social is conditioned by care for others. Anger has the capacity to bring people into collective life, for when one acts in anger it is also in defence of others – "one's friends." To not defend one's friends is, as Aristotle words it, "slavish."[12] Fisher calls this one of the most important elements of Aristotle's work: "The idea that the passions are incited by what occurs within a world of care and concern – parents, children, friends, those loved or close to us – as well as what happens directly to us."[13] The person struck with anger by an act of injustice committed against her or him or them, is often likely to respond even more forcefully when this act is committed against a loved one. Thus, self-worth and care for others are the two conjunctive forces at work in the scene of anger. Even the potential pleasure to be derived from the hope of revenge through anger should not be considered within the limitations of personal satisfaction, but in terms of the greater good.[14]

But anger has undergone dramatic shifts in meaning and judgment in its history. That the Stoic doctrine of *apatheia*, or the pursuit of the good life free from suffering, thereafter condemned anger altogether as a passion of excess and even evil comes as no surprise. In a response to his brother Novatus's purported question about anger, its causes and especially its cures, Seneca writes at length about this "foul and frenzied" passion.[15] His protracted indictment of anger summons all manner of examples of this passion's inflictions of violence and destruction. Contrary to Aristotle, Seneca was far less concerned with the causes of anger than with its harmful results. In a Freudian vein of "Verschiebung" (displacement) *avant la lettre*, Seneca articulates the danger of the displacement of anger's wrath that can result in unhinged violence and therefore undue punishment of the innocent. Various interpretations of the opening verse of Homer's *Iliad*, and the ominous threat posed by Achilles's incipient state of rage, what Peter Sloterdijk has referred to as "Europe's first word," frequently characterize anger as the pathos-laden genesis of absolute carnage and destruction.[16] If the world was formed through rage ("menis"), as Sloterdijk proposes, then it was the commission of the Stoics to work to contain this rage. One might argue that the figure of Christ subsequently became this containment of Western anger, the unconditional embodiment of forbearance and clemency. The church long after had a monopoly on the passions and ordered them along lines of virtuous and sinful. Anger occupied a place in the category of the latter. The Old and New Testaments are rife with dictates that preach against the use of anger: "Refrain from anger, and forsake wrath! ... It tends only to evil." (Psalm 37:8). From Job to

Christ, the Judeo-Christian pedagogy of sacrifice and forbearance in the face of injustice would haunt anger's future.

It is often with recourse to these two classical genealogies that modern and contemporary conceptualizations of anger in Western philosophy and politics are shaped. In adumbrated version: The first one traces its way back to Aristotle's praise of anger as a performance of justice in the face of injustice. The second takes recourse to Stoicism's doctrine of *apatheia* via a Judeo-Christian tradition that condemns anger as a passion of excess and destruction.[17] The early part of the eighteenth century, with its radical inward turn to the individual, witnessed a shift in focus from the collective power of anger to anger's explicit psychological effect on the ego. Immanuel Kant discusses the necessity of giving vent to anger for the health and soul of an individual.[18] Further, the advent of a discourse on feeling in the latter part of the eighteenth century did witness the echo and expansion of Aristotle's more affirmative approach to anger. Drawing on the writing of German Rationalist philosophers such as Ernst Platner, Johann Christoph Gottsched, and Ernst Karl Wieland, Johannes F. Lehmann narrates a historical transformation of anger as an affect newly endowed with a taxonomy of vital qualities, including productivity, energy, strength, and resistance.[19] Indeed, the "rage" or "wrath" (*Zorn*) that permeates the literature of antiquity, the Middle Ages, and the Baroque period is part of the privilege of the sovereign ruler. Gradually, with the fall of monarchial ascendancy and the subsequent rise of the bourgeoisie in the eighteenth century, the privilege of this affect is repossessed and modified, democratized, even. The bourgeoisie did not find itself in thrall to "rage," with its unconditional and violent desire for revenge, but instead given to "anger" (*Wut*) as a response to injustice and an assertion of subjectivity.[20] Noting this transformation in the historical discourse of anger adds a layer of complexity to a trajectory of anger affirmation that comes to bear on modern and even contemporary conceptualizations. But where Lehmann reads this as a critical break and a move away from Aristotle's concept, I understand this turn from the narrow to the broad in the eighteenth century as a chapter in the longer history of anger or rage (indeed, I use the two terms more or less interchangeably), which begins with Aristotle.

This trajectory transports us to the twentieth- and twenty-first centuries and to the political writing of African American scholars and authors, from James Baldwin and Toni Morrison to Audre Lorde and bell hooks, and finally to Australian British scholar Sara Ahmed, who have rendered a theory and politics of anger that informs present movements for social justice and civil rights. Justice is the arc that connects this particular history of anger. Drawing a direct line between Aristotle and Audre Lorde, Sianne Ngai writes that "[t]he observation that justice conversely requires anger, and cannot be imposed solely by reason, underscores the passion's centrality to political struggles throughout political history."[21] Through the work of thinkers and authors, like Lorde, I propose a methodology of anger that (in this chapter) I map onto artistic production, in particular on the theatre styles and movements, which anticipate the theatre of anger. In subsequent chapters, the theatre of anger comes under direct scrutiny through close readings. Without being impositional or hegemonic, and subscribing to some extent to Edward Said's notion of "travelling theory," a paired reading with contemporary US theorists and activists proffers a means of working through the less discursively undertaken realities of racialization and racism in Germany.[22] Such a transatlantic exchange is strategic and revealing because, as Fatima El-Tayeb adroitly articulates it:

> Rassismus als strukturelles Problem, das sich nicht als individuelle Abweichung vom gemeinschaftlichen Konsens lokalisieren lässt, sondern die gesamte Gesellschaft durchzieht, so die Überzeugung, existiert vielleicht in den USA, aber sicher nicht in Deutschland.[23]

> The conviction that racism as a structural problem that does not allow itself to be localized as an individual aberrance from societal consensus, but as something that pervades society as a whole, exists perhaps in the United States but certainly not in Germany.

This is gradually changing in many academic institutions in Germany. In the social sciences, for instance, postcolonial and postmigration studies are gaining ground, and questions of colonial history, migration, and social pluralism are being addressed in critical and important ways.[24] However, there remains a broader oversight and unwillingness to attend to racism as a societal and systemic problem in Germany and this in turn has posed considerable challenges to the attempts to fight its persisting existence. James Baldwin, who found respite in Europe from the virulent racism in the United States in the pre–civil rights era, called this nescience "European innocence," Stuart Hall the "internalist story," and El-Tayeb quite plainly, "colorblindness."[25] This denial has silenced many groups and individuals in their struggle for civil rights and liberties in Germany. That this struggle continues in the United States since the 1960s is an unassailable truth, but that it is still to a large degree only beginning to issue forth in Germany also cannot be denied.[26] For this reason, I rely heavily on the work of women-of-colour feminists based predominantly in the United States and in the United Kingdom, but I also remain aware of the locative specificity of such a move.

The Spectre of Aristotle: Anger and Justice

The Black Lives Matter movement formed in 2013 as a social media campaign in summary response to the pervasive practice of police brutality against African Americans, brought to surface with the tragic deaths of Michael Brown in Ferguson, Missouri, and Eric Garner in New York City.[27] It has since developed into an international social justice movement against systemic racism and violence inflicted upon communities of colour and Black people. The movement's founders, Alicia Garza, Patrisse Cullors, and Opal Tometi, have connected the broader Black Lives Matter movement to the civil rights movement, while also expanding its parameters in an effort to form a more inclusive action that is critically queer and intersectional. As Tometi notes:

> [W]e wanted to create a political space within and amongst our communities for activism that could stand firmly on the shoulders of movements that have come before us, such as the civil rights movement, while innovating on its strategies, practices and approaches to finally centralize the leadership of those existing at the margins of our economy and our society.[28]

With this movement, there has been a correspondent resurgence in general interest in the literature of authors kindred to the civil rights movement, particularly in the works of feminist and queer authors of colour. As a writer whose work speaks both to civil rights and gay liberation, James Baldwin has been reclaimed by many as a voice of the contemporary age.[29] His writing is as timely now as it was half a century ago. Although he has not written extensively on anger and its importance in the struggle for social justice, he did not balk at anger. Writing in the pre- and early civil rights era, Baldwin engaged the reality of his anger as a Black man in America. One cannot help but return (and one certainly does)[30] to a quote from Baldwin's collection of essays, *Notes from a Native Son*, about the inevitability of anger in the Black community: "There is not a Negro alive who does not have this rage in his blood – one has the choice of merely living with it consciously or surrendering to it."[31]

If rage thus inherits the qualities of an extended, even a more permanent ontological, state, is this not in contradistinction to Aristotle's account, which prescribes anger as a temporally and contextually subscribed response to an act of injustice? But Baldwin does not propose that "to be in rage all the time" is the state of a perpetually angry or, as Aristotle words it, "irascible man." Instead, Baldwin's statement is a powerful reckoning of the presence of racial injustice that confronts African Americans as a conditioning for both historical and everyday existence. When Lorde speaks of her anger in response to racism, she describes it as a lived experience. "My response to racism is anger. I have lived with that anger, ignoring it, feeding upon it, learning to use it before it laid my visions to waste, for most of my life [...] I have used learning to express anger for my growth."[32] The injustice of racism at once conditions existence and spurs instincts for survival against the ever-threatening negation of personhood and lived self-worth. To be angry is to refuse victimhood. As Morrison poetically words it in the epigraph that opens this chapter, "there is a sense of being" and "an awareness of worth" in anger that surges.[33] In her first novel, *The Bluest Eye*, Morrison's character, the young Pecola, struggles between anger and shame after a scene of implicit mistreatment by the candy store salesman. Unlike the sting of shame, anger empowers; it offers a sense of self and a sense that she has been wronged and not that something is wrong with her.

Although it emerges in response to the acts or words of another, anger is an active, not a passive, emotion. It is what Ahmed encourages us to read as a "speech act."[34] Such a reading of anger is part of a broader feminist tradition, which Ahmed importantly synthesizes in *The Cultural Politics of Emotion*. The notion of anger as speech act first arose in the writing of Marilyn Frye, who argues: "Being angry at someone is somewhat like a speech act in that it has a certain conventional force whereby it sets people up in a certain sort of orientation to each other; and like a speech act, it cannot 'come off' if it does not get uptake."[35] Thus, anger is performative; it can be both an action and a call for action. But as a speech act, anger requires felicitous conditions, such as an audience of willing listeners. Anger is relational. According to Ahmed, and this is one point where she carefully returns us to the insights of Black feminist discourse, one must also learn to listen to the speech act of anger and not to block it. If feminist discourse alerts us to the importance of anger for gender difference, more specifically, Black feminist discourse does so for both gender and race. What differentiates various instances of angry speech acts are their attribution, their articulation, and their audience. For anger is not absolute. It is not simply good or bad. The way that it is used and received determine its form and future. Used in the "right way," as an affirmative, anger can be powerfully dynamic; it can mobilize people in the pursuit of social justice.

As Baldwin succinctly presents it (at the dawn of the civil rights movement in the United States), sustained anger or rage holds the will and promise to mobilize collective political protest that incites awareness and change.[36] Needless to say, the expression of anger as a catalyst for movement and change has become, time and again, the resentment of those concerned with upholding the status quo, who believe that life is a zero-sum game. Throughout more recent history, the rage of the colonized has been pathologized and carnivalized, as a display of emotion most jarring and even outrageous. This aimed to subvert its threat. In her essay "Killing Rage," bell hooks writes: "To perpetuate and maintain white supremacy, white folks have colonized Black Americans, and a part of that colonizing process has been teaching us to repress our rage, to never make them the targets of any anger we feel about racism."[37] She adds that "[m]ost black people internalize this message well."[38] Briefly tracing this conservative backlash determined to undermine the link between "Black rage" and a passion for justice, hooks employs the famous example of Malcolm X. Often perceived as the aberrant, radical (Muslim) other, Malcolm X has historically been juxtaposed against the Christian, forbearing, nonviolent figure of Martin Luther King, Jr. hooks further charges that newer readings of Malcolm X bent on redeeming him as a figure not resolved to rage but (as Cornel West argues) to love, ultimately fall short because they fail to recognize the potency of rage in its entanglement with his commitment to justice.[39] Frequently vexed by his affirmation of rage (not to mention his unmitigated pessimistic vision of America), Malcolm X's public perception and legacy have, as hooks holds, also "set [him] apart from contemporary Black thinkers and leaders who feel that 'rage' has no place in anti-racist struggle."[40] That Black feminist thinkers, such as hooks and Lorde, have recuperated Malcolm X precisely for his important insistence on rage as a tool and mobilizer for social justice struggles, and not a bane of his character, is crucial.[41]

Anger unearths and confronts injustice; it invokes the realities and histories erased from view by majoritarian society, and it treads in the residue of these histories, reoccupying its spaces with bodies bent on attention and justice, kicking up dust, gathering strength and energy. Calling out its cause, calling out for action, anger moves us – *it becomes a movement*.[42] What might this movement of anger look like? In the case of Black Lives Matter, which later transmuted far beyond its social media presence to the collective power of bodies gathered in the streets, schools, cultural institutions, and spaces of worship, anger mobilizes the means of protest against systemic racism, and especially police violence, when other channels of expression are unyielding or closed off. There are many similar examples that can be named here and will be throughout this book. I evoke Black Lives Matter as one of the important collective manifestations of anger against injustice because it is both historically recent (and in many ways ongoing) and has an abounding reach – both in terms of geography and medium. This movement and others, both historical and contemporaneous, have come into existence through anger. It is a response to injustice and a tool of its eradication. As a catalyst for a movement, however, anger also pursues transformation and change. As Ahmed proposes in her killjoy manifesto, "[a] movement comes into existence to transform what is in existence," and as a result create new worlds of possibility.[43]

The conditions of possibility forged by anger also extend to art. In their collective pursuit of change through anger, Lorde, hooks, and Ahmed incite us to think about anger as a potentially creative process. The affectivity of anger as the articulation of both a personal and a social experience of injustice and the desire to transform this experience underpins this. According to Raymond Williams, an affective social experience, "lived, actively, in real relationships," infuses a structure of feeling to politics and activism that extends to art.[44] New creative and aesthetic forms thus unfold from the force of anger's manifestation in politics. Williams's concept of a structure of feeling articulates the critical mutability between art and emerging social processes; these are what he refers to as "social experiences *in solution*."[45] But these art forms do not merely register a shift in politics; instead, they merge the subjective and the social, the aesthetic and the political, and the past and the present. Although Williams does not engage individual feelings or emotions as such, his theory suggests that we read for tone, since different historical and present periods can hold to collectively felt experiences of sadness, joy, and, yes, anger, as a kind of affective zeitgeist.[46] If we live in the age of anger, this book aims to trace this anger as an affirmative affect in creative processes and production, and in theatre in particular.

Giving Anger Theatrical Form in the Laocoön's Image

Emotion is the thing of theatre. Even with Bertolt Brecht's contemptuous yet valiant attempt to purge the theatre of (many would claim) an overwrought pathos with the radical introduction of his epic form, theatre could simply not escape the full pitch of its repertoire of historically textured affects. Indeed, Brecht himself would later submit to the idea that feelings in theatre were inevitable.[47] The peril of the apparent false sentiment of the theatre is of course a well-trodden line of thought. Plato was notably sceptical of theatre both for its tendency towards mimetic deception and its potential for excessive emotionality. In Book III of *The Republic*, Plato describes how Socrates and his interlocutors engage in a long and earnest discussion about mimetic art with the resulting conclusion that imitation can only be permitted when the object of imitation is virtue. Therewith ended the possibility of theatre in an ideal society. Even Aristotle's famous defence of tragedy with its taxonomy of strong emotions, including especially pity and fear, but also surprise, suffering, and terror, perceived it in the service of a categorical catharsis of these selfsame emotions. Tragedy, and all forms of imitation more generally, assumed a valuable didactic purpose whereby the aim was the purgation of interior weakness facilitated via what Aristotle, in *Poetics*, calls "embellished language."[48] Theatre provided the necessary occasion of emotional release motivated by heightened, pathetic speech acts where the audience could have a good fright and a good cry and then set out homeward feeling emotionally cleansed and enlightened.

The aesthetic possibilities of emotions would enter neither philosophical nor theatre discourse in a serious way until the eighteenth century. Indeed, even with this entry emotions remained mired in a pedagogy of temperance, especially in the realm of the theatre. Moral codes held the theatre in a firm grip. For this precise reason, practitioners such as Friedrich Schiller, who famously placed the theatre on the level of "moral institution" (*moralischer Anstalt*) as a kind of church-ersatz, have long borne the burden of criticism from their later more radical modern counterparts. Yet the aesthetic and therefore formal treatment of emotions in theatre in the eighteenth century, while largely subsumed under a moral didacticism, did flourish. Gotthold Ephraim Lessing was the first figure to formalize emotions in relation to theatre and thus forge a critical link between theatre and the plastic arts. His 1766 aesthetic treatise, *Laokoon oder über die Grenzen der Malerei und Poesie* (*Laocoön: An Essay on the Limits of Painting and Poetry*), shaped early modern thinking about the mediality and legibility of aesthetic articulations of emotions, not dissimilar from what Eugenie Brinkema would much later call the "forms of the affects."[49] The ostensible crux of Lessing's *Laocoön* is, as the title immediately reveals, to delineate the limits of representation of emotion in poetry and in particular the plastic arts. The latter also included drama, as a medium likewise held in the grip of affectivity of material, living representation. In Lessing's account, strong emotions, such as rage and pain, may be treated without restriction in poetry because the impression is not as offensive and violently direct. Since the plastic arts must confine their representation to a singular moment, what Lessing famously calls "der fruchtbare Moment" (the pregnant moment), it is imperative that this moment is chosen with care. Although painting and sculpture have been emancipated from the rigid Gesetz der Schönheit (law of beauty), that is, any object may be the source of art, it is nonetheless the artist's responsibility to render even the ugly and disgusting beautiful through art. Such a task may be pursued through temporal choice. To represent a scene at the height of its affect would be too powerful an image for the viewer. Thus, to avoid affronting the viewer, the scene must be represented either in a pre or post state, when the physically distorting power of rage or pain has either not yet piqued or has subdued.

The statue of the Laocoön presents an anomaly to this schema. Its artists indeed capture the tableau of a father in the height of struggle as he futilely attempts to rescue his sons and himself from what is certain death in the violent clutch of two serpents, sent as punishment by Poseidon. Is this not that singular moment of rage and pain so eagerly avoided by artists? But it is beautiful. How is this possible? Lessing categorically circumvents rage and focuses instead on that more pitiable emotion, pain. Nonetheless, his vivid description of the body, and its contorted gestures, implicitly speaks to that unnamed emotion. Earlier readers of Lessing's account of the Laocoön have proposed semiotic and psychoanalytic approaches to deciphering the statue (see especially David Wellbery's analysis), in which it is argued that morphological deflection becomes an important compensatory measure.[50] In his treatment of the Laocoön statue, Lessing draws a distinction between the body and the face. While the face as the emotional centre must be rendered with expressive constraint, the representation of the body, as I see it, is permitted to assert an idiom of rage and pain. The gape of a wide-open mouth held in a scream is perceived as ugly. As Lessing writes: "The wide-open mouth, aside from the fact that the rest of the face is thereby twisted and distorted in an unnatural and loathsome manner, becomes in painting a mere spot and in sculpture a cavity, with most repulsive effect."[51] Held only slightly parted, the mouth of the father in the Laocoön statue eschews this risk of repulsiveness. Likewise, the gaze of the father, which in the state of rage and pain can be so disturbing to the viewer, is muted through the blindness induced by the venomous snake bites. However, the body's expressivity is not flattened. I argue that the affective miens absent or subdued from the face are carried out by the body. The centre of this pyramidal tableau of father flanked on both sides by his young sons is the paternal abdominal musculature contracting in pain. "To show [the physical effects of the venom and the pain] the vital parts must be left as free as possible and external pressure completely avoided, for this might change and weaken the activity of suffering nerves and laboring muscles."[52] In a phrase, interiority becomes exteriority and the visual problem of the former is resolved. What is so radical about Lessing's otherwise quite conservative approach to aesthetics is his emphasis on the body as a visual language that not only signifies the materiality of art, but constitutes its aesthetic and affective drive. By Lessing's account, the Laocoön demonstrates facial, and therefore emotional, restraint, but the body is given full expressive range. Similar to the chest, the vivid rendering of the hands of the Laocoön was imperative. Lessing writes: "Nothing is more expressive and lively than the action of the hands; especially when emotions are in play."[53] It is nothing new to propose that the body is the expressive interface in theatre, since the face cannot easily be seen at a distance. The body becomes, like in cinema discourse, "facialized;" in other words, it adopts signification.[54] Emotion, anger in particular, is re-enlivened on the body. It causes the muscles to contract, the heart to palpitate, the veins to distend. Such is the corporeal state of the father presented in the Laocoön. He is so corporeally vividly enraged!

That Lessing seems to place too much emphasis on the face is evident; that his reading of the statue of the Laocoön is, as Simon Richter words it, "euphemistic," follows.[55] Nevertheless, even in his possible misreading of the affective work of the Laocoön statute, he does not forsake affect's hold, nor insist on tempering it. Lessing instead transmogrifies the Laocoön's rage and inverts it. The result is the composition of the ideal pitiable scene, that is, the creation of the ideal pitiable subject. The arousal of pity that is so intrinsic to the work of catharsis in classical tragedy makes its return for Lessing, but this time with a distinct material and aesthetic form. What is significant to the present study is that at the heart of this ideal pitiable subject is the unsuspecting corporeal performance of rage. This is not simply the metaphysical rage invoked by a kind of tragic *anagnorisis*, but a very real, physically seething anger that threatens at any moment to burst through the surface. That the Laocoön statue becomes the aesthetic embodiment of pity for Lessing, and that this is effectively a pity founded on anger, begs the question of anger's obscured role in tragic aesthetics. In the case of theatre, *the* medium of the body, through which the body directly presents living moments of experience, Lessing imposes further limits on affective intensity. The ontological realism of the theatre makes it an unseemly site for the expression of strong emotions. Yet as we see in the case of the Laocoön, the violence, death, and the bodily pain these invoke may be presented materially and affectively on the exterior of the body without overwhelming the spectator – or by doing just that. I want to investigate the paroxysm of the Laocoön representation and especially the anger at its core and quite literally on its core, which I argue not only lies at the heart of the new aesthetics of media introduced by Lessing in the eighteenth century but also at the heart of theatre. Thus, repressed anger is the affective force against which the carefully controlled emotions of pity and fear of classical theatre dialectically work.

To propose that anger is always at work in some form in theatre may seem like an overextended claim. Since Lessing, anger has often been perceived as antitheatrical and antitragic. As seen in earlier sections of this chapter, anger stands in direct contradiction to Nietzschean *amor fati*. But it finds roots in Greek tragedy, whose Antigone and Medea figures present important prototypes of theatrical pursuits of justice through anger. Anger has a goal: it is about not accepting the situation at hand; it is about change and hope for change. Nico H. Frijda offers a fitting description: "Anger implies nonacceptance of the present event as necessary or inevitable; and it implies that the event is amenable to being changed."[56] The agonistic force of anger is teleologically optimistic. Yet a theatre of anger is not metaphysical, neither in the Aristotelian sense (of catharsis) nor in the spirit of Antonin Artaud, whose own radical call for a theatre that disturbs and provokes revolt in the early part of the twentieth century remained on the level of the virtual.[57] The goal of the theatre of anger is not cathartic release, but a materialistic, even ontological, confrontation, which presses itself on the audience. In this sense, the theatre of anger bears elements of Brechtian epic theatre that incorporates the role of the audience as co-players charged with recognition and aroused to action, but at the same time maintains an embodiedness and the force of affect that Brecht would only later come around to, and then just briefly, when he opened up the definition of epic theatre in "A Short Organum for Theatre":

> We need a type of theatre that not only facilitates the sensations, insights and motivations permitted by the particular historical field of human relations on which the action happens to take place, but also employs and produces those thoughts and feelings which help transform the field itself.[58]

The theatre of anger turns on the political as well as on the ontological. Much like the figure of the Laocoön, in the theatre of anger the drama is of the actors; it is the actors. And theirs is a reality called to life through theatre.

Beyond the Laocoön

The theatre of anger borrows from manifold traditions in theatre and performance that also extend beyond the historical traditions of the Western canon. The political subversiveness of Turkish shadow puppet performances under the Ottoman Empire in the late sixteenth century could also be a compelling distant forebear of the theatre of anger. Shadow puppet performances were a form of popular entertainment for children and adults alike, at a time in the context of traditional Islamic culture when representation was seen as heavily problematic and was essentially banned. The impossibly direct mimesis of the shadow puppets offered a way around this. Beyond the subversiveness of form and the elision of censorship, the central narrative structures taken up by these performances were also radically sociopolitical in their intentional inversions of power relations. The two main antagonists, Karagöz and Hacivat, who became synonymous with this form, reflected the class struggles among the rural, uneducated peoples and the urban intellectuals, an antagonistic juxtaposition that continues to inform modern Turkish cultural production. The story always proceeds thus: the rather brutish countryman, Karagöz, dreams of wealth and success but is ridiculed for his ignorance by the educated Hacivat. By the end, Karagöz typically gets his revenge through violence.[59] This performance tradition even has direct transnational ties that lead us to Germany. One of the first full-length plays to be written in German by a Turkish author was Emine Sevgi Özdamar's *Karagöz in Alamania* (*Black Eye in Germany*), which premiered in 1986 at the Schauspiel Frankfurt under the direction of Özdamar herself. The play transplanted Karagöz, the Turkish man from the country, into a migrant labourer in West Germany, who does achieve his dreams of wealth in a distant land, but loneliness and the fear of betrayal back home become his downfall. Although the play does not perform anger in its address of the experience of labour migration, through its commitment to new narratives, even counternarratives, it is an important antecedent to the work of postmigrant theatre more broadly and certainly bears mentioning here.[60]

Influences continue to abound with theatre and performance theories of the latter part of the twentieth century from what Jonas Barish has famously called antitheatricality (1981), against the artifice of theatre, as well as the multiple turns and returns to the audience with performative (Erika Fischer-Lichte) and postdramatic (Hans-Thies Lehmann) theatre and their attendant focus on the body. Yet the theatre of anger does not teleologically follow these precursory movements as much as it diagonally cuts across them. Similar to performative and postdramatic theatre, the theatre of anger is one that presses on the theatrical event and the presence of flesh-and-blood bodies onstage and in the audience. This theatrical event is a drama of confrontation by way of which the fourth wall collapses, and actors and audience meet. But it is also a political event in which the performance of the moment extends into the social sphere beyond the confines of the theatre, as discussion and debate continue. Confrontation, intervention, and critique mark the elements of the theatre of anger. Further, the relational quality of anger as an affective mode designates a feedback loop in the theatre. Anger is not simply a theme or a tone as much as it is a praxis (in the true Aristotelian sense of the word) here. The theatre of anger does not simply dismantle the apparatus of theatre; it takes control of it and recreates it both in its Ur-image of anger scorned (of the Laocoön statue) and as a process of refusal of one's set destiny.

Thematically, the theatre of anger draws most heavily on the influence of British theatre of the latter part of the twentieth century. Beginning in the 1950s and 1960s, the theatre movement "Angry Young Men" (including such playwrights as John Arden, Edward Bond, John Osborne, and Harold Pinter) made its mark on British stages, most famously with John Osborne's 1956 naturalist-style play, *Look Back in Anger*. The theatre of the Angry Young Men not only engaged with taboo subjects, such as class, sexuality, and violence, but did so with an aggression and a language of howling depravity, which one critic referred to as "verbal artillery."[61] The ultimate aim of this theatre was to shock the system and recast theatrical sensibility. Later decades witnessed a political and social opening up of this movement with the rise of women playwrights working in similar aesthetic traditions, in particular the radical work of the Women's Group Theatre active in the mid-1970s. But if the 1950s and 1960s ushered in a new theatrical aesthetics of anger, then the now-desensitized British audiences of the mid-1990s witnessed its postmodern recalibration with the rise of in-yer-face theatre and especially the plays of Sarah Kane. With a nod to but also a sense of redirectionality, this new wave of anger was aptly dubbed "look forward in anger" by theatre critic Sarah Hemming.[62]

Playwrights Necati Öziri and Sasha Marianna Salzmann have spoken of the impact of in-yer-face theatre on their work and the drive to "look forward in anger." Salzmann names Kane as a significant influence. Kane is undoubtedly the byword of British theatre of the 1990s and the in-yer-face movement, in particular. Similar to the effect of Osborne's 1956 play *Look Back in Anger*, in-yer-face theatre made its mark with the premiere of Kane's 1995 piece *Blasted*. It drew on a style that aimed to shock and confront the audience with an affective force of anger, but also crudeness and obscenity. Hemming writes, "We are looking for plays that burn with rage, that dislodge complacency, that disturb their audiences, and for young writers who have taken the batons handed on by more recent angry men – Brenton, Barker, Bond and Berkoff – and run with them, proving that theatre can still be a radical, shocking medium."[63] Distinct from the theatre of the Angry Young Men, in-yer-face theatre shed lingering naturalist remnants and found influence in the Theatre of the Absurd and Artaud's theoretical sundering with his cruel attack on the spectator's sensibility.[64] In-yer-face theatre is just that, a proverbial punch in the face. It not only staged subject matter hitherto prohibited from dramatic, and especially mimetic, representation, it did so with unadorned directness that aimed to disturb and unhinge the audience. The dictionary's definition of "in-your-face" is "something blatantly aggressive or provocative, impossible to ignore or avoid, and confrontational," which resonantly construes the nature of this theatre movement.[65] Aleks Sierz offers this vivid description: "The widest definition of in-yer-face theatre is any drama that takes the audience by the scruff of the neck and shakes it until it gets the message."[66] It follows that in-yer-face theatre did not simply provoke for provocation's sake alone. While it undoubtedly set about assailing the boundaries of aesthetic and dramatic permissibility, it was not only on the whim of formal experimentation; it had a point. In-yer-face theatre forced the audience to reflect on its own violent and cruel reality. Not altogether new in theatre, its means of shocking the audience into reflection were radically distinctive. The sensibility and techniques of in-yer-face theatre continue to ramify and pulse through contemporary European theatre, albeit with an increased infusion of political jolts. That is not to say that in-yer-face theatre was not political; it was without doubt predicated on issues of class in British society and challenged the socially homogeneous institution of the theatre. Whereas the theatre paradigms of Angry Young Men and in-yer-face were intent on transgressing the boundaries of theatrical representation and expectation with the grotesque, the theatre of anger is more direct in its attunement to the politics of migration.

Its directness and its unequivocal critique of politics of the present avow the theatre of anger's relationship to politicized street performances, or what Richard Schechner has called "direct theatre," a topic I take up further in chapter 4.[67] Indeed, the theatre of anger works within the institution of theatre but also draws influence from beyond its hallowed walls. Sustained movements such as Las Madres de la Plaza de Mayo (The Mothers of the Plaza de Mayo) in Buenos Aires, which consisted of a group of mothers and grandmothers who met every Thursday afternoon between 1977 and 2006 on the square to bring visibility to and demand information about the disappearance of their children by the military regime during the so-called Dirty War (1977–1983) are instructive in this regard. The collective presence of a diverse group of women, who had hitherto never been politically active, but who gathered to publicly and defiantly express their anger against state terrorism was a spectacle. Their use of images and ID cards, banners, and even symbols, such as white cloth diapers for kerchiefs, imbued their protest with performance and theatrical elements. The movement drew so much attention worldwide that it also influenced other like movements.[68] Similar to the Las Madres de la Plaza de Mayo, the phenomenon of the Cumartesi Anneleri (Saturday Mothers) became one of the most significant and sustained protest movements in Istanbul. Between May 1995 and May 1999, (mostly Kurdish) mothers met to protest every Saturday in the central neighbourhood of Taksim on the western side of the city. Their children had been arrested and then allegedly "lost under custody." These disappearances began in the aftermath of the 1980 military coup in Turkey. The period witnessed the emergence of the far-left militant Kurdistan Workers' Party (PKK), whose goals remain the pursuit of equal rights and autonomy for Kurds in Turkey. Until this day, anyone thought to be affiliated with this party can be arrested in Turkey. The mothers regularly met for sit-ins in front of the private French high school, Galatasaray, on the busy, commercial Istiklal Street. The location offered visibility and the possibility to interact with passers-by. The performance of the Saturday Mothers' protest was an important occupation of space with a synecdochical effect that became too much for the authorities, and the police began to violently crack down on the movement, which eventually led to its dissolution.[69]

Although the Saturday Mothers' actions were based on silent defiance, it was performative in its physical demand for information and justice. Both movements were about bringing presence to a disappearance; the presence of a mother for the disappearance of (usually) a son. Performative presence becomes an assertion of presence: we are here as mothers; dead or alive, our children exist. While Diana Taylor has analysed the protest of the mothers on the Plaza de Mayo as a performance of trauma, as opposed to a performance of anger, she offers insight on the importance of performance protest and its collective and political transmission. I would like to share three of her five points here:

- Performance protest helps survivors cope with individual and collective trauma by using it to animate political denunciation.
- Both make themselves felt affectively and viscerally in the present.
- They're always in situ. Each intervenes in the individual/political/social body at a particular moment and reflects specific tensions.[70]

Performance protest's pronounced capacity to "animate political denunciation," its affective and visercal presence, and its quality of intervention are critical. These dimensions of performance protest also inform the theatre of anger.

The theatre of anger is also performative. In many ways, it does things with gestures, as in the case of the mothers' sit-ins in Istanbul, and with words. Language does not simply name something; it performs that which it names. This is the case no matter if speech is uttered on the street or in the theatre. Judith Butler, drawing on J.L. Austin, has extended the scope of the performative not merely as that speech act which brings things into existence, but also as that with political and social capacity. In Butler's formulation: "[A] reconsideration of the speech act as an instance of power invariably draws attention to both its theatrical and linguistic dimensions."[71] Ahmed adds the affective and the political to the speech act's inventory and declares that emotions are also speech acts and can generate (political) effects.[72] Certainly, emotions such as hate, fear, panic, and anger have acquired striking faculties of iterability and mobilization in the contemporary political arena. Indeed, anger becomes a practice, and in the theatre of anger this practice, this affective speech act, comes often (though not exclusively) in the form of the monologue. Itself the quintessential theatrical speech act, the monologue performs anger beyond the limits of the rhetorical as it reaches out over the audience in its force of direct address.

The Raging Dramatic Monologue

The monologue is a relatively recent discursive phenomenon in theatre, but one that has enjoyed increased scholarly currency in the last few decades. Pinning down a categorical definition of the dramatic monologue beyond the elemental notion of "solitary speech" would be a tricky and, quite possibly, impossible pursuit. Even as a theatrical device, it may exist in a vast array of forms. However, most would agree that the dramatic monologue relies on a particular taxonomy of characteristics and conditions. These include, according to Beth Sessions, "speaker, audience, occasion, revelation of character, interplay between speaker and audience, dramatic action, and action which takes place in the present."[73] Employed as a mode of exteriority, by way of which the inner thoughts and feelings of a character are effusively expressed, the monologue exceeds representation. It permits an unmediated presentation of the character, whose authenticity and presence in the moment of the monologue intensify the connection between actor and audience. While the monologue might not always operate on the level of direct address (for it might be directed at an object onstage, express the contents of a letter, and so forth), the audience is frequently the explicit addressee. Throughout the plays examined in *Theatre of Anger* this is almost exclusively the case.

Like no other so frequently employed theatrical technique, the monologue has the possibility to rend asunder the fourth wall, that precarious threshold of permissibility, or at least what Erving Goffman refers to as the very "dramatic frame" of the performance.[74] The monologue has that disruptive candour that fixes the audience's attention in a way that forecloses distance and mediation, and in some cases even bids a response. During heightened moments of contact, the monologue slides into a performance that sparks the feedback loop. Fischer-Lichte famously describes the feedback loop in performative theatre as a dynamic, autopoietic system, which opens up the interaction between actors and spectators.[75] This aperture no doubt lies at the heart of performance and the performative turn in theatre. I propose that the monologue presents itself as a mode of performance that seems to rest as a form on the promissory sociality of speech acts. Even a brief verbal onslaught is relational; it requires a listener and always threatens to puncture the fourth wall.

The breaching of the proscenium at once puts pressure on the fragile fiction of the play, thus strictly avoided in European theatre of the late eighteenth and early nineteenth centuries (Georg Büchner's plays are one notable exception),[76] and conflates character and actor not in the striving for Stanislavskian perfection but by asserting the materiality and presence of the living, breathing, finite body that speaks. The actor qua flesh-and-blood human being intervenes in this moment, disrupts the mediated flow of the narrative, and throws the audience's expectations into a quagmire of ontological doubt. Only gradually during the later period of modern drama, from the late nineteenth to the early twentieth century, and with the eventual loosening of the rigid conceptual restraints of realist and naturalist theatre and its steadfast hold to the fourth wall, did the monologue begin to appear with more regular occurrence. Later Ibsen, Strindberg, and O'Neill began employing monologues, albeit sparingly. In spite of the fact that early monologue was almost exclusively put at the service of psychological revelation of the character, it nonetheless maintained its potentially disruptive effect.

In her comprehensive study on the postmodern monologue in theatre, Deborah R. Geis contends that the wayward quality of the monologue is a feature of postmodern theatre, which, in her words, "refuses the completion and coherence [of neatly sutured monologues] and opts for deconstructive explorations of its own resistance to pairing and linearity."[77] I would simply add a qualifier and propose that the intention of the monologue changes in more contemporary theatre, but its ontological structure of obtrusion was never absent; it was merely disciplined. Otherwise, why would it have been so adamantly elided by the neoclassicists, the realists, and the naturalists? The monologue interjects! By virtue of its structure and strategy of outward address, its literally "in-yer-face" quality, as it were, of aggression, provocation, and confrontation, the monologue is a critical element of the theatre of anger. In the context of German-language theatre, no exploration of the monologue and its weight of anger would be complete without a word about Peter Handke's 1966 "Sprechstück" (speak-piece, or a speak-in) *Publikumsbeschimpfung* (*Offending the Audience*). In this play, and for its entire duration, four actors speak, at times in chorus, at times in sequence, directly to the audience. These monologues begin with the self-reflexive troubling of the actor-spectator binary, not to mention the ontology of theatrical performance itself. Here is an example:

> Dadurch, daβ wir zu Ihnen sprechen, können Sie sich Ihrer bewuβt werden. Weil wir Sie ansprechen, gewinnen Sie an Selbstbewuβtsein. Sie werden sich bewuβt, daβ Sie sitzen. Sie werden sich bewuβt, daβ sie in einem Theater sitzen.
>
> Because we speak to you, you can become conscious of yourself. Because we speak to you, your self-awareness increases. You become aware that you are sitting. You become aware that you are sitting in a theatre.[78]

Not only is there a curious role reversal by way of which the spectators become the focus of the spectacle – that is, the performers – but as the monologue progresses, or better digresses, the spectators are mocked, even verbally abused. Two-thirds of the way through the text and the performance, the actors announce that they will now insult the audience: "Zuvor werden Sie noch beschimpft werden." ("But before you leave you will be offended.")[79] With that they switch into the informal second-person plural address, "ihr," and release a torrent of obscenities. They call the spectators everything from "Rotzlecker" (ass kissers) to "Nazischweine" (Nazi pigs), "Kabinettsstücke" (wax figures), and "Miststücke" (bastards).[80] But mostly, the spectators are insulted for their role in the theatrical event: "Ihr wart Vollblutspieler. Ihr begannt verheiβungsvoll. Ihr wart lebensecht. Ihr wart wirklichkeitsnah." ("You were thoroughbred actors. You began promisingly. You were true to life. You were realistic.")[81] During the premiere at the Frankfurter Theater am Turm, directed by Claus Peymann, some of the members of the audience, bathed in house lights the entire performance, become increasingly visibly agitated. There is persistent barking from the back of the auditorium. At a moment of peaked response, several members attempt to enter the stage, and at the end they rise to their feet to holler and boo emphatically.[82] Jonas Barish has analysed Handke's play as, perhaps, *the* antitheatrical project, in which not only is theatre ontologically dismantled from within, but "the theatricality of the moment is transferred from the stage to the audience."[83] This latter quality of the feedback loop is what I pair most significantly with the effusive energy of the monologue.

The anger that circulates through *Publikumsbeschimpfung* is not an affectively contagious or even phenomenologically animated one. The actors' performances are rather impassive. Their bodily gestures are economical. Though kinetically lively, the vivacity of their movements likewise fails legibility. Movement and language appear to be at odds. (The influence of early Brecht is unambiguously present.) Instead, anger is transmitted through the performance of language (injurious or not) and seizes its desired object of address. It is the audience that seethes with anger by the close of the play. The vigour of the monologue, its moving capacity, does not hinge on the affective spectacle of the actor (or actors) so much as it does on the stricken audience. Here the crossover from stage to audience is where the monologue boils over as a force of aesthetic, social, and/or political intervention. Treating the heavy labour (yes, those actors work hard in the name of drama) of the monologue in *Publikumsbeschimpfung* sets up a thinking about the wild yet conceivable extremes of monologue more generally. And yet it does not fully reach the potential I pursue in the name of the theatre of anger. The limits of the performance of the monologue here are drawn by the indifference and ultimate unmarkedness of the young, white, male actors in the roles of the nameless performers who offend the audience in Handke's play. What if the raging monologue not only disturbed but also asserted ways of being and even identity at the site of this disturbance?

There is a rich archive of theatre history that explores and engages the radicalness of the monologue and its noisy capacity to pull apart repressive social and political structures at their seams. The monologue has been taken up as a feminist device that extends Brechtian gestural possibility and challenges hegemonic significatory practices.[84] As Elin Diamond teaches us, "[f]eminist practice that seeks to expose or mock the strictures of gender usually uses some version of the Brechtian A-effect. That is, by alienating (not simply rejecting) iconicity, by foregrounding the expectation of resemblance, the ideology of gender is exposed and thrown back to the spectator."[85] But the matter of exposure and confrontation that most interests me here is not the alienation of text and body or its attendant strategy of de-essentializing gender and body; it is something much more basic than that. The performative qualities of the monologue become most striking when identities are not set at a distance but *are* the expressivities of a situation. This is not a Brechtian or even Handke-inspired performance of the actor as actor (playing the role), such as in *Publikumsbeschimpfung*, but a performance that also asserts the ontological effectivity of "I *am* here" and "I *am* speaking." For minoritized performers this is a powerful assertion. The theatre of anger is a space where under-represented voices are heard. As practitioners of postmigrant theatre repeatedly state, it does not suffice that theatres might have plays that touch on postmigrant topics in their repertoire; there also need to be postmigrant performers in their ensembles.[86] The same stands for the theatre of anger.

The monologue has re-entered the theatre (most prominently through the influence of performance art and cultural performance) as a tool of identity, subjectivity, and affirmation. To speak in monologue (both as a single actor or as a chorus, as in *Publikumsbeschimpfung* and in Salzmann's *Zucken*, explored in chapter 5) is to speak by and for oneself. If, as Geis holds, monologue has an autobiographical imperative insofar as it is both theatrical and personal, then I would add that it also has a political imperative.[87] It is about asserting an identity that needs constant asserting, because it is not white, cisgender, male, and heterosexual. Marvin Carlson contends that this was the incitement of early cultural performance. "The performance of identity, often with the use of autobiographical material, became one of the most common forms of performance art from the early 1970s onward. Its frequent concern with providing a voice to previously silenced individuals or groups often involved such work in social and cultural issues as well."[88] One paradigmatic example of this is Eve Ensler's 1993 episodic play *The Vagina Monologues*, which contains a series of monologues performed by women about their sexual history, desires, and their relationships to their vagina. Despite the play's representational problems, in particular with its focus on cisgender women and culturally determined depictions of sexual violence, it is premised on the powerful nexus of the theatrical, the personal, and the political that imposes and orients the present study on the theatre of anger. Indeed, Feridun Zaimoğlu and Günter Senkel's *Schwarze Jungfrauen*, discussed in chapter 3, has been called a radical Muslim remake of *The Vagina Monologues*. The dramatic monologue's concentration of performance's vociferous enunciatory force makes it a fitting place of analysis for the theatre of anger. It is on this site where identity is powerfully articulated and subjectivity is amplified.

In the first part of this chapter we explored anger and conceptions of it as a complex object of knowledge. We drew on sources ranging from early philosophical discourse to radical Black feminist theory to show that anger can be analysed and recovered for affirmative politics and the pursuit of social justice. The application of such a perspective led the chapter through an extant history of civil rights politics and protest. From protest to theatre, the latter parts of the chapter revealed the participatory relational aesthetics of anger – its commitment to both politics and art. Anger in theatre is also nothing new. It harks back to a long history of affective-political theatre and performance in the West and beyond. Its force of refusal and its push towards social justice in a transational context is what sets theatrical anger apart in important ways. Techniques such as the monolgue are reshaped and given new significance. This chapter has sought to offer philosophical, historical, and formal (theatrical) grounding to this study of the theatre of anger in a manner that makes way for close analyses of its plays.

Bringing anger and the raging monologue into the context of contemporary transnational German theatre gives it shape and definition within and beyond the politics of identity. The following chapter proceeds with an analysis of *Get Deutsch or Die Tryin'*, which manifests the ethos of the theatre of anger in its performance of a young Turkish man who attempts to obtain German citizenship. In one long monologue, the protagonist lashes out in anger at his absent father. But the tentacles of his anger reach much further than this singular narrative of generational conflict. The play ushers in a thinking with and a commitment to a broad scope of transcultural performances of anger in postunification Germany. This contextualization reads the theatre of anger in a longer tradition of political art and performance. The art and performance network Kanak Attak may be cited as the more overtly political and mixed performance precursor of the theatre of anger. A comparison of the two throws the nuanced affective and political tenors of the latter into relief. As a means of setting up subsequent chapters, which focus on specific plays and artists by way of individualized themes and forms of anger, the following chapter offers a more localized context with an exploration of recent historical developments and political influences within the German space.

Chapter Two

Get Deutsch or Die Tryin'; or, Confronting a History of Exclusion and Violence

You should be angry. You must not be bitter.
Bitterness is like cancer. It eats upon the host.
It doesn't do anything to the object of its displeasure.
So use that anger. You write it. You paint it. You dance it.
You march it. You vote it. You do everything about it.
You talk it. Never stop talking it.

Maya Angelou[1]

Necati Öziri is an angry playwright. Anger is his creative power, his affective-political impetus. If he is the "Angry Young Man" of Germany, then his 2017 play *Get Deutsch or Die Tryin'* is his pièce de résistance. With this play Öziri transports his anger towards Germany and its treatment of migrants onto the stage. The imperative of the title of Öziri's play speaks to a long postwar transnational history of the challenges and vicissitudes of migration, citizenship, and integration. Until 2000, obtaining citizenship as a non-ethnic German was almost inconceivable, as citizenship laws had been hitherto based on the principle of *jus sanguinis* (the right of blood). If one was not ethnically German, one could not be German. In the exclusive construct of national identity, being German presented itself as an impossibility to most migrants. The proposal to adjust this law in 1999 by the Social Democrat Party (SPD) to allow long-time residents of Germany to obtain citizenship through *jus soli* (the right of soil) was met with intense, widespread debate. Even at the turn of the twenty-first century, many Germans did not want to give up their ethno-national notion of what it meant to be German.

The denial of citizenship is the denial of rights: it is the denial to vote and participate in the political life of a country, a state, and a community; it is the denial of free movement; it is the denial of the right to assemble and associate; it is the denial of unrestricted access to the job market; and it is the denial of the right to become a civil servant. In an official capacity, noncitizens living in Germany were legally, politically, and socially marginalized and excluded not only from the national fold, but also from universal human rights. For large groups of migrant workers, who went to both East and West Germany in the postwar decades and chose to stay, the impossibility to become naturalized citizens was a hindrance that they had no choice but to pass on to their children. This became the stigma of being a "migrant," a national status underpinned by a certain transitoriness, a perceived otherness. Fatima El-Tayeb explains it as a systematically ascribed "flat, one-dimensional existence in which she or he always has just arrived."[2] The terms second- and third-generation migrant are still commonly used to describe children and grandchildren of migrants. How can someone who is born in a country and has lived nowhere else be conceived of as a "migrant" to that country?

This chapter begins with this history as it is dramatized by Öziri's *Get Deutsch or Die Tryin'*, in a production by director Sebastian Nübling. The play takes up the struggles of Arda Yılmaz, a so-called second-generation migrant in Germany and son of Turkish parents. This premise already calls to mind a thick history of structural discrimination and criminalization.[3] At the age of eighteen, Arda undertakes the daunting challenge of obtaining citizenship. In the meantime, his older sister moves out and his friends gradually disappear. Bojan is deported, Danny goes underground, and Savaş tragically dies. Arda is thrust into a state of loneliness and loss. He is angry. *Get Deutsch or Die Tryin'* is the first play I take up in this study because it accounts for the history of migration and marginalization from which the theatre of anger emerged and to which it responds. Here this response is in the form of an angry energy that is also sonic. The play is framed by the pounding of a drum. From *Get Deutsch or Die Tryin'* I explore the 1990s, that decade between German unification and the relaxation of citizenship laws, when things came to a head. The pogroms against migrants throughout Germany in the early 1990s, to which many politicians turned a blind eye, and which I will address in detail later in the chapter, exposed the deeper issues of racism and its ramifications. In my contention, if the theatre of anger draws influence from earlier cultural production, it is especially the political performance work of Kanak Attak, a loosely connected hip-hop, media, art, and performance group of mostly second-generation "migrants," which foregrounded confrontation in a response to the violence of the early 1990s and the gnawing presence of racism in postunified German society. This teleology of politics, violence, and cultural resistance brings us finally to the emergence of postmigrant theatre, and to the theatre of anger in particular.

Within this context, *Get Deutsch or Die Tryin'* both sets up this broader study and is opened up as a performance of anger that speaks to a history of exclusion and violence in Germany. If any play sets the tone for a study about the theatre of anger, then it is this one. Taking its title from American rapper 50 Cent's 2003 debut album, "Get Rich or Die Tryin'," which was also later made into a film by the same name, *Get Deutsch or Die Tryin'* is a theatrical album of hip-hop, soul, and violence. So much is encapsulated in this title alone: the ironic injunction of German citizenship is a privilege apparently worth dying for, yet almost impossible to achieve. This play offers an incisive portrait of a life of frustration and anger. It is about living in a country and in a language that do not belong to you because that is what you have consistently been told. The American title's influence also has a bearing on the play's overall structure and form. In Öziri's text, each scene is referred to as a "track" – a song.

The promotional image for *Get Deutsch or Die Tryin'* features the main actor, Dimitrij Schaad, who plays Arda, banging on a broken drum (figure 2.1). On his face is a scowl. He is wearing an old-fashioned suit, and behind him is the Berlin downtown cityscape with high-rises and advertisements, among them Checkpoint Charlie featured prominently. The allusion to Günter Grass's renowned postwar novel *Die Blechtrommel* (*The Tin Drum*), and Volker Schlöndorff's film adaptation thereof, is evident. Schaad's own reputation as the enfant terrible of the Maxim Gorki Theatre is notable in this regard. From his role in Yael Ronen's *The Situation* (premiere 2015) and *A Walk on the Dark Side* (premiere 2018) to Sasha Marianna Salzmann's *Wir Zöpfe* (*We Braids*, premiere 2015) and *Meteoriten* (*Meteorites*, premiere 2016), and András Dömötör's adaptation of Maxim Gorki's play *Die Letzten* (*The Last Ones*, premiere 2018), Schaad is a celebrated ensemble member known for his angry characters and his ability to deliver scathing monologues, not to mention his penchant for improvisation and angry asides. The picaresque figure Oskar in *Die Blechtrommel*, who uses his drum to resist and subvert in the Nazi period, fits Schaad's angry performance of Arda Yılmaz in *Get Deutsch or Die Tryin'*. Is Arda an Oskar for the present? Perhaps. But such an interpretation does not speak to the complex layers of the play and its critique of the ideologically impenetrable bulwark of German national culture and identity. Beyond Grass, echoes of Brecht remind us that drumming can be both subversive and militaristic in the theatre.

2.1 Promotional poster for *Get Deutsch or Die Tryin'*. Image © Esra Rotthoff.

The Mise-en-Scène of Anger

The drum kit is one of the few fixtures on the otherwise sparse set, which keeps with the minimalist leanings of set designer Magda Willi. One of the principal set designers for the Maxim Gorki Theatre, Willi is also responsible for the set designs for *Verrücktes Blut*, *Aufstand: Monolog eines wütenden Künstlers* (*Rebellion: Monologue of an Angry Artist*) and *Zucken*, three plays I consider later in the book. In *Get Deutsch or Die Tryin'* the set consists of almost labyrinthine walls painted in faded lounge colours and unevenly set together to create a deep, cavernous space reminiscent of a shabby underground club, which ensconces the mise-en-scène in a claustrophobic feel. Upstage on a leather armchair, set back in this deep space, Schaad/Arda sits in the shadows with legs crossed and observes. A muted industrial beat can be heard from an unknown source. Another performer enters and takes a seat at the drums and immediately begins to play. The performer, Almut Lustig, is the drummer and has no other role in the play. Thus, sonically, the play begins with a three-minute-long drum solo. The upbeat tempo of the hi-hat and the bass drum make the drumming sound like club beats, giving it a '90s house music energy that reflects the space of the set. The changing but repetitive beats on the snare drum break the monotonicity. But there is otherwise no accompanying sound. This powerfully minimalist beating of the drums is then followed by a minute-long pause, and then the drumming begins again for another two minutes. During this rhythmic introduction, performers appear in energetic bursts and then disappear offstage again. In ritualistic manner, Arda's drunken mother, Ümran, played by Pinar Erincin, crawls to the minifridge positioned stage left and takes a gulp from a clear bottle, each time increasingly agitated by the fridge door, which stubbornly refuses to close. Erincin is also known in the contemporary theatre world for her sharp tongue and angry performances (*Schwarze Jungfrauen* [*Black Virgins*], *Jenseits – Bist du Schwul oder bist du Türke?* [*Beyond – Are You Gay or Are You Turkish?*, 2008], *Verrücktes Blut*, and *Schepperende Antworten auf drohende Fragen* [*Clashing Responses to Threatening Questions*, 2012]). This high-intensity opening sets the tone of aggression, energy, and anger so characteristic of Nübling's style. An in-house director at the Maxim Gorki Theatre since 2013, his plays routinely foreground the energy of bodies and their kinesthetic possibilities. Dancing, running, jumping, and corporeal violence saturate the stage with physicality and potential. Nübling lets bodies speak through movement. He is, according to one critic, the "Körperkommunikator" (body communicator).[4] Anger is legibly enlivened on the body in a manner that echoes the Laocoön. Muscles are taut and gestures often appear jerky. There is no fluidity to Nübling's choreography. The performers are something akin to the Laocoön on speed. Nübling's direction provides Öziri's angry text with a raging bodily performance and praxis. Further, it reminds us that history can be embodied.

Roughly six minutes into the performance, an epically long monologue begins, what the daily newspaper *Berliner Zeitung* has referred to as another "therapeutische Wutrede" (therapeutic monologue of rage) at the Maxim Gorki Theatre.[5] Öziri has likewise referred to his play as one long monologue of rage. Indeed, the play consists almost entirely of monologue with only occasional moments of dialogue and fictionalized flashbacks, as Arda, on the eve of his eighteenth birthday, attempts to piece his life together. But while this extant speech act of rage may offer some therapeutic release, it is by no means cathartic. If anything, Arda becomes increasingly angry as the play progresses. If anger is a speech act for social justice, then the raging monologue is the sustained performance of assertive political subjectivity that confronts. I am here. I am speaking. I have a bone to pick. You will listen or you will leave.

Dressed in a magenta velour suit with a purple undershirt and pointed-toe dress shoes during the entirety of the play, Arda's self-presentation seems at first tongue in cheek. Is he not a walking cliché of a young Turkish man? Early on, a random series of physical attacks on Arda as the expression of a history of hate and violence, causes the seam in the crotch of his pants to rip. Whether this was intentional or not, it breaks down the cliché and demonstrates its superficiality as it literally comes apart at the seams. More than anything, though, Arda's monologue cuts in a manner that often overtakes humour. "Stell dir vor, du bist tot" ("Imagine you are dead") is the first line uttered. "Stell dir vor, du bist tot und ich bin auf deiner Beerdigung" ("Imagine you are dead, and I am at your funeral") follows.[6] Uttered with a tone of scathing abjection, the opening of the monologue rhetorically confronts Arda's absent father Murat, played by Taner Şahintürk, who only appears fifty minutes into the play and has minimal lines. But *Get Deutsch or Die Tryin'* is not simply about personal, familial, or generational conflict. Nor is it a long, embittered, filial monologue to a father as an indictment for his absence and neglect. What several critics have called the "Bitterkeit" (bitterness) of the play, I reassess as anger.[7] In Maya Angelou's powerful epigraphic charge above, a clear distinction is drawn between bitterness and anger, in favour of the latter as a creative and mobilizing force. In Angelou's words, anger incites creative processes, such as writing, painting, and dancing, as well as political processes, such as marching, voting, acting, and speaking. Bitterness, on the other hand, hinders; it becomes *ressentiment*, that hostile sense of frustration that is categorically displaced and repressed. While, according to Friedrich Nietzsche, *ressentiment* can also be a creative force, it is ultimately a negative one, and incapable of addressing the source of injustice.[8] Pankaj Mishra offers an updated definition of *ressentiment*:

> An existential resentment of other people's being, caused by an intense mix of envy and sense of humiliation and powerlessness, *ressentiment*, as it lingers and deepens, poisons civil society and undermines political liberty,

> and is presently making for a global turn to authoritarianism and toxic forms of chauvinism.[9]

But Mishra does not distinguish between *ressentiment* and anger. Perceiving the injustice that lies at the roots of *ressentiment*, he fails to recognize anger's capacity to also address this and to take us in directions that do not lead solely to "toxic forms of chauvinism." This is not the path taken by Arda. Despite the broader political issues that weigh on his fate as a German-born Turk, sans-papiers, with an absconded father and an alcoholic mother, this play refuses to pathologize Arda's anger.

Sadistic encounters with immigration officers at the Ausländeramt (immigration office) underscore the reality of what it means to be Turkish (and without a passport) in Germany. Arda applies for German citizenship. In one scene during the play, he is questioned by the immigration officer Herr Kozminski. The officer is played by three different actors, who tirelessly assault Arda with questions in an attempt to catch him unawares and without all of the necessary documents. They individually enumerate documents *ad absurdum* that Arda should provide, and all demonstrate frustration at his preparedness. Among these required documents is even an "eidesstattliche Verschollenheitserklärung" (sworn declaration of presumed death) of his father, which Arda must sign. "Ich habe dein Leben für meine Staatsbürgerschaft getauscht" ("I traded your life for my citizenship"), he declares to his absent father.[10] Yet all three sets of interrogation end with the oblique statement, uttered gleefully by each immigration officer, that "da fehlt noch etwas" ("something is still missing").[11] The scene is humorous in its absurdity and elicited laughs from the audience, in particular when one officer asks Arda some general knowledge questions, such as "Wie oft wird Deutschland in der Bibel erwähnt?" (How often is Germany mentioned in the Bible?) The answer: "Tausend sechs hundert achtzig mal in der Form des Paradies" ("One thousand six hundred and eighty times in the form of Paradise").[12] Yet the veiled truth that this scene bears in its depiction of the ludicrous challenges certain communities face to become legal, political, and social subjects in Germany is altogether enraging.

Finally, Arda is granted his citizenship, but only once he offers written evidence of his linguistic abilities in German. He speaks his written statement in the form of a self-evidently presented monologue:

> Ich ficke deine Tochter bis sie arabisch spricht. Ich mache deinen Sohn drogenabhängig, klaue ihm den Praktikumplatz und verkaufe seine Organe auf dem Turkenmarkt. Ich breche nachts den Stern von deinem Benz und trage ihn zu meiner Halbmondkette. Ich will kein Arzt oder Anwalt

> werden. Ich werde Superstar oder arbeitslos. Ich bin der deutsche feuchte Traum deutscher feuchter Frauen.[13]

> I will fuck your daughter until she speaks Arabic. I will make your son addicted to drugs, steal his internship spot, and sell his organs on the Turkish market. I will break off the star from your (Mercedes) Benz at night and wear it with my half-moon necklace. I don't want to be a doctor or a lawyer. I will become a superstar or unemployed. I am the German wet dream of all wet German women.

A barrage of clichés is pounded out in one breath. All Turkish men must fit the stereotype before they can be recognized by the state. Criminalized, hypersexualized, objectified, they must confirm the prejudices to which they are constantly subject. Arda comments at one point that the troubles he faces at the *Ausländeramt* are part of "sein Erbe" (his inheritance), the same way that the label "migrant" is the inheritance of second and third generations in Germany. History and trauma of discrimination can be inherited.

The play sets up a confrontation between Arda and his father, who in all likelihood is still alive, and the assignment of accountability. Arda's father, an alleged leftist asylum seeker from Turkey, goes to Germany after the 1980 military coup, where he meets Arda's mother. They marry and have two children. Before the second, Arda, is born, the father, Murat, returns to Turkey, where he faces certain imprisonment for his involvement in a failed terrorist attempt. Why does he abandon his family in Germany and his ill-paid work on the assembly line of a slaughterhouse? Why are prison and torture better options? This open question becomes stuck in our throats. Perhaps Arda's father did not want to "get Deutsch or die tryin'." Arda's father is presented as a rather sad figure in the play. In a closing encounter between father and son, an attempt at reconciliation on the part of the father is thrown back in his face. His gesture of embrace is repelled by a violent shove from Arda. It is in fact the father who is abandoned onstage at the close of the play. Seated at a table alone, his eyes are visibly moist as he attempts restraint. The drumbeat returns. Then there is a gradual fade-out and finally a cut to black and silence.

Despite its humorous moments, its energetic playfulness, and its range of sartorial silliness, from Arda's magenta suit to the carnivalesque New Year's costumes, *Get Deutsch or Die Tryin'* is an angry play that explores a history of political, social, and physical violence. In many ways, it is also deeply personal, despite Öziri's professed abhorrence of autobiography as a genre. Öziri's father was also a political refugee from Turkey who fled to Germany and later abandoned his family. Despite being born in Germany, Öziri, like Arda, also did not become a citizen until he was eighteen. This meant that he could not travel freely and regularly encountered problems with public authorities. He never felt at home in Germany. As the former artistic director of the Studio Я and active predominantly as a dramaturg at the Maxim Gorki Theatre and at the Berliner Festspiele, where he directs the International Forum of the *Theatertreffen*, Öziri finds creative outlets for his anger and his politics. *Get Deutsch or Die Tryin'* emerged within the collaborative framework *Flucht, die mich bedingt* (*Flight that Determines Me*), a writing project initiated by Maxi Obexer and Sasha Marianna Salzmann through the New Institute for Dramatic Writing (NIDS) and in collaboration with the Maxim Gorki Theatre and the Studio Я.

Although *Get Deutsch or Die Tryin'* is one of the more recently produced plays explored within this book's frame, its narrative speaks to the historical, political, and cultural influences of a theatre of anger, which I pursue in the balance of this chapter. The theatre of anger is a response to historical and contemporary conditions of injustice, in particular the injustices faced by "noncitizens" or minoritized subjects in Germany. It is a response to a history of denied rights, marginalization, and violence. It is a refusal to go along with this course of history, and it is a demand for change. In *Get Deutsch or Die Tryin'*, the question of why one would willfully return to a place from which one flees, what poet Warsan Shire has powerfully called "the mouth of a shark,"[14] or more specifically, why one would leave West Germany in the 1980s to return to a post-coup Turkey and face seventeen years of prison and torture cuts like knife. At the close of the play, Arda offers the suggestive response that what is seventeen years in prison compared to a lifetime of flight. But the anger that courses through this play is not entirely negating; the play even concludes manifesto-like in its forbidding affirmation of change:

Es kommt der Tag, da werden wir gehört.
Es kommt der Tag, da sind wir frei.
Es kommt der Tag, da werden wir gebraucht.
Es kommt der Tag, da kommen wir an.
Es kommt der Tag, da werden wir gehört.
Es kommt der Tag, da sind wir frei.
Es kommt der Tag, da werden wir gebraucht.
Es kommt der Tag, da sind wir zu Hause.[15]

The day will come when we are heard.
The day will come when we are free.

> The day will come when we are needed.
> The day will come when we arrive. / The day will come when we are home.

There is a revolutionary tone to these words and their structure of repetition. Delivered hastily, almost frantically by Arda, the performance combines a sense of anger, energy, and hope. It is a call for resistance and confrontation, but also a potential call for change to the dominant narrative of nonarrival. However, onstage Arda does not utter these words with repetitive conviction. He cites a slightly shortened version of this text and frames it with the qualifying line "Ich denke immer" ("I always think"), so that the hopefulness of this proclamation is caught in suspension, not unlike Lauren Berlant's neoliberal concept of cruel optimism, which she defines as "a projection of sustaining but unworkable fantasy."[16] The theatre of anger does not trade anger for hope, and certainly not for some kind of cruel optimism and its deceptive apparatus of lateral agency. Hope is part of anger, and the promise of this play and of others in this repertoire lies in staying with one's anger and giving it breathing space.

Art Given to Angry Politics (1): Kanak Attak

I trace the history and the development of the theatre of anger in Germany, which, I reiterate, is not synonymous with all postmigrant theatre, back to a historical moment. The early 1990s was ushered in both with a newly unified Germany and a period of intense, racialized violence. Migrant and minority communities came under attack, and the rest of the nation responded with relative indifference. This was a moment when the hope of migration was thrown into crisis. Not only was it proven that playing by the rules of majoritarian society does not bring one into the national fold, but "noncitizens" were flung into an unbounded state of nonsovereignty and precarity. Minoritized Germans and second- and third-generation "migrants" struck back with political art and performance. As I explored in the previous chapter, anger is always attributive; it always responds to something. This creative snap of anger in the 1990s crystallizes the inception of a movement that would later incite the work of the theatre of anger.

Without reducing this theatre paradigm to a singular enunciation of embittered historical reception, a brutish negating of *ressentiment*, or just plain old bad faith, the political attribution of anger helps to avert the risk of losing sight of the cause and reason of one's anger, so frequently read and undermined by others as unreasonable, unattributed, and ex nihilo. Sara Ahmed reminds us that even attributed anger in response to racism and sexism can be dismissed as unreasonable and motivated not by real issues but simply as anger for anger's sake.[17] The theatre of anger works against this. Indeed, "anger," as Sue J. Kim writes, "is historically situated. Just as no one is afraid, happy, or sad in a vacuum, nobody is ever just angry in a vacuum."[18] Situating these moments of crisis and violence in recent German transnational history, when anger can certainly be deemed a justified affective response to hate, the following locates and contextualizes art and theatre within the sociopolitical movements in Germany from which they also emerge. On offer is a brief overview of the creative inception of the theatre of anger as influenced by the political performance art movement Kanak Attak, and read with a series of national and historical events from the 1990s to the present.

The period following German unification was a tumultuous one. Contrary to much international media coverage, these were not excessively celebratory times for all. As history readily reveals to anyone who bothers to look, there was a surge of right-wing, racialized violence scattered throughout the newly established republic. Between 1989 and 1994, arson, vandalism, physical brutality, and murder seethed through political and affective promises of a unified Germany. One trace of this taxonomy of violence and hate that haunts the national narrative can be seen in a photograph of a burned-out shell of a two-storey family home resting in the bucolic, unsuspecting village landscape of Solingen, in the industrial Ruhr Area (figure 2.2). This haunting is something akin to Marx and Engel's proposed aporia, as something that is in fact omnipresent yet goes unheeded – that which is blindingly visible and deafening loud. But the real spectre of this photograph in Solingen is the conservative Chancellor Helmut Kohl, Germany's father of unification, who was absent. A sign that this event was unworthy of real political regard, or perhaps too incongruent to the dreams of a united Germany of the future, Kohl's absence is documented. The home, once occupied by Turkish migrants, was destroyed in an arson attack by neo-Nazis on May 29, 1993. Five people died; three were children under the age of twelve. But this scene was no anomaly. The town names Hoyerswerda (1991), Rostock-Lichtenberg (1992), Mölln (1992), Solingen (1993)[19] (and these are just the best-known) have become reminders of hate and violence, what many have attempted to explain away as vagaries of a historical narrative of modern nationhood and national identity and not its crucible. In the same year the horrors of Solingen occurred, Kohl's Christian Democratic Party (CDU) passed two anti-immigrant laws. The first was to uphold, with only nominal latitude, the citizenship law of *jus sanguinis*, which, as mentioned earlier in this chapter, decreed

2.2 Racially motivated arson attack in Solingen, 1993. Image © Rainer Henkel / CC BY-SA 4.0 (via Wikimedia Commons).

by law the incompatibility of non-ethnically-German Germans.[20] This was followed by the infamous *Asylkompromiss* (asylum agreement) in 1993, which placed even more severe restrictions on asylum claimants in and to Germany.[21] While parts of civil society responded to the violence in Solingen and other places with mass demonstrations and candlelight vigils across the republic, this support failed to bring about any kind of real change.

The explosion of hate crimes that ushered in the history of a new era for Germany regalvanized the sense of precarity among migrants, asylum seekers, and Germans of colour (at the time more than twenty per cent of the population). In her celebrated poem "blues in Schwarzweiß" (1995), May Ayim gave voice and another perspective to this historical moment when one border (the border between East and West) was replaced by another internal one:

das wieder vereinigte Deutschland
feiert sich wieder 1990

ohne ImmigrantInnen flüchtlinge jüdisch und schwarze Menschen
es feiert in intimem kreis

a reunited Germany
celebrates itself in 1990
without its immigrants, refugees, Jewish and Black people
it celebrates in its intimate circle[22]

As articulated in this stanza, the heady mood of history turned a blind eye to these cumbersome new fault lines in society. But this period of right-wing violence and the official disregard of it did force a reckoning among first- and second-generation "migrants," who bore the shock of this extant hate in a land they had hoped to call their own. Étienne Balibar has written extensively about the internal borders within postnational Europe, put in the service of stigmatizing, repressing, and containing the "populations whose presence within European societies is nonetheless increasingly massive and legitimate."[23]

In the postunification era, Kanak Attak was one of the first and more visible countercultural movements against racism to emerge from within culturally diverse communities. Tom Cheesman notably described this phenomenon as the linkage of cultural action and political consciousness, which broke with identity politics.[24] But at its core was the drive for the self-empowerment of migrants.[25] Kanak Attak was a loosely knit Germany-wide activist network consisting of mostly second-generation "migrants," including Manuela Bojadžijev, Imran Ayata, Mark Terkessidis, Nicola Duric, Micho Willenbrücher and many others, whose principal aim was to engage in antiracist performance and artistic acts in order to raise awareness. These ran the gamut from culture jamming to television-style infotainment, cabaret, performance, readings, music, discussion, and subversive documentary literature. Most resonant was the discursive work of the group effected in its name, which was an important speech act of subversion, recuperation, subjectivity, and an angry rejection unto itself. The term "Kanak" is a pejorative and racist term used to connote people of Turkish and Middle Eastern background, but it has been used as a derogatory term for "foreigner," more generally. Fatima El-Tayeb and others have untangled its etymological history.[26] The term is a residue of German colonial presence in the South Pacific in the mid to late 1800s. Its use in German vernacular came as the equally negative appellation of Pacific Islanders, apparently co-opted from local vernacular. It entered more mainstream slang with a broadening of its semantic scope in the 1960s, contemporaneously with the arrival of labour migrants from southern European countries and Turkey. The recuperation of this harmful speech as performed by Kanak Attak demonstrates an act of disidentification, what José Esteban Muñoz has described as "a critical negotiation in which a subject who has been hailed by injurious speech, a name, or a label, reterritorializes that speech act and the marking that such speech produces to a self."[27] Reterritorializing language is an emancipatory act of self-determination with a long and rich tradition. The author Feridun Zaimoğlu, who was loosely associated with Kanak Attak, and has been called the Turkish Malcolm X in Germany, percussively sums up the operative role of reappropriating "Kanake" as a mechanism of political community and power, albeit via a negative dialectic:

> The feeling of playing in the league of the damned has united all of them [immigrants] in the conviction that they must stand up for themselves against the culturally hegemonic expectations. The foundation of this community is still negative self-confidence as it articulates itself superficially in seeming self-recrimination: Kanake! This derogatory term becomes a word of recognition and identification that binds these *Lumpenethnier* [lumpen ethnos] together.[28]

Marxian in its tone and choice of vocabulary, the language applied by Zaimoğlu also invokes postcolonial discourse from Frantz Fanon to Achille Mbembe with a dash of performative irony.

The weight and density of "Kanake," as a word that at once wounds and empowers, certainly calls for address. But what draws my interest to Kanak Attak is the anger that effervescently rises and resists. The act encapsulated in the word "Attak," which is not simply a synecdoche for this labour of reterritorialization, nor simply a rhyming addendum to "Kanak," offers its own display and exertion of aggression that directs itself outward. This effusive application of such a combative verb transmuted into a noun of action invokes the anger at the heart of so many antiracist struggles. Yet the charge of this discursive anger, which certainly never exploded in physical violence or aggression, is nevertheless frequently skirted by supporters and disparaged by detractors. Indeed, the causal link between the hate and violence that rocked early unification and the radical antiracist backlash of Kanak Attak is seldom drawn. Admittedly, the network was only conceived of in 1997, seven years after unification and, as El-Tayeb observes, through the medium of hip-hop music.[29] Further, the playful subversiveness of Kanak Attak, most famously conveyed through their "Kanak TV" performances and so-called man-on-the-street interviews, does not ostensibly operate through a politics or an aesthetics of anger in the way that direct activism might. This is most evident when we compare Kanak Attak to activist movements, such as the militant anti-fascist group "Antifa" (Die Antifaschistische Aktion) or the Kreuzberg SO 36 gang "36 Boys."[30] The latter group did form in direct response to the rise of extreme right-wing violence that swelled in the early 1990s. By contrast, Kanak Attak presented a much more subtly sophisticated approach that was routed through culture and performance:

> [W]e compete for a new attitude of migrants of all generations that we want to bring on stage, independently and without compromise. Whoever believes that we celebrate a Potpourri out of Ghetto-Hip Hop and other clichés will be surprised. We sample, change and adapt different political and cultural drifts that all operate from oppositional positions. We go back to a mixture of theory, politics and cultural practice. This song is ours.[31]

Yet Kanak Attak speaks from a place of existential experience of racialization and discrimination that does not undermine the critical action of mass bodies protesting in the street, but bears an ontological realism where the biological, social, cultural, linguistic, and ritualistic converge. A lived experience of racism and violence is placed at the centre of their work, a centre that pulses with anger. The affectivity of Kanak Attak is not played out as raw emotion; in fact this approach is even ironized. On the contrary, it is affectively distilled through a complex feedback loop of presentation, expectation, projection, and re-presentation, in which performers also subvert accusations of overproximity and irrationality. Kanak Attak uses anger to expose and respond to the realities of violence and racism. And it refuses to let go of anger so that white Germans may simply forget and move on. Ahmed would call this the labour of the feminist killjoy, one who does not let people off easily.[32] She indirectly links the feminist killjoy to the figure of the "melancholic migrant," whose "anger, pain, misery (all understood as forms of bad faith insofar as they won't let go of something that is presented to have gone) become 'our terror.'"[33] An angry migrant all too easily becomes a "would-be-terrorist" in the national imaginary. Kanak Attak not only refuses to forget or move on; it also throws these invidious fears back in the faces of the white majority.

In 1997, the popular weekly magazine *Der Spiegel* ran a provocative cover story, with the egregiously racist title *Gefährlich fremd: Das Scheitern der multikulturellen Gesellschaft* (Dangerously Foreign: The Failure of the Multicultural Society). The cover image featured a woman of colour holding aloft a large red flag – indistinct, but likely Turkish. Her fierce attention is directed before her, and she seems to be shouting vociferously. Her mouth is agape; the veins on her neck stand out as she is caught mid-utterance. She likewise appears to be captured in movement, in a protest march. This person appears angry. Coupled with the titular headline and additional background images of purportedly delinquent male youths brandishing a weapon on one side and young girls in headscarves studying what appears to be the Qur'an on the other, the figure of the woman becomes an unequivocal figure of danger and rage. This figure is reminiscent of Ahmed's feminist killjoy, an important component of Ahmed's treatment of anger in both *The Promise of Happiness* and *Living a Feminist Life*. For Ahmed the feminist killjoy is someone who is not afraid of calling out people and institutions for antifeminist (or other oppressive) behaviour or language, even if this means creating uncomfortable situations, disturbing the peace, or going against the status quo. The feminist killjoy is not afraid of being recognized as a feminist, that is, as someone who doesn't just go along to get along. But she is not simply a killjoy in the face of antifeminism; she is also a killjoy within feminist circles. She is not afraid of killing "feminist joy" when it is exclusionary or supports forms of racism. Often unpopular, and sometimes reviled, the feminist killjoy seeks a more just world, in which everyone can flourish.[34] The image of the protesting woman of colour on the cover of *Der Spiegel* appears to be all of these things. However, there is an attempt to use this identity against her, to read her motivations and goals otherwise. In Ahmed's words, the woman is presented as "fantasy figure that produces its own effects," and is inspired by the errant notion, which I raise here again, that something is wrong with this figure and not that something is wrong.[35]

In 1999 Kanak Attak resignifies this blatantly racist and criminalizing cover and creates a poster to advertise a film series event in Kreuzberg SO 36 (figure 2.3). In this recasting, objects in the images are circled, including the prominent vein exuding from the woman's neck and her fist clenching the flag pole. By reemploying this cover page, and deliberately drawing attention to the magazine's emphasis on the gestures of the woman that would indicate her anger and portray it as something "dangerous," something that indeed *endangers* the homogenizing logic of multiculturalism, as indicated in the magazine's original issue title,[36] the creative work of Kanak Attak not only critiques but also recalibrates the original message with added aggression. Now framing the entire cover image in black and white is the title "Kanak Attak," where the name of the magazine would normally be. Set here visually, Kanak Attak offers a performative promise that effectively reappropriates, subverts, and confronts hurtful discriminatory messages that all migrants are violent, religious fundamentalists, and ultimately in

2.3 Kanak Attak 1997 *Der Spiegel* cover reproduction, May 27, 1999. Image courtesy of Michael Willenbücher.

thrall to unattributive anger. The new version criticizes *Der Spiegel* for its representation of anger as simply motivated by a failure to integrate and a failure to adjust to a multicultural society that suits majoritarian opinion, and not by a corroborative sense of injustice.

While Kanak Attak as a network is no longer active, its angry purport continues to offer momentum and purpose to artists such as Öziri, who has referred to his work as "Kanak Attak."[37] The term has entered regular speech and continues to offer a radical label to activist art that is self-determining, angry, and in-yer-face in its approach, in particular from a Turkish German perspective.

Art Given to Angry Politics (2): Theatre of Anger

Shermin Langhoff has spoken of the influence and role of Kanak Attak as a political and performative precursor to postmigrant theatre. Developing as a part of postmigrant theatre, the theatre of anger appropriates this significant teleology of political confrontation and empowerment of minoritized Germans through art and performance. As much as contemporary German theatre, broadly speaking, has a politically leftist, avant-garde, and confrontational history (something I examine at greater length in chapter 4), up until quite recently it has been a culturally specific institution built by white artists and organizational leaders (mostly cisgender, heterosexual, and middle-class males) and for white audiences.[38] As Meropi S. Peponides describes it in the Euro-American context, theatres have long "trade[d] in white culture (which is actually often the absence of culture – a flattening and neutralizing of traditions), and therefore, by default, [have been] socially and politically engaged in upholding the values of white supremacy."[39] This needed to be undone.

Langhoff eventually moved to Berlin in the mid-1990s, via Bursa, Turkey and Nuremberg, Germany, and gradually made the transition from film and television to theatre in the early 2000s. In 2004, with the support of Matthias Lilienthal she curated her first major theatre project at the Hebbel am Ufer (HAU), titled "X Wohnungen Migration," which was the second project of an extensive performance series featuring theatre plays and concerts. For the next four years Langhoff stayed on at the HAU, where some of the initial critical postmigrant plays were produced. These included Feridun Zaimoğlu and Günther Senkel's *Schwarze Jungfrauen*, directed by Neco Çelik (which I explore in the next chapter), and Nurkan Erpulat and Tunçay Kulaoğlu's *Jenseits, bist Du Schwul oder bist Du Türke* (*Beyond – Are You Gay or Are You Turkish*, premiere 2008). The first premiered as part of the 2006 cultural festival *Beyond Belonging*[2] at the HAU, the event that is perceived to have launched postmigrant theatre and, I argue, also the theatre of anger. This new theatre eventually found a more permanent (albeit infrastructurally precarious) space at the Ballhaus Naunynstraβe in 2008 and later at the Maxim Gorki Theatre in 2013 under Langhoff's artistic direction (in collaboration with Jens Hillje). Over the past two decades, other theatres around Germany have also worked to diversify their repertoires and ensembles in important transnational and postmigrant ways, in particular the Schauspielhaus Bochum, which not only has a history with Emine Sevgi Özdamar (1979–1984), but is also one of the few theatres throughout Germany with a culturally diverse permanent ensemble. (This is, for instance, where Dimitrij Schaad got his start.)

Characterized by Langhoff as a "Kampfbegriff" (fighting concept) in its earlier days, postmigrant theatre has been and continues to invoke an aggressive and even confrontational purport that I propose turns on a politics and aesthetics of anger. Many practitioners have since offered the corrective that this theatre is not simply a "Kampfbegriff" or a polemic, but truly a "Kampf" (a fight, a struggle).[40] The incited language of battle aptly distils social truths and calls for a transformation of the theatre space into a metaphoric battlefield, where the ruse of social and cultural homogeneity comes under attack. It echoes and reconfigures

2.4 A promotional pin with the Ballhaus Naunynstraβe logo. Photo by Olivia Landry.

Muñoz's assertion of the significant relation between stage, battlefield, and the social: "the social is both a stage and a battlefield."[41] To paraphrase Langhoff's pugnacious description, the theatre of anger is the dog that barks from the third row.[42] This description also became and remains the visual logo for the Ballhaus Naunynstraβe.

Accounted for in Langhoff's metaphor of the barking dog is the marginalized position of the Ballhaus Naunynstraβe, "in the third row," the place where postmigrant theatre found its footing. Since its reopening in 2008, the Ballhaus Naunynstraβe has survived on nominal financial support from the city of Berlin. The figuration of the barking dog is one of agitation and even anger, unwilling to quietly and unobtrusively recede into the background, unwilling to fall from sight and sound. Also a kind of killjoy, the barking dog disturbs the peace. It loudly reminds us, without ceasing, about the hate and social violence that so often goes unremarked, neatly tucked away from view. As much as this is part of postmigrant theatre's history in Berlin, it is also part of what shapes the theatre of anger. The theatre of anger quite literally confronts its audience with an anger that refuses to accept the conditions of the present and aims to redirect the path of the future voiced in the closing declarative words of Arda in *Get Deutsch or Die Tryin'*. In this sense, the theatre of anger performs political interventions. But its political capacity extends to its spatio-mediality, by way of which theatre becomes an agora, a forum for information and discussion of cultural, social, and political issues within the institution of theatre, that paragon of cultural conservatism and elitism, and outside of theatre in the lived social world of the historical present.

If Kanak Attak was a response to marginalization and racialized violence, which reached a crisis in the decade following German unification, the theatre of anger continues in this tradition. My pursuit of the theatre of anger speaks to Lawrence Grossberg's theory of radical contextualization insofar as I seek to offer a framework to examine the complex set of relations and events that surround and interpenetrate the moments of this theatre's emergence and development in order to understand its significance and effects.[43] From the late 2000s to the present, several national events have impacted the course of the theatre of anger. On the face of it, the 2010 release of Thilo Sarrazin's book *Deutschland schafft sich ab* (*Germany Abolishes Itself*), hardly seems to count as a national event of significance. However, this racist, pseudoscientific book, which egregiously postulated the demise of German society through migration and so-called Islamification, had vast ramifications. Sarrazin's hateful treatise quickly rose to the top of the national bestseller list and was taken up as the mouthpiece for a silent majority.[44] By example, it made open racism socially acceptable. Its detractors justly called it hate speech and some even compared it to Hitler's *Mein Kampf*. Nurkan Erpulat and Dorle Trachternach responded to the book and its national popularity with a play called *Clash*, produced in 2011, which premiered at the Deutsches Theater in Berlin. Similar to *Verrücktes Blut*, which will be examined in chapter 3, *Clash* is a youth play that thematizes integration as a pedagogy by bodily force. The play is a biting satire set in the future at a time when Sarrazin's augury has become reality. Germany has been converted into a planet of the apes. Ironically, Sarrazin himself in the form of a life-size doll is the leader and deus ex machina of this fictional planet, who is literally lowered down to the stage to whisper divinations to his people, which are subsequently interpreted at will. When he is lowered a third and final time, he is apparently dead. This event elicits the indifferent response "shit happens."

One year after the release of Sarrazin's "new National Socialist manifesto," the racially motivated murder series of the self-titled National Socialist Underground (NSU) was uncovered.[45] From 2000–2007 an extreme right-wing terrorist cell murdered ten people: eight Turkish Germans, one Greek German, and a policewoman. In addition, they committed numerous other crimes, including arson and the detonation of nail bombs in immigrant neighbourhoods. The group's declared aim was to kill "foreigners" and "citizens of foreign origin."[46] What was most disturbing about the discovery of this group and their crimes was that for over a decade the local and federal police and the Federal Intelligence Agency did not recognize these crimes as terrorist acts of hate. As a result, individual murders not only went unsolved but were frequently also falsely attributed to the alleged criminal activity of the so-called Turkish mafia of which the victims were indirectly accused of being members. The recognition of this long series of hate crimes and the absolute lack of institutional efficacy to get to the bottom of things, or even care to do so, sent a shockwave through the Turkish German and other minority communities in Germany. Adding insult to injury, the treatment of the murder series in mainstream media was laden with racist language. The series of murders was dubbed both the "Dönermorde" (döner murders) and the "Bosphorusmorde" (Bosphorus murders), expressions that served to both dehumanize and objectify the victims and their families further. From the uncovering of the crime series to its five-year-long trial, which finally came to an end in 2018, much more media attention has been paid to the terrorist group and its three main members (two of whom are now dead) than the victims and their families.

As chance would have it, 2011 also marked the fiftieth anniversary of the arrival of the first Turkish postwar labour migrants to West Germany, in 1961. By the close of 2011, it was evident that even half a century was not sufficient time to transform postwar German society into an open one where diversity could thrive. The Maxim Gorki Theatre has confronted this series of events in various ways. Most significant among the theatrical responses to the NSU and this historical imbrication was the re-production of Nurkan Erpulat and Tunçay Kulaoğlu's 2010 musical play *Lö bal Almanya* as *Lö Grand Bal Almanya: 57 Jahre Scheinehe* (*57 Years of Fictitious Marriage*) in 2018 at the Maxim Gorki Theatre. If the original version addressed fifty years of migration and integration history, the re-production extended its account by nearly a decade to show the historical continuity of marginalization and violence that eventually led to the NSU murders. Despite the play's tone of frothy satire and song, the tragedy of its content and this inveterate through-line to the present (the NSU murders were no anomaly) accosts its audience with moments of anger.

A final devastatingly significant event occurred in October 2017 when the extreme right-wing party, the Alternative for Germany (AfD), took ninety-four seats in the German federal parliament and became the largest opposition party. This was the first time the party even made it into federal parliament. The party line is predicated on racism, anti-Semitism, Islamophobia, and identitarianism. Often referred to as a neo-Nazi party, its presence in parliament continues to be enraging to many, and to the Gorki team in particular. If in 2013 the ostensible ethos of the theatre for a new era was one of common ground, as Langhoff herself has stated,[47] then in 2017 the Maxim Gorki Theatre took a different turn. From November 11 to 26, 2017, it presented its third biannual Herbstsalon (Fall Salon) to usher in a new theatre season. The slogan and theme of this Herbstsalon was "*Desintegriert Euch*!" (De-integrate yourselves!). The fifteen-day event comprised a remarkably wide range of performance pieces, visual art, and discussion panels prepared by roughly 100 artists and artist groups. The salon even left the spatial confines of the theatre and swept through the centre of Berlin. The theme of this salon was not only political, it was about a refusal to participate in the brutal reality of the present. In particular, "*Desintegriert Euch*!" addressed neofascist tendencies in contemporary Germany and Europe. Highlights of the salon included, for example, Banu Cennetoğlu's "Die Liste" ("The List"), which contained information about the 33,293 registered deaths of asylum seekers, refugees, and migrants who lost their lives between 1993 and 2017 in their attempts to find safety and a better future, precisely as a result of the ever-restrictive politics of immigration of Fortress Europe. Forty-eight copies of this long list were posted throughout Berlin. In the Maxim Gorki Theatre proper, the *Tribunal NSU-Komplex auflösen* (Unraveling the NSU Complex), which is an activist alliance dedicated to presenting the missing narratives of the NSU murder series, presented a lengthy bill of indictment. One floor down was an installation piece of a living room by Heinrike Naumann called "Das Reich" ("The Reich"), a mise-en-scène designed to recreate the physical ideology of the so-called "Reichsbürger" (Reich Citizens) of Germany.[48] *Desintegriert Euch!* presented both a protest against the swell of contemporary right-wing politics in Germany and Europe and a refusal to reconcile oneself to this deleterious present as well as to an inheritance of hate, violence, or even simply indifference. If integration is that well-worn path to a homogeneous society in accordance with a single dominant culture and way of life, then *Desintegration* is its dissenting deviation, a physical act of heterogeneity and divergence. Indeed, how does one integrate into a society in which such harrowing acts and politics against humanity are in play? Thus, *Desintegration* is a performance of protest; it is anger showing itself against a fanfare of hate and injustice swelling in our present with the likes of the Alternative for Germany (AfD), Patriotic Europeans Against the Islamization of the Occident (PEGIDA), National Socialist Underground (NSU), and so forth.

The theatre plays that emerged during the season of *Desintegration* at the Maxim Gorki Theatre not only carry the impulse of refusal and confrontation, they perform its labour, for *Desintegration* is not a simple task. It is a mechanism of upheaval and a reseizure of one's culture and history from majoritarian society. Between 2017 and 2018 a welter of plays premiered, which directly or indirectly addressed and performed themes of *Desintegration* and anger, such as Öziri's *Get Deutsch or Die Tryin'*, Sasha Marianna Salzmann's *Zucken* (directed by Sebastian Nübling), discussed in chapter 5, Max Czollek's *Celan mit der Axt* (*Celan with the Axe*, directed by Sapir Heller), Oliver Frljić and Ensemble's *Gorki – Alternative für Deutschland?* (*Gorki – Alternative for Germany?*, directed by Oliver Frljić), Sibylle Berg's *Nach Uns das All – Das Innere Team kennt keine Pause* (*The Universe after Us – The Inner Team Knows No Break*, directed by Sebastian Nübling), Falk Richter's *Verräter* (*Traitors*, directed by Falk Richter), and Suna Gürler and Ensemble's *Stören* (*Bothering*, directed by Suna Gürler). All of these plays inventory histories of failed integration as a refusal to see past or let go of past and recent memories of racism and hate; they represent a refusal to participate in the national game. Many of them are predicated on acts of protest against histories of hate and violence, against histories that hurt. They could all be taken up as important recent examples of a theatre of anger and therefore as further objects of study for the present book.

That such a response to a history and politics of exclusion and violence arrives by way of the theatre and theatrical performance is not to suggest that it becomes simply representational, lost in mimesis. Performance in theatre, compared to performance in real life, has been dismissed as fiction. Focusing on the particularity of language, J.L. Austin argues that performance in theatre should not be taken seriously because it has no illocutionary force.[49] However, others have certainly taken a more inclusive approach to performance in theatre. As Bert O. States proposes, following Jean-Paul Sartre, "[p]erformances may well go on in the theatre but they are *transitive* in nature."[50] That is, in the context of theatre, performance can bear a purpose beyond itself. Considered thus, anger and politics in the theatre might not be taken seriously. Yet theatre, as States further points out, "is [distinct from the other arts] most like life as it is lived in the real world."[51] To be "lived in the real world" is also to assert bearing on the real world. And the theatre of anger has a weighty bearing. It regularly and methodically takes up events and politics of life within and outside the theatre. Inasmuch as this theatre is not a place of escape from the real world, it is also not merely representational. The theatre of anger is not positioned outside of the institutions it seeks to change; it stands in the centre – starting with theatre itself and moving outward. If this theatre were not to be taken seriously beyond its walls, then the Alternative for Germany (AfD) would not have so vehemently sought to have the Maxim Gorki Theatre's funding cut, not to mention that of other theatres with diverse ensembles and repertoires, when it entered the federal parliament.[52] The theatre of anger is a force to be reckoned with.

This chapter's overview of anger as a confrontational affect with a distinct historical, political, social, aesthetic, and performance art lineage in Germany is intended to offer a localized formal framing to this study. A rejoinder to a migration history of exclusion and violence, Öziri's *Get Deutsch or Die Tryin'* offers a tangible and illuminating example of the theatre of anger's project. The chapter exposes and registers the harm and injustice wrought by hate, exclusion, and social violence and calls for change. Germany's postwar migration history gives shape to a heritage of both politics and protest that has had far-reaching consequences. The themes of Öziri's play directly link to the political impulses of Kanak Attak. Presenting Kanak Attak as the precursor of the theatre of anger, the chapter demonstrates the use of anger in art and theatre of the contemporary as a tool that confronts and disturbs. Beyond *Get Deutsch or Die Tryin'*, the theatre of anger is comprised of an important repertoire of plays and performances that demand our attention and closer analysis. With distinctive thematic focus, successive chapters further bring into relief and concretize anger's radical and creative undertaking in a selection of theatrical performances, beginning in the following chapter with the most eminent plays of the theatre of anger, Feridun Zaimoğlu and Günter Senkel's *Schwarze Jungfrauen* and Nurkan Erpulat and Jens Hillje's *Verrücktes Blut*. These plays draw us into a more culturally specific discussion of Islam in Germany.

Chapter Three

Staging "Muslim Rage"

Who gave anyone expertise
over the meaning of feelings
of injustice?

Lauren Berlant, "The Subject of True Feeling"

In September 2012, *Newsweek* magazine sank to sensationalist, not to mention virulently Islamophobic, levels with its now infamous cover bearing the title "Muslim Rage," accompanied by an image of a group of Muslim men, wide-eyed and mouths agape in anger. The image had been apparently taken during a protest against the Islamophobic video *Innocence of Muslims,* which had been uploaded to YouTube in July 2012. The magazine cover added insult to injury and renewed outrage across Muslim communities. This cover image was accompanied by a similarly toned article by the Somali Dutch American politician and scholar Ayaan Hirsi Ali, an open critic of Islam, titled "How I Survived It / How We Can End It."[1] "Muslim rage" is presented as attributed only insofar as it is culturally determined. That Muslims are read as quick to rage becomes part of a fantasy that asserts a cultural prevalence of irrationality and even threat. The incident of this *Newsweek* cover exemplifies how, in Sara Ahmed's words, "[f]eelings can get stuck to certain bodies in the very way we describe spaces, situations, dramas."[2] The sticky affect of anger can determine the way bodies move through the world and are perceived by others. That anger is frequently, hostilely affixed to Muslim male bodies in Germany, and in the West more generally, on the woefully fallacious premise that Islam, contrary to a supposedly peaceful and enlightened Christianity, cultivates violence and aberrant behaviour, must continue to be troubled.

An outpouring of messages on Twitter responded to the image and article in *Newsweek* via the hashtag #muslimrage, with overwhelmingly funny and sometimes even endearing rebuttals, such as images of children playing or comments about food and clothing: "When my falafels don't turn out crispy" or "When my hijab doesn't match my outfit." These sought to dispel false perceptions that Muslims are more prone to anger than other religious or nonreligious communities; however, the responses also dismissed rage as a negative and unattributed emotion, and upheld the notion of anger as bad faith and (re)asserted that rage is linked to irrational behaviour and violence. What if the majority of comments had not attempted to diffuse emotion but affirmed the significance of rage as a political tool to challenge the hate and injustice perpetrated against Muslims? That the *Newsweek* edition and the flood of responses occurred in the wake of the terrorist attack by Islamic militants against an American diplomatic compound on September 11, 2012, in Benghazi, Libya, bears noting in the context of the question posed. As a matter of course, rage becomes connected to terrorism and violence as though they were not only interwoven but also interchangeable. Much contemporary discourse on anger is refracted through hate and violence. For instance, Pankaj Mishra assumes an implicit connection between terrorist violence and anger that can be found in any community. Without denying the potential causal relationship of anger and the violence of hate, I want to argue that it hardly forms a cause-and-effect narrative. As explored in chapter 1, anger has a complex history and discursively dense pulse, which calls for an understanding of context, speaker, and listener.

Yet thinking about anger and Islam carries its own unique set of questions and entanglements. To propose that anger and Islam are in some way inherently intertwined is not the intention of this chapter. Rather, the nature of anger that incites this exploration is one that responds to hate and the abuses committed out of hate and discrimination. Thus, it elides and critiques a tendency in the West to portray Muslim communities as excessively sensitive and prone to violent overreaction, as portrayed in *Newsweek* magazine and elsewhere. The 2012 incident of the Islamophobic YouTube video, which derogatorily portrayed the prophet Mohammed, was preceded by a similar incident in 2005 when equally disparaging cartoons of Mohammed were published in the Danish newspaper *Jyllands-Posten*. In both cases, there was an uproar in Muslim communities across the globe. But the reaction was overwrought in Western media for both sensational purposes and as a means to deflect guilt. Audiences were not given to understand the controversy as an act of cultural insensitivity and even hate on the part of the newspaper, but that Muslims were not only killjoys who cannot take a joke, but even irascible.

This chapter reflects on anger's utility both as outrage against the injustice of Islamophobia and as a declaration of personhood in line with what bell hooks posits as "the assertion of subjectivity, that colonizers do not want to see."[3] The theatre of anger does not position itself against anger but within it. Two plays that get at anger in a culturally directed way are *Schwarze Jungfrauen* (*Black Virgins*, premiere 2006) and *Verrücktes Blut* (*Mad Blood*, premiere 2010). Among other things, these plays address the contemporary moment in German politics and society and the troubled place of Islam. Indeed, the question of whether or not Islam has a home in the national fold is still publicly debated. This moment harks back to the emergence of the religious category "Muslim" in German public discourse, which replaced the ethnonational category "Turkish" in the early 2000s as a public reimagining of a community suddenly interpellated with new tenets, as Yasemin Yıldız has observed.[4] Building on Yıldız's observations about the locutory shift from "Turkish" to "Muslim" in the early 2000s, Fatima El-Tayeb also draws attention to the racialization of Islam, especially since 9/11. "Islam," she writes, "at times appears as a signifier almost as empty as race, ascribing a combination of naturalized cultural attributes to 'Muslims' that has little to do with religious beliefs or even with being a believer."[5] Without suggesting that discrimination did not exist prior to these discursive shifts, the category of "Muslim" became an assignment of identity that served to further marginalize many migrants in Germany.

A paired reading of *Schwarze Jungfrauen* and *Verrücktes Blut* under this rubric opens them up to new possibilities of interpretation. The problems, struggles, and contexts from within which and to which the theatre of anger responds become highlighted in the thematic relationship of these plays without reducing them to this one direct relationship. Both also (re-)create spaces of antagonism, provocation, and dissolution. Not to be read as hopeless tales of failure and regret, and rife with bad faith, *Schwarze Jungfrauen* and *Verrücktes Blut* are performances of anger that respond to Islamophobia and the dismal estimation (by many) of an interfaith society in Germany that is often already a projection of contention.[6] One further point of connectivity between these plays, and much of the theatre of anger, is their attack on the culture and aesthetics of theatre in Germany that speaks to an anti-dramatic or antitheatrical discourse. Anger thus takes form by taking *on* form. Theatre is critiqued. Representation is critiqued. Illusion is critiqued. Theatrical form is recast.

Yet the respective theatrical structures of these two plays diverge significantly. The raging monologue is elemental to *Schwarze Jungfrauen*, which is composed solely of monologues and resists all conventions of dramatic plot and development. *Verrücktes Blut*, on the other hand, is structured much more in the style of a naturalist play and presents the audience with a realistic drama à la Chekhov and Ibsen. *Schwarze Jungfrauen* is without doubt more conceptually radical than *Verrücktes Blut*; however, the complex layers of performance of the latter and its (albeit modest) application of the raging monologue secure it a place within this study of the theatre of anger. Stretching the parameters opened up by *Get Deutsch or Die Tryin'*, both *Schwarze Jungfrauen* and *Verrücktes Blut* employ blatant and confrontational, even violent, language that serves to shock and offend. In the spirit of in-yer-face theatre, this flagrant language provokes in unexpected ways: "Because," as Aleks Sierz argues, "humans are language animals, words often seem to cause more offence than the acts to which they refer."[7] The unsettling force of language as performance has been well established, but while J.L. Austin has argued that language in theatre sheds its performative capacity, Sierz proposes that in its liveness, theatre's act of breaking taboos becomes all the more shocking compared to other art forms. "Live performance," he observes, "heightens awareness, increases potential embarrassment, and can make the representation of private pain on public stage almost unendurable."[8]

Language's force is thus intensified by the sheer reality of bodily acts of direct encounter in the theatre, something these plays underscore with cultural awareness and weightiness. That certain affects become attached to already interpellated Muslim bodies in the German public sphere is prodded and challenged in these plays. But bodies do not attempt to diffuse or relinquish the anger projected; rather, they seize its performative power and energy and project it back. The performers assert their right to feel angry in the face of a society that at once induces their anger and denies its worth. Following its Ur-form in the Laocoön (itself an unsuspecting resistance and revision of the theatrical body), the body of anger in *Schwarze Jungfrauen* and *Verrücktes Blut* also asserts itself beyond representation. Whereas Elin Diamond draws on Brecht in her reading of the feminist theatre theory to emphasize that "the body...by entering the stage space, enters representation," these plays urge us to experience the ecstatic presence of the body onstage.[9] For not only does the affective presence of indignant bodies in their unrestrained performance in these plays trouble representation, the moment of performer-spectator encounter, or what Peggy Phelan might call the principle of presence-to-presence interaction,[10] they also lead us to the heart of the theatre of anger.

Black Virgins Talk Back

It is safe to say that the exuberantly curious audience that filled the Hebbel am Ufer Theatre (HAU) in Berlin-Kreuzberg on March 17, 2006, for the opening night of *Schwarze Jungfrauen* – a play co-written by Feridun Zaimoğlu and Günter Senkel and directed by Neco Çelik – was in for a shock. Although the play premiered midway through the month-long transnational festival, *Beyond Belonging – Migration²*, *Schwarze Jungfrauen* pummels the audience with an assertive, sexualized, politically incorrect, even radically Islamic set of speech acts performed by young self-proclaimed Muslim women – something not witnessed before in the theatre. Indeed, there are no appalling acts of physical violence, explicit sex, or even nudity onstage, but the language employed and the manner in which it is delivered by young Muslim women is highly provocative, even well-nigh pornographic in its sex positivity. For instance, in one monologue, a paraplegic woman (identified simply as "The Woman in the Wheelchair") describes in detail the first time she fellates her caretaker:

> [E]r steckt ihn mir in den Mund, nein falsch, ich schnappe gierig nach seinem Schwanz. Das erste Mal, dass ich einen Schwanz schmeck, das ist ein Geschenk für einen Krüppel, und weil ich noch ungeübt bin, gibt er mir Anweisungen: Nicht so fest, und du must auch atmen, sonst erstickst du, ja, jetzt ist es toll. Ich habe geleckt und geschluckt. Was macht er dann? Er kommt mir nicht mit der Schmusenummer, nein, er zieht sich an, aber lächelt dabei fies, er denkt, er hat einen Islamistenkrüppel geschändet, und ich bin so abartig, dass es mir gefällt, mir gefallen seine harten und gemeinen Gedanken. Der Pfleger war mein unanständiger Engel. Ich war selig, ich habe nach dem Blowjob eine Kraft gespürt, das kann ich nicht beschreiben.[11]

> He sticks it in my mouth, no wrong, I snap voraciously for his dick. The first time that I taste a penis, that's a gift for a cripple, and since I am still inexperienced, he tells me what to do: Not so hard, and you have to also breathe, otherwise you'll suffocate, yeah, now it's great. I sucked and swallowed. What does he do? He doesn't try to get all cuddly, no, he gets dressed, but also smiles in a nasty sort of way, he thinks, he defiled an Islamist cripple, and I'm so deviant that I enjoyed it, I enjoyed his hard and

mean thoughts. The nurse was my obscene angel. I was blessed, after the blowjob I felt a sort of power, I can't describe it.

The obscenity of the monologue lies both in its content, a raunchy narrative of fellatio that thrills, and its performance, delivered by a devout Muslim woman in a wheelchair. Already the idea that a pious Muslim woman would practise oral sex seems shocking; that this woman is also differently abled breaks yet another taboo, for as many disability scholars have asserted, in public discourse disability and sexuality seldom merge in the context of pleasure.[12] Instead, if sexuality and disability become entangled, it is often on matters of abuse and victimization. The assertion of pleasure at once denies victimization and proclaims the socially unacceptable. To utter these words live and onstage heightens their effect and the force of their obscenity, their potential shock value. Shock is of course always a form of confrontation that seeks to distress and even enrage the interlocutor. As Sierz asserts, "[s]hock is an essential part of a confrontational sensibility."[13] It goes without saying that confrontation is a significant component of the theatre of anger. Speech is frequently rebarbative. In the spirit of self-reflexiveness, the same performer adds in acid tones:

Stört es euch, dass ich so offen rede? Wollt ihr euch abwenden? Was treibe ich hier für ein kleines billiges Spiel? Ich weiβ doch, dass ich Zumutung gegen Vermutung setze, ihr glaubt, zu wissen, wie ich bin, und ich spreche dagegen an, um einen richtigen vulgären Eindruck zu hinterlassen. Aber – ich bin tatsächlich so, und es ist alles wahr, fast alles ist wahr.[14]

Are you disturbed by how openly I speak? Do you want to turn away? What kind of cheap game am I playing here? I know that I impose rather than suppose, you think you know what I am, and I try to be something I'm not in order to leave a really vulgar impression. But – I am in fact like that, and it's all true, almost all of it.

As the play that notably initiated what has come to be called post-migrant theatre, *Schwarze Jungfrauen* is also an exemplary case of the theatre of anger. It consists of monologues performed by five Muslim women in contemporary Germany. Written as a collection of ten first-person texts by Zaimoğlu and Senkel, *Schwarze Jungfrauen* was then condensed by Insa Popken and Tunçay Kulaoğlu into a series of monologues and premiered under the direction of (the film director) Neco Çelik. The characters featured in the play are nameless but are portrayed as follows: (1) The Bosnian, (2) The Party Girl, (3) The Student,

(4) The Convert, and (5) The Woman in the Wheelchair. These identifications are not inserted in the original text by Zaimoğlu and Senkel but were added by Popken and Kulaoğlu and included in the playbill accompanying the performance. Each character delivers several monologues over the course of the evening. While there is narrative continuity throughout the monologues delivered by a singular character, they are delivered in a manner that is theatrically self-contained. No one is interrupted or directly intersected. The performers only briefly speak in chorus at the conclusion of the play.

Based on a series of ten interviews that Zaimoğlu conducted with Muslim women about their relationship to their faith and to their sexuality, the play has been largely (though not exclusively) analysed within its status as semi-documentary theatre. Though, as Claudia Breger makes explicit, such a tendency slides into the quagmire of sociological interpretation and relegates the play's aesthetics to the sidelines.[15] Further, the play's overall dearth of documentary elements in the form of film, slides, graphics, and so forth, as notably employed by Erwin Piscator, or what Carol Martin refers to as the "tripartite structure of contemporary documentary theatre: technology, text, and body," belies this generic classification further.[16] Heavy use of media and archival documents is eschewed in favour of a modern minimalist mise-en-scène. Further, the actual "authenticity" of the monologues has been called into question. The biting style and content of the monologues are reminiscent of Zaimoğlu's larger corpus of writing and his foundational work with the political art activist group Kanak Attak, explored in chapter 2. *Schwarze Jungfrauen* is often read as the theatrical derivative of Zaimoğlu's 1998 text *Koppstoff*, also a collection of literary monologues with Turkish German women about their private lives. Elements of documentary form the generic underpinnings of some of the plays examined in this book. But the extent to which we can call this play documentary has scant bearing on my analysis.

The theatre of anger takes many forms. *Schwarze Jungfrauen* can also be classified as an episodic play, formally and thematically comparable to Eve Ensler's *The Vagina Monologues*. Yet it would be amiss to refer to *Schwarze Jungfrauen* simply as a Muslim version of *The Vagina Monologues*. Indeed, the 2003 Dutch play *De Gesluierde Monologen* (*The Veiled Monologues*), written by Adelheid Roosen, which gained much more international fame than *Schwarze Jungfrauen*, already achieved this in its essentialist and ideological representations of European Muslim women as victims of Muslim men's violence.[17] *De Gesluierde Monologen*, like so many European representations of Muslim women, perpetuates the long-held colonial fantasy narrative of "white men saving brown women from brown men,"[18] or to paraphrase Beverly M. Weber in the case of Roosen's play, as "white women saving brown women from brown men,"[19] and what Jasbir Puar has more recently referred to as "white women's burden."[20] *Schwarze Jungfrauen* offers different performances of self, which reject narratives of victimization. Through this explicit rejection of troubling dogmatic narratives, the figures in *Schwarze Jungfrauen* express their anger in an undoing of theatre.

> Die Deutschen schauen sich das Schlampentheater an, sie füllen die Zuschauerränge bis zum letzten Platz, auf der Bühne wird ein Dorfstück gegeben. Und was ist das dramatische Element? Das Moslemmädchen kommt in die europäische Metropole, es lässt sich den Wind der Freiheit um die ungepuderte Nase wehen, das Mädchen bekommt eine groβe Sehnsucht – es will in die Diskothek, es will einen Freund, es will einen Job, es will den Discount-Schund kaufen, und es will sich endlich auch die Nase pudern. Da kommt das Moslemmädchen auf die Idee, dass es sich ein wenig ausziehen muss, um als tolle fremde Frau zu gelten. Also geht der Krieg gegen die Eltern und gegen die Männer los. Am Ende darf das kleine fremde Mädchen ein Proseccoglas in der Hand halten und irgendwelchen anderen deutschen Mädchen seine Befreiungsgeschichte erzählen: Ja, ich war so schlimm unterdrückt, und jetzt, da ich alles Islamtürkische zum Teufel gejagt habe, darf ich mir die Nase pudern. Doch am Ende seiner Geschichte kommt immer die gleiche Pointe: Der Islam is schlimm. Die westliche Freiheit is toll.[21]

> The Germans watch this slut theatre, they fill the audience tiers to the last seat, onstage a village play is performed. And what is the dramatic element? The Muslim girl arrives in the European metropolis, she lets the wind of freedom blow around her unpowdered nose, the girl develops a great desire – she wants to go to the disco, she wants a boyfriend, she wants a job, she wants to buy discount trash, and she wants to finally powder her nose. The Muslim girl gets an idea that she has to undress a bit to be a cool, foreign woman. Thus begins the war against the parents and against men. In the end the foreign girl may hold a glass of sparkling wine in her hand and tell some German girls about her story of liberation: Yeah, I was so terribly suppressed, and now that I've chased away everything Islamic Turkish, I can powder my nose. At the end of the story it's always the same punchline: Islam is bad. Western freedom is great.

So much anger seethes and simmers in just this one monologue voiced by "the Student" and in the Fifth Text of the longer published version of the monologues. The "Schlampentheater" (slut theatre), to which the speaker refers, is contrasted with the present theatre experience: *Schwarze Jungfrauen*. "Slut theatre" is the condemning classification of the popular and popularized conversion (or better: integration) narrative from Islam to a kind of Western Christian atheism. This condemnation responds to the cultural and historical context preceding the opening of the play. The year *Schwarze Jungfrauen* premiered in 2006 also marked the first annual Deutsche Islamkonferenz (German Islam Conference), initiated by the Federal Ministry of the Interior, ostensibly with the intent of stimulating dialogue between representatives of the federal government and members of the Muslim community. As Yıldız notes, "[t]his institutional framing effectively designated 'Islam' and 'Muslims' as primary subject categories and objects."[22] Ultimately, the work of this institutionalized dialogue has been a unidirectional discussion about the "integration of Muslims" into German society, through assimilationist strategies and the imperative adoption of German/Western values and practices and the departure from Muslim traditions. In Weber's account, from the beginning the Islam Conference has given priority to the voices of public figures in Germany who have criticized Islam, most famously Seyran Ateş and Necla Kelek, to speak for and ultimately shape the public position of Muslims in Germany. Both have written best-selling memoirs about so-called self-liberation narratives and their paths away from Islam, which follow the basic premise of conversion, condemned in the citation from the play above.[23] Not dissimilar to Ayaan Hirsi Ali, cited at the beginning of the chapter, these Turkish German women have characterized Islam as an antifeminist, backward, and violent religion and culture that must be rejected.

As Katrin Sieg has demonstrated, *Schwarze Jungfrauen* not only comes on the heels of this dominant public discourse that renders women mere victims of Islam tout court, it also responds with militancy and, I add, a sense of outrage that breaks with taboos of representation.[24] In the same blow, it attacks the audience, "the Germans who watch this slut theatre." The verbal artillery of the play has numerous targets, but the audience as both the physically present body of interlocutors and the still overwhelmingly white, non-Muslim, German majority in the room is most frequently and deliberately targeted or caught in the line of fire.[25] While critics gave the play an overwhelmingly favourable reception, and it was even featured on the cover of the auspicious German-language theatre journal *Theater heute*, the general public reacted with anger and irritation. In an interview with Lizzie Stewart, in 2012, Çelik describes the audience members as "so irritated that even when there was no post-show discussion they didn't go home. They waited in the foyer and forced you into discussion."[26] In a post-show discussion I attended in 2014, the audience was still fraught by the play, and Çelik, who was briefly present, was visibly impatient. It is seldom the case that eight years after the first performance (of the same production) there is a necessity for a post-show public discussion, but *Schwarze Jungfrauen* still has the power to irritate its audience. Its effect remains forceful.

Agitation is stirred both by the sparring and scandalous content and nature of the monologues, to which I will return in greater detail, and the aesthetics of the performance itself, the mise-en-scène, and the blocking. Much has been written and discussed about the curious staging of *Schwarze Jungfrauen*, which has incited all manner of interpretations, from the sexually exploitative to the science-fictional. The highly experimental set, designed by Mascha Mazur, consists of six self-contained LED boxes, three on the bottom and three on top. Some critics have likened the structure to a set of display windows through which the women are ogled (like objects).[27] Sieg has suggested that the boxes are similar to small claustrophobic compartments reminiscent of the cramped apartments inhabited by migrant workers in Germany in the 1960s and 1970s.[28] Most notable, however, is that the structure looms over the audience in a manner that a mere row of individual compartments could not. Taking up the entire stage and positioned not as a backdrop but downstage, its sheer height and mass dominates the space. Originally performed in smaller theatres (HAU and the Ballhaus Naunynstraβe), without a balcony, this effect of magnitude was particularly prominent. The performers present an aggregate force that towers over the audience. Upon first viewing of the play, I was in the parquet close to the front, and I was compelled to constantly tilt my head up to view the performers. But if the structure elevates, it also distances. Breger's reference to a Brechtian or possibly a post-Brechtian aesthetic with regard to the mise-en-scène is astute.[29] Distanciation as alienation assumes many guises in *Schwarze Jungfrauen*. By way of the set design, the performers are also alienated from one another, physically cut off and isolated in the individual compartments.

But this extends beyond the mise-en-scène. If, according to Marx, the labourer in the capitalist system experiences multiple levels of alienation, self-estrangement at its crest, then in Brechtian theatre such alienation becomes inscribed on the bodies of the performers and the manner in which they communicate with each other and with the audience through self-awareness. Brecht writes: "The actors openly choose those positions that will best show them off to the audience, just as if they were acrobats. A further means is that *the artist observes himself* ... he will occasionally look at the audience as if to say: isn't it just like that?"[30] Such aptly illustrates the provocative opening of *Schwarze Jungfrauen*. Onstage darkness is punctured by flashes of coloured light: a looping of red, green, and blue. Electronic music pulsates to the rhythm of the beaming coloured lights in the LED boxes. The image onstage is blurred by a translucent curtain, a scrim, reminiscent of an Arabesque veil that is gradually lifted. The performers, clad in black overcoats and headscarves, their backs to the audience, eventually become visible. In unison, these bodies strip down. Even their long black tresses are revealed to be wigs that can be easily shed. Yet the potential peep-show effect of this preamble is less sexualizing than it is estranging. It projects with more than a dash of self-awareness the desires of the audience – that is, the Orientalizing desire conjured by the veiled women, whose concealed bodies are presented as an enigma awaiting discovery by the penetrating Western gaze. The stripping away of the veil at the beginning of the play, however, should not be read as a direct act of submission to Western fantasy of "unveiling" or an elaborate spectacle of conformation to its corollary politics, but instead as a stripping down of loaded tropes. It is what Joan Copjec calls the "sartorial matter"[31] and not the body itself that is often eroticized.

Roland Barthes's brief but evocative account of the striptease supports this claim and transports it into a broader context. While the atelic action of stripping epitomizes the sexualized spectacle, the resulting phenomenon of the naked woman is its inverse, for as Barthes contends, a "[w]oman is desexualized at the very moment when she is stripped naked."[32] Just as Meyda Yeğenoğlu reads the act of unveiling as a drama that incites intrigue and fear insofar as it exposes the fantasized other, Barthes similarly reminds us of the striptease's oscillation between attraction and fear. The contradictory nature of the striptease, its ultimate desexualization of the body, is echoed in *Schwarze Jungfrauen*. Stripping here takes an unexpected turn – a turn that is realized through the performers' synchronized physical turn towards the audience. For what is revealed are not naked female bodies but ones garbed in neutralizing, even masculine, vesture – salmon-toned long underwear. Likewise, the performers' hair (considered part of a woman's sexuality, certainly not just in Islamic culture) has been tightly tucked away under a cap and make-up, giving the uncanny impression of baldness (see figure 3.1). It is as though the female characters point and say: "Ha, so this is what you expected; well, here you go!" The suggestive striptease denaturalizes social relations by theatricalizing them – making them seem strange. The self-awareness or consciousness expressed through Brechtian acting is thus not only class consciousness,

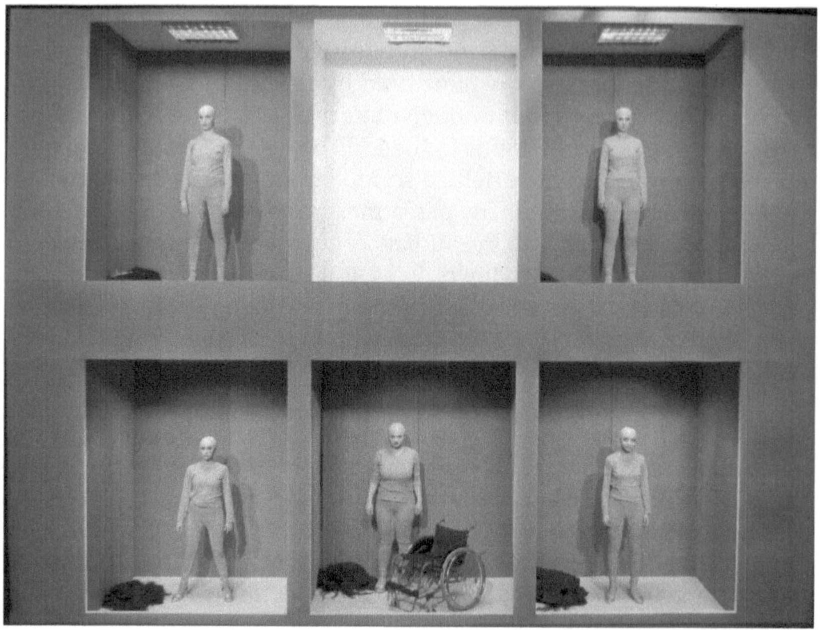

3.1 The striking staging of *Schwarze Jungfrauen* post striptease. Image © Ute Langkafel MAIFOTO.

but here also a feminist and anti-colonial consciousness that is impelled by the power of anger. I am inspired here by the words of Adrienne Rich, who so fittingly writes in the final stanza of her celebrated 1972 poem "The Phenomenology of Anger," "[e]very act of becoming conscious ... is an unnatural act."[33]

Sieg and Stewart have further noted the allegorical nature through which Çelik addresses issues of alienation by literally playing with science-fictional overtones of an alien encounter.[34] The opening sequence's spectacle of flashing lights and futuristic electronic beats seem to beam the performers onto the stage like alien beings.[35] With their hairless, slightly cone-shaped heads, and matching nondescript garb, these so-called black virgins appear strange, otherworldly. The nature of their monologic speech does something similar. Linked to both madness (from *Macbeth* to *A Streetcar Named Desire*) and alienation (particularly in the case of Eugene O'Neill's plays), the monologue presents itself as an apt form for the expression of these alien-like and alienated figures. For even though the monologue opens up interiority, the result here is neither insight nor character development. The private is simply narrated and theatricalized.[36] This dramatic opening has an eldritch effect that persists throughout the performance. At various intervals, there are longer pauses between the monologues. The opening music returns and the empty centre top compartment is illuminated. Only shadowy outlines of the performers in the darkness remain visible. During these extended moments of silence and strange spectacle, I recall the unease of fellow spectators made tangible through the shifting in seats.

The performers embody the Brechtian *Gestus* (that socially encoded behaviour) and propel it further into the arena of the post-Brechtian, or perhaps into what Stanton B. Garner Jr. limns in other contexts as "the postmodern radicalizing of Brechtian aesthetics."[37] Socially encoded behaviour is not only exposed onstage, its act of exposure is exposed and repurposed. But the play's Brechtian influence is placed under duress once the monologues commence. That the ontology of the traditional theatrical monologue troubled Brecht's approach to theatre and politics, because it inhibited communication and, by extension, theatre as such, is evident. Brecht had no problem with actors addressing the audience. What was to be avoided was the traditional psychological connectivity with the audience that often forged empathy by way of the monologue. Insofar as the actor must become alienated from the character portrayed, the rhetorical possibility of the monologue was thrown into crisis.[38] Thus, the soliloquy in the tradition of Shakespeare's *Hamlet* disappears from Brechtian theatre altogether, because there is to be no interiority or space for existential moralizing; the actor should only cite in expository manner the social and political traits of the character played. However, monologues were still employed in Brechtian plays with a new function: to emphasize the dialectical conflict between performance and text (or theatre and play). In its performative ambit, the monologue in the theatre of anger formally comments on the fissures between performance and text, but it also retrieves elements of authenticity of the self-revealing soliloquy that inversely calls for an alignment of body and text. *Schwarze Jungfrauen* at once restores the possibility of stage language to express the inexpressible, and it occasionally slides into *Gestus* by throwing into question the weight behind the monologue and its tendency towards mere citation.

The monologues in *Schwarze Jungfrauen* are personal and defiant. They reveal desire and rage. They break taboos. Simply put, they are in-yer-face. But what distinguishes the raging monologue aesthetically from the violent assault on the senses of the in-yer-face tradition is that in the theatre of anger, rage and provocation do not rely on visceral provocations of disgust and shock through sex and violence alone. Instead, the raging monologue is also about talking back. bell hooks defines "talking back" as speaking when not spoken to, as speaking out of turn.[39] It is about moving from silence into speech for the oppressed. In particular, women within oppressed groups often do not speak and contain their feelings of despair, rage, and anguish, as hooks writes, citing Audre Lorde, "'for fear our words will not be heard nor welcomed,' coming to voice is an act of resistance."[40] Such willful speech acts both represent a coming to voice and a rebellious addressing of authority figures as equals. That these black virgins embrace the Black feminist tradition of "talking back" is evident. Although the use of informal language in direct audience address is not uncommon in contemporary theatre,[41] in the case of *Schwarze Jungfrauen* this resonates even at the level of pronominal address, in which the informal "ihr" for the plural "you" is employed throughout. Further, the inherent performativity of the monologues of *Schwarze Jungfrauen* actually dispels concerns that these female characters simply ventriloquize the male voices of the authors. The force of the monologue imparts to the play a narrative voice that emerges at the moment of utterance. As Geis in like manner writes: "Monologic language not only takes on the power to alter time and space despite the absence of a malleable printed text (as in a novel) or of editing (as in a film), but it also achieves a dramatic resonance and potential for creative manipulation all its own."[42] With a focus on performance and play as spectacle, postdramatic approaches attest that the text itself becomes malleable. For, as Hans-Thies Lehmann asserts, "in theatre the text is subject to the same laws and dislocations as the visual, audible, gestic and architectonic theatrical signs."[43] This is not to say that the text becomes emptied and equivocal, vanquished by sheer utterance, but that the performative function of language and its affective force come to life when spoken onstage by angry young Muslim women.

If the voices of any community and identity in recent history have been silenced in Western discourse, they are the voices of Muslim women, who are so frequently spoken about but seldom given the space to speak for themselves. Yeğenoğlu has described Muslim women in Western discourse in Foucauldian terms as *the* embodiment of docile bodies "who have been trained or corrected, classified, normalized, excluded, etc."[44] With minor exception, representations of Muslim women in film, popular media, television, theatre, and literature have perpetuated this image of objectified submission – one that, as Maha El Hissy observes, only began to fray in the early 2000s in Germany with performances such as *Schwarze Jungfrauen*, which radically upset the status quo.[45] What is formidable about this performance is the simmering orchestration of voice, body, audience, and verbal aggression. In many ways, this also sums up the theatre of anger as a whole. *Schwarze Jungfrauen*'s drama of five angry young women, who talk back (to a white German audience) about Islam, sexual desire, and politics through the exclusive deployment of monologue, is paradigmatic of the project of the theatre of anger.

From the moment the first performer begins to speak, an uncontained verbal avalanche inundates the auditorium. Language flows with a robust force and plenitude that is overwhelming. The self-declared "Convert" begins with a tragic anecdote about the death of a friend (who out of politeness held in her sneezes until she had a brain aneurysm) that is told with cynicism and angry indifference. *Schwarze Jungfrauen* opens with a callousness that cuts. Even death is deemed ridiculous and trivial. Gestural language tells an angry tale, too. The performer stands with her legs apart, arms half-raised, then folded tightly across her chest. Her posture is informal but profoundly tense. The first monologue is brief. The stage is then eclipsed in complete darkness. A light appears just below in another compartment. The second monologue begins. Pinar Erincin, who also plays the mother in *Get Deutsch or Die Tryin'*, is the second performer and plays the "Bosnian" character. With the exception of Meley Erenay, Erincin is one of the only original cast members to continue to play in Çelik's production. Erincin's monologue is not as radical or shocking as some of the others, but it is the bawdiest and the most rancorous. Hate speech pervades her monologue with heavy intention. She spews homophobia, antifeminism, racism, anti-Semitism, and xenophobia with virulent conviction. Relaying the speech of an acquaintance, an apparent nasal-spray junkie and homophobe, the "Bosnian" articulates condemning words only loosely impersonalized in the third person:

> Der sagt: wir im Westen verschwulen unser System heiβt Homokranz der Arschficker stell dir n Kreis aus Homos vor jeder hat ihn drin und spurt dass er ihn drin hat der perfekte geschlossene Kreis die schönste Homoharmonie. So ist es bei uns und die Liberalsten von uns sind die Homos die wolln so viele Ausländer wie möglich aber Männer damit sie den Homokranz der Arschkficker erweitern können. Stell dir vor ne Lesbe lobt mein Schleier ich habe das Spiel mitgespielt und gelacht die dumme Lesbe hat gedacht: Die lacht weil ich auf sie Eindruck mache und dann macht die öde Tante mich an wie n Kerl die lud mich zum Vaginalutschen ein. Da habe ich laut geschrien es warn ja viele Leute auf der Geburtstagsparty ich hab laut gerufen: WAS? DU WILLST DASS ICH DIR DIE VAGINA LUTSCHE? MEIN GOTT DIESE LESBE MOCHTE DASS ICH IHR DIE VAGINA LUTSCHE!!![46]

> He says: here in the West we are queering [derogatory] our system it's called the homo wreath of ass fuckers imagine a circle of homos everyone's got it in and feels that it's in it's the perfect self-contained circle the most beautiful homo harmony. This is what it's like here and the most liberal among us are homos and want as many foreigners as possible but men so that they can expand the homo wreath of the ass fuckers ... Imagine that, a lesbian praises my veil I played along and laughed the stupid lesbian thought: She's laughing because I make an impression on her and then the boring broad comes on to me like a dude she invited me for some pussy sucking. I screamed loudly there were lots of people at the birthday party and I yelled loudly: WHAT YOU WANT ME TO SUCK YOUR PUSSY? MY GOD THIS LESBIAN WANTS ME TO SUCK HER PUSSY!!!

The sting of these words reverberates. A lack of punctuation in the original text already offers a paratactic ejection of language that carries all the qualities of a rant. Even the process of writing them again here, not to mention translating them, has both a confusing and a bristling effect. While the audience might not feel addressed by this hostile verbal onslaught, ensconced in theatre, linguistic specificity, and the stoic self-defence mechanism of not allowing oneself to feel at risk, one still easily becomes caught in the crossfire of malevolent language. As Denise Riley writes, "those words were directed at me, but it wasn't especially me who was hated, I just accidentally got in that speaker's way."[47] But hate speech is often scalar; it has a tendency to stick, to linger with heaviness, even if the intent and direction appear ambiguous. The audience cannot escape its affective repercussions. Arising from anger, hate speech hardly seems comparable to the acceptable reaction of anger articulated in Aristotle's account and set in motion by the event of being wronged. As I indicate in chapter 1, anger should not be conflated with hate, as it lays claim to a sense of justice and retribution that is attributable, what Jean-Paul Sartre has referred to in the context of colonial reprisal as "violence on the rebound."[48] Yet the theatre of anger can also be cruel and can give life to forces of anger that seem to merely want to provoke. Provocation, however, is not happenstance; it calls for felicitous conditions in order to be effective: speaker, audience, context, content.[49] This character's hate speech at once cuts right through the liberal establishment in all of its vacant rhetorical political correctness and strikes down the constraints imposed on theatre as a space where the interests of this mostly liberal, elite, white, and bourgeois audience are perpetuated. It upends expectations.

The question of the relationship between the text and the body that utters it comes to the fore when that body is female. Jill Dolan reminds us that "the female body is not reducible to a sign free of connotation. Women always bear the mark and meaning of their sex, which inscribes them within a cultural hierarchy."[50] Geis adds that this is particularly evident in the act of monologic speech.[51] And in the case of a Muslim woman, this cannot ring true enough. *Schwarze Jungfrauen* takes on these expectations and subverts them. Young Muslim women deploy the most hateful and violent language and the audience's shock arises doubled in the purported disconnect of text and body. Witnessing men use this kind of language onstage might have been less shocking, but young Muslim women, girls even, present another matter altogether. The same can be said of the provocative statements of "The Student," whose fervour for radical Islam and willingness to pursue jihad in the name of political Islam shocks and disturbs.

The monologues of "The Student," who curiously always speaks in the collective "we," often sound more akin to propaganda speech than to a theatrical monologue. Premiering just five years after 9/11, this speech was and continues to be so startling in its impassioned conviction, even love, and support for Islam and the Taliban. The final monologue of the play, also performed by "The Student," concludes with a quasi-Islamist call to arms: "Islam wird populär werden! Jihadfront steht!" ("Islam will become popular! Jihad front remains!")[52] While the other four performers gather in the top centre compartment, which had remained empty throughout the performance, "The Student" maintains a solitary position in the top right compartment. Leaving the audience with a question, the four gathered performers speak in choral monologue as a collective: "Wer hat Angst vor den schwarzen Jungfrauen? Wer hat Angst vor uns?" ("Who's afraid of the black virgins? Who's afraid of us?") This final line subversively alludes to the racist German children's tag game "Wer hat Angst vorm schwarzen Mann?" (Who's afraid of the Black man?), in which the "Black man" is imagined as the ultimate "Kinderschreckfigur" (frightful figure to children). There is a tendency throughout the play to mix and borrow from popular German culture. But this final line is also possibly a decisive nod to the title of Edward Albee's famous play *Who's Afraid of Virginia Woolf?* and its vital question about the fear of looking beyond the surface, that is, of "living without false illusions."[53] These characters are not simply angry misfits, exceptions to the rule, young women gone astray; they are, as one character, asserts, "die neue Realität" (the new reality), a self-assertive neo-Muslim reality, and as such a force to be reckoned with.

And yet the theatre of anger is not just about theatre bodied with angry characters. A troupe of five Muslim women does not immediately resonate in a Western collective imaginary with a tone of anger, whereas "young Muslim men" or "young white men" or "young Black men" might. *Schwarze Jungfrauen* assaults our expectations. The theatre of anger is thick with ambiguity and complexity. As I write throughout, this theatre delivers an aggressive response to injustice. *Schwarze Jungfrauen* broadly attacks Islamophobia. The play not only counters an upsurge of hate across the West in the wake of 9/11, it also indirectly addresses national politics of injustice with regard to, for example, the so-called Kopftuchstreit (headscarf debate), which erupted when a young Muslim teacher, Fereshta Ludin, went to the supreme court in the late 1990s because she was denied a position due to her hijab. Weber, who has written extensively on this topic, holds that this incident unleashed vehement debate in Germany because the case "disturbed understandings of Muslim woman victimhood."[54] The persisting discourse about oppression and violence against women in Muslim families and communities becomes linked to an assigned submission and victimhood of Muslim women. In Germany and elsewhere in the West, Muslim women are frequently discussed but are rarely participants in the discussion. As a result, racism explains violence as an expression of culture. The incompatibility of Islam and Europe is predicated on the notion of the protection of rights for women and the importance of gender equality. The entanglement of racism and religion gained purchase in the early 2000s, and as Fatima El-Tayeb writes, "the *hijab* worn by some European Muslim women has become a highly charged symbol of racial, cultural, and gender, as much as religious difference."[55] *Schwarze Jungfrauen* implicitly address this history and context; it talks back. It asserts subjectivity, willfulness, and desire both in the face of dominant discourse and by means of shock and alienation.

Maaaad Blood (Need I Say More)

If *Schwarze Jungfrauen* inaugurated a new wave of anger and audacity in Berlin theatre in 2006, then Nurkan Erpulat and Jens Hillje's *Verrücktes Blut* gave it stamina and proof that the theatre of anger had come to stay. When the play opened at the Ballhaus Naunynstraβe at the start of the new 2010 theatre season, it instantly struck a chord. This new theatre was "durchgeknallt und unverschämt" ("crazy and shameless"),[56] as one critic pithily wrote. Not as radical as *Schwarze Jungfrauen* in terms of form and aesthetics, *Verrücktes Blut* employed more conventional methods to address the fraught politics of the present, still with a raging critique, and found enormous success. In 2011, it was invited to the prestigious *Theatertreffen* in Berlin, and that same year, it also received the illustrious accolade of *Stück des Jahres* (Play of the Year). The play brought prominence to its writers, its director, and the Ballhaus Naunynstraβe. Despite its prominence, *Verrücktes Blut* should not be treated as the bellwether of the theatre of anger, and indeed at moments it presents itself formally as an outlier. This play is nonetheless an important object of study in this book and especially in this chapter, insofar as it performs anger in response to social injustice, in particular Islamophobia.

One prominent target of the play's timely criticism was the integration debate, which publicly reemerged full force in 2010 with the publication and startling success of Thilo Sarrazin's racist and ideological book, *Deutschland schafft sich ab* (*Germany Abolishes Itself*), also discussed in chapter 2. With its egregious premise of cultural demise in the face of mass immigration from non-European, and particularly countries where Islam is the dominant religion, Sarrazin's hateful manifesto stimulated a new culture of racist panic and fear that focuses on religion. Sarrazin's condemnation befalls so-called delinquent male Muslim youth in particular. With an alarming gesture of ignorance and hate, he warns of the purported unwillingness of Muslim youth, the children and grandchildren of Turkish and Arab migrants, to assimilate into dominant culture, and adumbrates the resulting dramatic shift in cultural and social life in Germany – an Islamification of Germany.[57]

Loosely based on Jean-Paul Lillienfeld's 2008 French film *Journée de la Jupe* (*Skirt Day*), about disenfranchised second- and third-generation French high school students in the Paris banlieues, *Verrücktes Blut* was remade as a two-act play about a German theatre lesson in a high school in Berlin that turns violent and violently didactic. Similar to the narrative frame of the film, the students in *Verrücktes Blut* are out of control and the teacher struggles to maintain some semblance of order. Then, a dramatic break of truly theatrical proportions transpires. A gun falls out of one student's bag and into the teacher's hands. She decides to use it against the students as a tool of power to make them obey her and to learn the works of Friedrich Schiller, beginning with his treatise *Über die ästhetische Erziehung des Menschen* (*On the Aesthetic Education of Man* [1793]). Unlike the film, though, the play makes room for irony and complexity and refuses the easy lapse into sentimentality and melodrama. *Verrücktes Blut* is as much about the struggles with theatre aesthetics and traditions as it is about identity politics.

Perhaps more than any theatre practioners associated with the theatre of anger, Erpulat's directing style and Hillje's dramaturgy are expansive. Erpulat received his training at the prestigious Ernst Busch Academy of Dramatic Arts in Berlin,[58] whose capacious "East European" theatre pedagogy draws on the traditions of Brecht, Stanislavski, Meyerhold, and Eisenstein.[59] Hillje, on the other hand, pursued cultural studies in Perugia, Hildesheim, and Berlin. A sophisticated engagement with theatrical form and history is brought forth in this play. While *Verrücktes Blut* has frequently been described aesthetically as bearing out a naturalist-style play and the actors as keen Stanislavskian subjects, such a description does not hold for the entirety of the play, whose layers are sundry. What drives the present consideration of *Verrücktes Blut* are these distinct breaks and crossovers in dramatic style. By tracing these breaks, anger is not only brought into relief, it is revealed as an element of the play that is consistently and violently redirected. If anger is a tone that for an entire evening spitballs towards the audience through the monologues of the "black virgins," then *Verrücktes Blut* allows anger to circulate within and outside of the diegetic space onstage. The youthful characters that populate this play move through a circuitous course of anger. They are angry at the audience, the teacher, each other, themselves, and so forth.

Verrücktes Blut opens with a lengthy prelude. This is Brechtian in its demonstrative display of "getting into character." The actors enter the auditorium and begin to change their clothing. Five young men don muscle shirts, hoodies, and sweatpants; one of the two girls wraps her head in a hijab. A slightly older actor changes into a formal outfit of skirt, jacket, and pearls. Finally, she adjusts a blond wig on her head. Set designer Magda Willi's minimalist, pared-down set, around which the actors prepare themselves, consists of an elevated square platform that doubles as a stage and physically resembles a boxing ring. Struggle assumes a visible form, not to mention an architectural structure. Following Shermin Langhoff's delineation of "postmigrant" as a "Kampfbegriff" (fighting term), the theatrical stage as boxing ring takes things to another level – to the fight itself. The set is also perfectly Brechtian insofar as it "shows the machinery" of the play.[60] According to Brecht, the dramatic struggle contains the logic of the boxing ring. *Verrücktes Blut*'s mise-en-scène thus reflexively underpins its own tendency to discipline unruly young bodies. A hulking grand piano also hangs threateningly overhead.

Once changed, the actors gradually climb up onto the stage platform and there they remain throughout the performance. The act of "getting into character" continues onstage. Chairs are lugged up and placed in a row at the back of the platform. There is a brief pause in action as the young performers take a seat and stare out at the audience. Gradually, one by one, each performer stands, walks downstage, and strikes a menacing "gangster" pose at the audience. Their bodies positioned in a row form a corporeally hostile tableau vivant of anger and aggression that is held for roughly fifteen seconds. Then the expectorating begins.

Silence is finally broken, not with puncturing words, but with a chorus of vulgar, hoarse, guttural rasping of the throat before it releases a vertiginous ejection of spittle. Words are replaced with the palpable spray of bodily fluid directed at the audience. Although no actual spit is ejected, the sonic effect of slimy ejection becomes so visceral that it motivated many audience members, particularly in the first few rows, to physically recoil, even duck. This is followed by a frenetic and collective adjustment of genitals, until language finally arrives in the form of a barking spew of epithets. Once the spectators are thoroughly abused for ten seconds, they are then sexually harassed with verbal solicitations and suggestive bodily gestures. Finally, each performer pulls out a cell phone and begins to scream into it. This sequence of antisocial behaviour is then repeated in variation several more times until the character of the teacher climbs up into the ring. The play as such begins. In Erpulat's words: "Das ist ein Stück über den Blick auf uns" ("This is a play about how we are seen [by others]").[61] The actors playing these roles are young and mostly second- and third-generation and minoritized Germans. However, this introductory act of assuming these roles is publicly displayed, made part of the performance even, and therefore puts all certainty of identity under duress as it calls expectations into question.

This theatrical prelude of getting into costume and character, accompanied by the quasi warm-up performance of a repertoire of vulgar gestures, exhibits the adoption of a definitive role, one that may not be confounded with the identity of the actor playing the role. But this is not the whole of it; that is, this is not an opening ascribed wholly to a Brechtian performance of transparent representation through a gesture of alienation. Gesture can do other things, as well. José Esteban Muñoz asserts that "gesture ... signals a refusal of a certain kind of finitude."[62] For Muñoz, gesture as performance inheres in the ontological imperative of perpetual becoming. There is much to be said about the fact that these youths assume the roles that are frequently already attached to their bodies both inside and outside the theatre and neatly summed up by the play's title – "mad blood." *Verrücktes Blut* is indeed an appellation, even an interpellation, whose Turkish equivalent "delikanlı" is typically applied to macho young men.[63] Dulled by common usage, in standard Turkish the term simply means "young man" or "lad;" however, the compound, suffix-affixed word "delikanlı" demands further reading. Considering all components, deli (adjective), kan (noun), and lı (prepositional suffix), the word literally means "with mad blood."

In the context of the play, we cannot deny the exhortation towards literal meaning and interpellation. To possess "mad blood" is to have madness in one's blood, to be predisposed to mad behaviour. In the context and history of race, the conception and figuration of "blood" is onerous. That racial difference was not only essential but also somehow ascertainable through blood was a long-held belief. As Achille Mbembe describes it in the context of colonial history, "[t]here were indigenous qualities inscribed in the blood of each race. In the blood of the Black race ran instinct, irrational impulses, and primal sensuality."[64] As explored in the previous chapter, blood, too, was long the determining factor for citizenship in Germany, *jus sanguinis* (or, the law of blood), and still remains partially in effect. "Mad blood," as a term, no doubt semantically invokes these weighty strains. But I propose that we can also consider "mad blood" as an affective metaphor. Although *Verrücktes Blut* also translates as "crazy blood," it is frequently referred to as *Mad Blood*.[65] The double meaning of "mad" as both crazy and angry in English is a felicitous coincidence but one that comes alive in the weave of the play. To have mad blood might also evoke the idiomatic term "to have boiling blood." And here one's blood boils with anger.

In one performance of *Verrücktes Blut*, in March 2012, following the tragic murder of the seventeen-year-old African American Trayvon Martin in Florida and the acquittal of his murderer, the performers all donned hoodies in solidarity with Martin, who also wore a hoodie the day he died, and which had quickly become a provocative symbol of anger and resistance against the systematic criminalization and dehumanization of people of colour, in particular young men of colour, in the United States and elsewhere. Regarding the subversive performance of interpellated identity, Muñoz's concept of disidentification again becomes illuminating. Not an inextricable quality or corollary of practices of disidentification, anger is also no stranger to the management of an identity that works against majoritarian opinion. As demonstrated in the prelude of the play, anger is manifested through aggressive and antisocial behaviour. It is focused outward; it is directed towards the audience.

With the prelude over, the play begins, and for the time being the audience is more or less left in peace and the fourth wall is in place. *Verrücktes Blut* shifts into the realism of naturalist theatre with only minor disturbances, in the form of musical interludes of a medley of German folk songs. An almost predictable study of human psychology and behaviour sets in: disenfranchised youths act out in school and the teacher struggles to control them. Once the desperate teacher, Frau Kelich, seizes the gun and takes the class hostage, she not only forces her students to learn Schiller and to perform roles from his plays *Die Räuber* (*The Robbers*, 1781) and *Kabale und Liebe* (*Love and Intrigue*, 1784) at her armed behest, she also indirectly teaches them the Stanislavskian system of acting, of shedding their ungainliness and "becoming" their noble roles. At one point, Frau Kelich even reprimands a student for employing artifice, "that *theatre* tone of voice," as she is sick of it.[66] Thus, this pedagogy of violence, literally teaching with a gun, not only marks a profound critique of the German classics but also one of classical and modern theatre more generally. What is at stake here in the adherence to a naturalist aesthetic is the (dis)placement of anger. Theatre, and the plays of Schiller in particular, become a redirection of social and political anger that contains it and even turns it inward towards oneself or each other. With a freshly bloodied nose, one student, Bastian, proclaims: "Mann, sie will uns nur gegeneinander aufhetzen, merkst du das nicht, mit ihrem Scheißtheater." ("Man, she's just trying to get us to fight each other. Don't you get it? With her fucking theatre.")[67] Although Schiller's earlier plays reflect the period of *Sturm und Drang* ("Storm and Stress"), one which stood out as young, male, and anti-authoritarian theatre of the eighteenth century, it was hardly the place to arouse action and the possibility for *Realpolitik*. As such, we approach the significant disparities between dramatic theatre and Brechtian epic theatre. According to Brecht, Schillerian theatre "wears down the spectator's capacity for action;" it only functions as a cathartic release within theatre's confined compounds.[68]

Two episodes are particularly illustrative in the redirection of anger orchestrated through Schiller's texts and Stanislavskian acting. Both instances occur when Frau Kelich seeks to teach the students scenes from Schiller's first drama, *Die Räuber*. A play about sibling rivalry, rebellion, and violence, it furnishes an evocative theatrical mise en abyme. Scenes are handpicked by the teacher for the purpose of dramatic performance and apparently social reflection. In the extract from scene 3 of act 2, Karl Moor is enraged to learn that his band of robbers has desecrated an entire village and killed innocent people. The character, Musa, dexterously embodies his assigned role.

MUSA: (*reads*) "Oh, the poor, miserable creatures! Children, you say, the old and the sick?" –

BASTIAN: "Yes, let the devil take them! I happened to be going past a row of cottages there, and heard a howling and peeped in, and when I took a good look, what was it? A baby, lying there under the table, and the table just about to catch fire – Poor little bastard! I said, you're freezing! And threw it into the flames" –

SONIA: Now if it had been men; but it was only women and children and babies!

MUSA: (*goes towards Bastian, embodies the role*) "Did you, Schufterle? And may those flames burn in your breast until the day eternity grows great! –

Away, monster! Never let me see you in my group again!" – (*Bastian wants to keep him at a distance, Musa pushes his hand away*) I'm gonna throw up, don't touch me!

BASTIAN: Why're you so aggressive, man?

MUSA: "What, are you mumbling? Are you hesitating?" – Damned dog!

Musa hits Bastian on the head with the text.

BASTIAN: Damn it, why did you hit me? Musa beats on Bastian: punches to the stomach, Bastian falls to the ground. He wants to stand back up, but Musa kicks him in the stomach.[69]

At Frau Kelich's ("Sonia's") prompting, the scene quickly escalates into a violent confrontation as Musa fully embodies and extrapolates on the role of Karl Moor and turns on Bastian's character "Schufterle." This excessive adaptation of the role reveals an anger that seethes and results in sanguinary explosion. If, according to Erpulat, "[the students are meant to] learn that they shouldn't use violence through *Die Räuber*," then this is a gradual pedagogical process, which first witnesses an inward turning to violence.[70] A trajectory from Schiller's earlier, protorevolutionary plays, such as *Die Räuber* and *Kabale und Liebe*, to his later classical, aesthetic treatise *On the Aesthetic Education of Man*, which firmly condemns revolutionary violence and the French Revolution, in particular, becomes a questionable method of diffusion of violence. Schiller's latter work actually perpetuates an implicit violence of law that is brought to bear on the institution of theatre. If, as he indicates, the very basis of our ontology as humans is that we "play," for "man only plays when he is in the fullest sense of the word a human being, and he is only fully a human being when he plays," it must be noted that this "playing" also demands a set of rules.[71] With rules comes a structure of authority. Being human, subjectivity as such, thus hinges on the adherence to a set of rules, especially rules of sociability.

First, Paul de Man reminds us of the principle of law at the heart of Schiller's notion of "play";[72] second, a return to Walter Benjamin's "Critique of Violence" demonstrates the ineluctable link between law and violence. "For the function of violence in lawmaking is twofold, in the sense that lawmaking pursues as its end, with violence as the means, *what* is to be established as law, but as the moment of instatement does not dismiss violence; rather, at this very moment of lawmaking, it specifically establishes as law not an end unalloyed by violence, but one necessarily and intimately bound to it, under the title of power."[73] Thus, it requires no epistemological sleight of hand to perceive this impact on the Schillerian theatre as a rule-based establishment of "play." The machinery of the theatre itself is built on this lawmaking and its structure of violence. Brandishing a gun, Frau Kelich enacts this violent authority; she literally calls the shots. And that violence begets violence is an inescapable truth. The range of violence employed by Frau Kelich is not limited to the presence of the physical weapon; she also unleashes a scathing torrent of invectives. She calls the students everything from losers, to fuckups, to cunts. With the power of the gun in her hands Frau Kelich becomes a language monster and reveals the depraved and grotesque nature of authority.

This performance of redirection and displacement of her students' anger and the unleashing of her own becomes an altogether depoliticizing act. At no moment is this more palpable than when Frau Kelich declares that Mariam, a Muslim girl in her class who wears a hijab, is suppressed and must be liberated. The character of Frau Kelich and her name resonate with the public figure Necla Kelek, whom Erpulat directly criticizes in his slightly earlier musical comedy with Tunçay Kulaoğlu, *Lö Bal Almanya* (2010).[74] Kelek's tendentious criticism of Islam as a repressive and fundamentally antifeminist religion and the hijab as a symbol of this repression has spurred and supported Islamophobic views in the public sphere. Frau Kelich believes that by playing the role of Amalia in the first scene of the third act of *Die Räuber*, a scene in which Amalia powerfully rebuffs the sexual advances of Franz Moor, Mariam will be guided to "liberation" and as a matter of course will shed her hijab.

> SONIA: Yes, I think so, too. So, Franz feels good, because he's taken over his father's position. He's the king of the city, Hasan. And now, forget your sad Kurdish fate. Throw it away. I can't hear all of this trauma anymore. Now you're Franz. And that's good, because Mariam is going to play Amalia. (*to Mariam*) Come, stand up. Mariam wants to learn how to rebel. And you're going to help her, OK? You've come to conquer Amalia's heart. You just got the position of king. But the position of queen is still free and without pussy, he's got nothing, OK?
>
> ...
>
> HASAN: "By your hair I will drag you into the chapel with my sword in my hand, force the oath of matrimony out of your soul, take your virgin bed by storm, and conquer your proud innocence with my greater pride."
>
> MARIAM: "Take this first!" (*pushes him away*)
>
> SONIA: (*pushes her from behind towards Hasan*) He wants to drag you into the chapel. Force you into marriage, pull your hair, with his sword in his hand. Force the oath out of your soul. Get on top of you! – What kind of

Muslim are you? Didn't you hear what he said? And he said it so well. Hit him! Slap him!

MARIAM: "Take this first." (*embodies the role, slaps him*)

SONIA: He wants to pull your hair. He wants your virginity.

MARIAM: "Take this first."

SONIA: Hit him! Yes, again. Defend yourself. Take revenge.

MARIAM: "Take this first." And this! And this!

SONIA: Yes, Hasan, the text. Franz!

HASAN: (*forced into the corner*) "If not my wife – my mistress –"

SONIA: Miiissstresss!

HASAN: "You shall be my mistress. Come – come with me to my room – I am burning with desire."

SONIA: He wants to force you into his bedroom!

MARIAM: Yeah.

SONIA: He's burning with lust. He wants to fuck you and call you his mistress.

MARIAM: Yeah. (*kicks him in the crotch hard*)

SONIA: Mariam let it all out. LEEETTT IIITTTT OOOOUUUTT! Go on!

MARIAM: (*She continues beating Hasan*) "Do you see, villain, what I can do with you?"

SONIA: Keep going!

MARIAM: "I'm a woman, but I'm a powerful woman!"[75]

The anger that the performance of this scene invokes in Mariam is powerful. Not unlike Musa, Mariam lets herself be swept away by the role she is playing and by Frau Kelich's coercion. She embodies the character of Amalia fully and again the result is displaced violence against Hasan as Franz. If the goal of the performance exercise is some kind of co-opted Boalian plot, by way of which theatre becomes a revolutionary means of liberation, then it fails. Frau Kelich gives Mariam to believe that not only is she oppressed, but that the source of her oppression is patriarchy, and Muslim men in particular. Hasan is made to stand in for this oppression against which Mariam is expected to turn her anger. However, Hasan himself must similarly be taught how to embody a fantasy of "Muslim male patriarchy." Throughout the scene, Sonia (Frau Kelich) instructs him to "grab his balls" as a means of asserting and ascertaining his masculinity, his "mad blood." The sum of these measures taken reveals the artifice of Frau Kelich's theatre exercise. Mariam's anger becomes contained in her role as Amalia and displaced. Theatre reverts back to an apolitical cathartic event in which action and violence, at least for the audience, are safely set at a distance.

Throughout *Verrücktes Blut*, performing Schiller provides a depoliticized outlet for anger that pulls it back in on itself, inverts it, and dilutes its range. Frau Kelich's notion that her students can work through their problems, and their anger, even correct their actions with the help of Schiller, becomes an utterly naïve enterprise. Yet the play demonstrates that theatre pedagogy may be taken in two different directions: first, as release; and second, as preparation for real action. Here a confluence of Schiller and authoritarian violence becomes transformative. By the second scene of the second act, the students appear to be fully converted to the ideology of enlightened humanism when they refuse to violently punish Musa, the class bully, despite Frau Kelich's insistence. This protean narrative is vivified through an alternative tableau vivant in which the group embraces, and in chorus they smile blithely at Frau Kelich. As verbal assurance, Mariam adds: "We've changed." Yet this is not some kind of insidious conversion narrative, rendered through harsh educational conditioning. The image of this motley crew, bloodied and disheveled, appears off. What is this change? What brought them there? Did the means justify the end? The latter is of course the question that violence always poses. Frau Kelich responds in disbelief and anger with a final strike of verbal assault. "You, you ... You cunts ... machos ... retards ... ass fuckers – Sizi, zavalli Aptallar!"[76] A peripety in the distilled form of a linguistic switch from German to Turkish shows signs of a disturbance in the flow of the play. Frau Kelich not only outs herself to her students as "one of the them," a German with Turkish roots, she also steps out of character. Antitheatricality marks this shift from German to Turkish, insofar as there is no translation and the audience (assuming many spectators do not speak Turkish) is thrown into a state of confusion and becomes disconnected from the spectacle.

The antitheatricality of the scene reaches its crest in the final minutes of the play when Frau Kelich begins to address the audience in a kind of monologue. Now switching between German and Turkish, she declares that she is tired, hungry, and that there is no point in going on with play because the audience didn't understand anything, anyway. Theatricality is transferred from the stage to the audience and the pedagogical performance of the play is redirected. Who was being instructed here? But before the actors can abruptly exit into the world, Pirandello-style, Hasan picks up the gun and forces them to remain. Distinct from *Schwarze Jungfrauen*, *Verrücktes Blut* has only one true monologue, which arrives at the end of the play. As its grand finale, however, this monologue bears unbounded significance. Throughout the play, Hasan is bullied and abused by his classmates and patronized by the teacher for not hewing to the charge of machismo and for his cultural difference, as a Kurd. If in fact the other characters learn to relinquish their anger, are broken down by the structural violence of authority, then Hasan actually moves in the opposite direction. He taps his simmering reservoir of anger through "playing" and demands an encore performance. It is not a matter of having lost himself to the role of Schiller's Franz Moor, no longer capable of distinguishing between himself and the character, between reality and play. Instead, Hasan delivers a raging monologue that quite literally assaults the audience. For in his hands, Hasan holds the gun. At first, he waves it threateningly, then he eventually aims it point-blank at the audience.

> HASAN: And I'll play Franz. I'm Franz and I'll stay Franz ...
> "I have every right to be angry at nature. Why did nature give me this ugliness? These Hottentot's eyes?"
> What do you see in me? An actor or a Kanake? Still?
> "Very well, then! I will crush everything that stands in the way of my becoming master."
> Who denied what to whom? Who's guilty?
> What do you want from me? The only thing that works in this school is the stage.
> The theatrical stage! We act. But what's going to happen to me when this is over?
> Become an established secondary-school teacher like you Miss Kelich? A real model Kanake?
> Or commit an honor killing on a TV show. Hmm, sorry, we've reached our capacity for model
> Kanakes, the role of the Kanake inspector on the detective show has already been filled.
> How many model Kanakes will our country tolerate anyway?
> "Whoever can float, will float. And whoever's too fat will sink!"
> As long as we act, everything's OK. This is the only place where that works. And it's soundproof.
> Soundproof! Can anyone hear us?[77]

His monologue crisscrosses between lines from Schiller's *Die Räuber*, from the character Hasan, and from the actor (Murat Dikenci) himself. It emerges as a clamorous entanglement of past and present, theatricality and reality, art and politics. The anger expressed by Franz Moor becomes Hasan's own. It is anger formed relationally and directed at the audience, which refuses to accept Hasan as an actor first and a Turkish German second. His use of the derogatory term "Kanake" brings into relief the injurious and negating gaze of the audience that weighs on the play, but also a performance of disidentification that throws it back, as explored in chapter 2. If the opening scene of crude tableaux vivants – projections of the audience's gaze – can be laughed off as physical comedy, then the attack of this final monologue cannot be so easily skirted. "Who's guilty?" Hasan roars. This close is much franker than a Brechtian epilogical turn to the audience in search of answers for unresolved matters evoked by the play, such as at the close of *Der gute Mensch von Sezuan* (*The Good Person from Szechwan*, 1941). Hasan is not searching for answers; he is angrily indicting the audience. With manifest confrontation, he opens up a discourse about the reality of institutional racism in German theatre, film, and television. Theatre, in particular, remains an intransigent bastion of cultural homogeneity and conservative ideals. Hasan's heady plaint that as an actor of colour he has no future in Germany – for only as a play within a play is the audience willing to accept him as an actor capable of performing Schiller's illustrious Franz Moor – has an effect that hews like an axe. These words echo Erpulat's own, as though he might be speaking through Hasan in this final monologue. In conversation about the play and its motivation, Erpulat elaborates on this:

> In all other countries, the theater is more progressive than the government. Twenty-five percent of the people in this country [Germany] have *Migrationshintergrund* [migration background]. That's one in four. Germany had been dealing with this for a while but the theater scene hadn't. It was already happening in dance and opera, usually much more conservative forms. Asian dancers have been around for 20 years, but there's still no Gretchen in *Faust* that has black hair.[78]

Erpulat potently speaks to the reality of most German theatres as exclusively white institutions, which not only trade in white culture but also do not reflect society. *Verrücktes Blut* and especially Hasan's final monologue address the need for German theatre to take stock of the myriad ways in which they uphold systems of oppression. This ending is not simply a rhetorical gesture.

Hasan's assaulting monologue also exposes a body that threatens. For, as Stanton B. Garner Jr. contends, "the human body threatens artistic control, breaks form into panic, through a physicality that stands outside and consumes."[79] From beginning to end, *Verrücktes Blut* exposes the physical excess of bodies onstage and the contingency they yield. If theatre is about bodies, it has traditionally been invested in the drama of controlling these bodies. In the theatre of anger, bodies resist control. Wielding the gun, blood smeared around his mouth, blackened eyes bulging, Hasan jerks his body around the stage with a rage that cuts. He is the Laocoön – the rage machine. He physically sets himself against both his fellow performers and the audience. If there was any doubt in the efficacy of the monologue to condemn, the shot fired into the auditorium rounds it off. The guilty party is indicted and violently struck. Not only is the performance transferred to the audience space, violence in all of its sinuous forms crosses over the threshold. The gaze is returned in the form of a bullet. Each time I attended the performance in the intimate Ballhaus Naunynstraβe theatre, a backward jolt passed over the audience at the moment of the shot. Just having the gun pointed in one's direction was enough to cause distress. Anger frequently slides into violence in *Verrücktes Blut*, both in its verbal and physical forms.

While *Schwarze Jungfrauen* disarms its audience with the manifestation of anger from an unexpected source, that is, young Muslim women, *Verrücktes Blut* explores the complexities of an anger frequently ascribed – to young Muslim men – but seldom probed. Theatre presents itself as the space and medium through which anger, in its corporeality and relationality, can be exerted and explored against hurtful tales of the present. Both plays roil against Islamophobia in a manner that strikes like a bullet into the auditorium. Inveterate theatrical codes are split, anatomized, reshaped, and hurtled forward through performance. Language in its performative capacity to damage is subversively reappropriated and flung back at the audience. It seems theatre and theatre society are assaulted with the weapon of their own invention. Here the unsettling, aesthetic protest of the theatre of anger lies in its recognition and confrontation of ubiquitous Islamophobia in Europe and theatre's tacit role in upholding these structures of discrimination, possibly even overextending them. The social justice bent to the theatre of anger offers a sparring resistance against multiple structures of hate and violence. The effectiveness of theatre as resistance and protest is explored head on in the following chapter as it links documentary theatre with active protest movements. The walls of the theatre are made permeable, and the political hold on the theatre of anger bears itself further.

Chapter Four

Documentaries of Outrage

It's time to take over! It's time to get angry!

Stéphane Hessel, *Time for Outrage*

Is theatre a significant forum for civil resistance and disobedience? Do theatre and performance simply offer aesthetic forms of resistance or do they also offer active protest?[1] The theatre of anger responds to these questions in the affirmative. But perhaps more than any other form of theatre affiliated with the theatre of anger, documentary theatre is a place where these questions are palpably taken up. Once explicitly linked to leftist politics (particularly in the German space), documentary theatre now seems to serve more experimentally diverse purposes. With a focus on the power of form, this chapter addresses two diverging examples of documentary in the repertoire of the theatre of anger. Despite their differences, Anestis Azas and Prodromos Tsinikoris's *Telemachos – Should I Stay or Should I Go?* (premiere 2013) and Mely Kiyak's *Aufstand: Monolog eines wütenden Künstlers* (*Rebellion: Monologue of an Angry Artist*, premiere 2014) both scrutinize and perform anger through transnational dialogues of protest. Rhetorically following the Maxim Gorki Theatre's programmatic theme of transnational exchange from the local to the global and back again, in this chapter Berlin "calls" both Athens and Istanbul. In other words, theatre and performance become part of a relationality that moves in geographically and culturally different directions. Both plays ask what is happening elsewhere, not simply from the perspective of the here and the now but also through the insight of the then and the there.

If the theatre of anger emerges as a response to earlier histories of marginalization and violence in Germany, as explored in the previous chapters, the plays in this chapter reveal the development of the theatre of anger alongside the extensive protest movements on the squares and in the streets across the globe that shook the dawn of the 2010s: Arab Spring (2010), Syntagma Square protests in Athens (2011), Occupy Wall Street and beyond (2011), the protests on the Plaza de Catalunya in Barcelona (2011), Refugee Tent Action in Berlin (2012), Idle No More throughout Canada (2012), the Gezi Park protests in Istanbul (2013), the Umbrella Movement in Hong Kong (2014), and the Ferguson protests (2014) that ignited the America-wide movement Black Lives Matter. Whether challenging that omnipresent cult of indifference, as argued by TINA ("There Is No Alternative"), which unapologetically asserts that neoliberalism is the only solution, or protesting social injustice and the threats to civil rights and freedom more broadly, these protest movements shaped the early years of the 2010s as a brief but monumental time of anger. Human rights activist, Stéphane Hessel has articulated this juncture as "the time for outrage" ([2010] 2011) in his brief treatise by the same name, in which he appeals to his young readers to "look around you and you will find the themes to justify your indignation."[2] Such a galvanizing message is shared by the project of the theatre of anger. With its commitment to social justice, its challenge to national theatre cultural traditions, and its confrontational tenor, the theatre of anger speaks to and asserts the contemporaneous ethos of outrage on the "public stages" of the city, which also make their way back to theatre. This chapter is especially animated by the points of encounter between street and stage, where the youthful protest spirit of the early part of the decade intersects with art.

For decades, this crossing from theatre to street was unidirectional and captured by Antonin Artaud's call in the 1930s for a theatre that could revive the agitation of the masses and send the people out on the streets.[3] Indeed, if radical theatre found its way back to the streets in the early part of the twentieth century, there it persisted. Although street theatre in the style of agitprop or guerrilla theatre has become less frequent, the theatricality of street protests, such as in the examples of the Las Madres de la Plaza de Mayo and the Cumartesi Anneleri considered in chapter 2, is still widely recognized. Richard Schechner calls this "direct theatre." "In 'direct theatre,'" he writes, "large public spaces are transformed into theatre where collective reflexivity is performed, fecund and spectacular excesses displayed."[4] The dramaturgy and choreography of street protests can be theatrical and carnivalesque in their mass display of bodies desperate to be seen and heard. Within this same line of thought, Baz Kershaw holds that politics left the theatre and became restaged on the streets in the late 1960s, and this is where it has remained.[5] This echoes the words of Peter Weiss, in 1968, who declared at the apogee of the student protests in West Germany and across western Europe that the new theatre belonged in the streets and the university lecture halls.[6] But with the theatre of anger, we witness the return of politics and protest to the theatre.

To suggest that politics and protest had abandoned the theatre altogether would, however, be inexact. According to Harry J. Elam Jr., in the 1990s in the United States, "oppressed peoples and new political movements ... turned to the theater as a means to articulate social causes, to galvanize support, and to direct sympathizers towards campaigns of political resistance."[7] Since the pathbreaking work of Augusto Boal, theatre's role as an empowering tool of emancipation, resistance, and solidarity cannot be overstated. Opening *Theatre of the Oppressed* ([1974] 1985), Boal declares, "[t]he argument about the relations between theater and politics is as old as theater and ... as politics."[8] Theatre has always provided a space for enacting, exploring, and interrogating concurrent struggles. In the wake of 9/11, British playwright David Edgar boldly announced the return of political theatre: "The war on terror brought politics back on the world stage, and it's no surprise that politics returned to theatrical stages as well."[9] Recorded as the epigraph to the introduction of Alison Forsyth and Chris Megson's edited book *Get Real: Documentary Theatre Past and Present* (2009), Edgar's observation opens up a rich study on the sudden upsurge of documentary theatre and politics. Coinciding with this pronouncement, Carol Martin similarly observes that "[i]t is no accident that [documentary] theatre has reemerged during a time of international crises of war, religion, government, truth, and information."[10] Such remarks may also serve to articulate the protest movements of the early 2010s, and the simultaneous development of the theatre of anger, especially its instances of documentary theatre. But I add this variation: if the post-9/11 era had reintroduced politics to the theatre, then the post-2010 period reintroduced active protest to the theatre (at least to the German theatre), in affective-political form.

Documentary has a notable history and tradition in the German-language space. From the early agitprop style of Erwin Piscator (and to some extent Bertolt Brecht) in the 1920s to the tribunal plays of Rolf Hochmuth, Heinar Kipphardt, Rolf Schneider, and Peter Weiss in the 1960s, documentary theatre has evolved as a theatrical form inextricably linked to leftist politics. Dubbed the "Theater der Unruhigen" (Theatre of the Agitators),[11] documentary theatre of the 1960s cohered with the revolutionary ethos of the student revolts in West Germany. In his seminal but brief fourteen-point treatise on documentary theatre, "Notizen zum dokumentarischen Theater" ("Notes on Documentary Theatre" [1968]), Weiss elucidates the important crossover between documentary theatre and political activism: "Das dokumentarische theater is nur möglich, wenn es als feste, politisch und soziologisch geschulte Arbeitsgruppe besteht und, unterstützt von einem reichhaltigen Archiv." ("The documentary theatre is only possible if it exists as an organized political working collective that has studied sociology and is capable of scientific analysis based on a capacious archive.")[12] What developed simultaneously was an abandonment of the theatre space to the street and subsequently the beginning of what became called "street theatre" in 1968. Although I do not propose that street theatre and documentary theatre are one and the same, their parallels are clear, particularly in the context of their inception in West Germany. Another subsequent development was the rise of "freies Theater" (independent or fringe theatre) in the early 1970s, which officially sought to reckon with the revolutionary spirit and desire for reform at that time with the theatre practices and traditions in West Germany.[13] "Freies Theater" might be marked as a break and the genesis of a new theatre free from the conventions of state or municipal theatre, in which new and radical forms and themes (particularly political theatre) could be pursued more freely.

In West Germany, freies Theater thrived on the margins, but it also gradually began to cross-pollinate with more traditional theatre, and distinctions between state and municipal theatres (that is, theatres directly supported by the government) and freies Theater became fuzzy. Manfred Brauneck observes that in the late 1970s and 1980s, many state or municipal theatres had adopted the innovations called into existence by independent theatre movements.[14] However, others have noted that the incendiary politics associated with the earlier phases of independent theatre was troubled throughout the West in the wake of postmodernity and the end of the Cold War. In its apodictic adherence to the left, political theatre had fallen on hard times. It came to be perceived as too ideological. With some exception, the late 1970s, 1980s, and 1990s witnessed a hiatus in political theatre. From the long era of Thatcherism in the United Kingdom to the protracted incumbency of conservative leader Helmut Kohl in West Germany and then in united Germany (1982–1998), the political climate had also radically changed since the late 1960s.

Ushering in a new era of political theatre in Berlin and beyond, the theatre of anger also relies on the documentary as a form particularly suited to the political in its probing nature and concern for real-world narratives.[15] Shermin Langhoff's description of the role of documentary in postmigrant theatre more broadly is instructive here:

> Aesthetically we are oriented towards, among other things, documentary theatre, researching real situations, putting real protagonists on the stage. We go outside the theatre, presenting not only in the theatre but

performing, for example in Anatolian cafés frequented only by men and on stage in the Naunynstraβe. It's about gaining access to new producers and stories as well as acquiring new recipients. This happens when people can identify with stories, and here we are especially successful with the Ballhaus.[16]

In Langhoff's formulation, documentary permits access to the real – real situations, real protagonists, real locations. It also mounts itself on the threshold between the theatre and the street, as well as between what Arthur Sainer describes as "life in its theatricality and theatre in its lifelikeness."[17] The documentary of the theatre of anger, what I call the documentary of outrage, is contemporary in its political investment but also rooted in a much older history of theatre's kinship with the street and protest. It brings forth the nature of protest inherent in the tradition of documentary theatre. For already in 1968 Weiss had proposed that documentary theatre not only works against a politics of repression in its drive to reveal alternative and truthful accounts of an event, but that it is also a direct medium of public protest: "Wie spontane Versammlung im Freien, mit Plakaten, Spruchbändern und Sprechchören, so stellt das dokumentarische Theater eine Reaktion dar auf gegenwärtige Zustände, mit Forderung, diese zu klären." ("Just like the spontaneous assembly out in the open, with placards, banners, and chanting, documentary theatre constitutes a response to the present state of things, with demand that these are clarified.")[18] Attentive to the politics of the present, the plays taken up here draw on this important tradition as they reawaken the spirit of protest in the theatre.

The play that will form the focus of the first part of this chapter, Azas and Tsinikoris's *Telemachos*, stands between the theatre and the streets of Athens. It researches real situations and puts "real people" onstage. As one of the explicitly inter-European plays to be performed at the Ballhaus Naunynstraβe, it interrogates the Greek debt crisis, the emergence of civic outrage, and the resurgence of emigration. This play develops as a continuity of protest. It takes up the performative anger inherent in the acts of resistance and protest and transports it to the theatre. In the balance of the chapter, I will consider Kiyak's *Aufstand*. This slightly later play stages the outrage in the wake of the Gezi Park protests in Istanbul through the perspective of a Kurdish artist from Diyarbakır and currently in Berlin. To call *Aufstand* a documentary play might seem misleading. It uses actors and fictionalized text and explores a more personal account of recent history. However, the play works with factual reports (Weiss) and presents truthful portrayals of real-life events and people (Martin). *Aufstand* is based on Kiyak's own eyewitness account of the Gezi protests as a journalist reporting for the German weekly *Die Zeit*. The production and performance of *Aufstand* as part of the festival "Voicing Resistance," in which contemporary artists' voices from conflict zones are collected, also bring it ideationally closer to documentary, a form that speaks to and explores an ongoing issue, not dissimilar in mode to a news report. Through almost exclusively monologic performance, *Aufstand* observes and resists the complex structure of power and citizenship in Turkey against the backdrop of the Gezi Park protests and recent Kurdish history.

Both plays seek transnational dialogue between Germany and Greece, and Germany and Turkey, respectively, as they dig up and scatter the damaged remains of historical entanglements wrought by dispossession and violence. "Calling," a term I apply here, becomes a gesture and genre of communication, which has already been instituted by Studio Я in the form of creative podium discussions between Berlin and other cities worldwide. It has become a forum for open discussions with Berlin-situated migrants, asylum seekers, and first- , second- , and third-generation and minoritized Germans who can speak as eyewitnesses to current resistance movements internationally. This chapter extends the concept of the theatre of anger by pursuing its possibilities through a focus on form. Documentary, protest, and anger form a resounding nexus of witness and uprising that blur stage and society and draw out a reflexivity of the relationality of theatre and politics so critical to the theatre of anger.

"Berlin Calling Athens," or Telemachos – Should I Stay or Should I Go?

Greek words, nothing less than a recitation from that paradigmatic tome, Homer's *Odyssey*, are spoken in whispered tones. Co-director and co-writer, Prodromos Tsinikoris, stands downstage left at a microphone. Translations of these words appear in German and English on the large black screen upstage. The set, designed by Lina Fey and Angela Konti, is configured like a Greek balcony in summer, complete with tiled floor and plastic patio furniture consisting of a long table and chairs. To the far left, upstage, is a DJ's turntable. The recitation ends. A grainy home video featuring a man, woman, and young child is projected on the screen. Prodromos turns to the screen and briefly watches. This is him as a toddler with his parents in their home in the once-industrial city of Wuppertal in North Rhine Westphalia. Finally, he turns towards the house and wishes the audience a good evening in Greek, German, and English. This unique mix of media, literature, language, and family memories open *Telemachos* as a layered narrative and performance.

Following its successful premiere in January 2013, *Telemachos* ran for nearly two seasons as part of the repertoire of the Ballhaus Naunynstraβe theatre in Berlin and then later at the Onassis Cultural Centre (OCC) in Athens. Co-written and directed by Anestis Azas and Prodromos Tsinikoris and Ensemble, *Telemachos* explores and performs, on the one hand, the story of the post-2010 financial crisis in Greece and the resulting emigration of many young Greeks, the so-called crisis migrants.[19] On the other hand, it offers a glimpse at Greece's postwar political and economic relationship to Germany through the encounter of Greek migrants to (what was then West) Germany during the span of active labour migration in the 1960s to the period of the financial crisis at the dawn of the last decade. The play thus situates new Greek migration to Germany in a historical continuum. A series of intersecting personal narratives of loss, migration, and displacement are performed through monologues, interspersed with dialogue, collective reminiscing, the exposition of Super 8 home videos, old photographs, and documents, dancing, and citations from Homer's epic Greek poem *Odyssey*, about travel and return, from which the play's main title is derived. (Telemachos is the son of Odysseus, who struggles to choose between going in search of his father or staying in Greece with his mother.) A kind of modern-day Telemachos narrative, the titular question is posed and given the charge of this narrative thread: "Should I stay or should I go?" Much more than just a riff on the famous Clash song, this question was also the banner name of the 2011 national public media debate about emigration: "Should I stay or should I go in crisis-ridden Greece."[20] *Telemachos* depicts real-life stories of protagonists caught up in and shaken by agonistic transnational politics. It is direct, confrontational, and personal. Performers play themselves and present their own lived histories. *Telemachos* is a rousing performance of memory and experience and its attendant challenges. If remembering personal experience is tricky enough, how might one possibly present this memory in mimetic form? As Martin might put it, this play is "a struggle to shape and remember the most transitory history – the complex ways in which men and women think about the events that shape the landscapes of their lives."[21] These words express the challenge of shaping and remembering that bears out this theatrical representation of Greece in a period of crisis.

Active in the theatre scene in Athens, with collaborative plays such as *Journey by Train* (2011) and *Epidauris: A Documentary* (2012), Azas and Tsinikoris are also no strangers to Berlin or the Berlin theatre scene. Azas even studied at the Ernst Busch Academy of Dramatic Arts. Both also collaborated with the Berlin-based performance and new-documentary group Rimini Protokoll on the project *Prometheus in Athens* (premiere 2010), whose premise of civic society and precarity bound up in Greek mythical ethics was thematically influential on *Telemachos*. The inception of *Telemachos* came as an invitation by director Nurkan Erpulat to return to Berlin in the summer of 2011 in the swell of Greece's devastating financial crisis and the ensuing Syntagma Square protests. The invitation arrived in the form of a proposal to create a play about contemporary Greece, the debt crisis, and Greek migration to Germany. Azas and Tsinikoris had participated in the protests in Athens and seized this opportunity to reflect on what they could bring to the theatre from the street and from political movement to art, in order to share their experiences with a German audience and to continue their political protest on the stage. The transnational point of contact is not incidental. Germany was a major destination for new Greek migrants, as it had been in postwar times. Paradoxically, as the eurozone's most powerful nation, Germany is also the country held responsible for the harsh austerity measures imposed on Greece as a condition of its bail-out package. Suffice to say, antagonism against the German government emerged with great fervour during the period of the protests. This was thrown into sharp relief when angry protesters in Athens brandished placards portraying Chancellor Angela Merkel as Hitler.

Mounting a play on the small proscenium stage of the Ballhaus Naunynstraβe that could capture the complexity of the revolutionary drift of the events in Athens without resorting to narrative mimesis posed a challenge. Simply transplanting the protests from the streets of Athens to the Berlin stage was not an attainable nor even desirable goal.[22] *Telemachos* had to also speak to a new encounter – between Greece and Germany. In lieu of offering a reconstruction and re-performance of the street protests, Azas and Tsinikoris conceived a play of documentary-style dramaturgy that unearths historical entanglements and recasts political and social relations between Germany and Greece from the perspective of the personal and the outraged.[23] The aggrieved Greeks onstage could confront the German audience head on, and the German audience members became drawn into an experience of direct encounter with individuals, who previously may have only been present to them as an angry throng of protesters and through mediatized sources or as bloodless statistics. *Telemachos* does not relinquish its protest mode: it makes it more intimate; it brings it into proximity.

Calling Athens: In a tangled replaying of history and politics, *Telemachos* revisits the protests that took shape on Syntagma Square in central Athens, upon which Greek citizens challenged the dispossession and the precarious conditions to which they have been subject under the pursuits of neoliberal capitalism and the subsequent austerity measures imposed on Greece by its European lenders. The economic thrall that settled on Greece, one of the countries with the highest financial growth rates in Europe between 1995 and 2007, was the result of massive privatization and spending.[24] There was a sudden influx of wealth and unhinged spending. For over a decade, life in Greece was largely comfortable and yielding in its short-term economic promises. But the situation was not sustainable. Lauren Berlant has articulated this narrative in broad terms as the "dawning of good-life-fantasy attrition," by way of which the pursuit of wealth and prosperity becomes precisely the path of its undoing, one of instability and precarity.[25] Massive spending and privatization reached a tipping point with the worldwide financial crisis in 2008. Suddenly thrust into the throttling clutches of unemployment, without health insurance, and the possibility of being without permanent shelter, dissensus rapidly spread. Many Greek citizens rallied around their damaged present and most uncertain future. The place of this rallying, the original public stage of protest – Syntagma Square – was transformed into a site of direct theatre. This transformation of the Syntagma Square, like so many urban squares at the time (Tahrir Square, Plaza de Catalunya, Taksim Square, Oranienplatz, to name just a few), recalls Ngũgĩ wa Thiong'o's assertion that any site of "social, physical, and psychic forces of society" can be a performance space.[26] Yet Syntagma Square was hardly an unmarked space. Flanking the Greek Parliament (also known as the Hellenic Parliament) building in central Athens, Syntagma Square was named after the Constitution of 1843. Initially mounted as a public space for strolling and sitting, by the mid-1990s it had become the symbolic site of the glorified "Strong Greece," and as a result it was transformed into an increasingly regimented space of control and surveillance where only "carefully orchestrated and controlled events organized by the authorities" were permitted to take place.[27] Thus, the act of physically entering this space en masse was a form of protest in and of itself.

Long a stage for national politics in flux, Syntagma Square provided both a geopolitically and symbolically charged site for the 2010–2011 austerity protests, which demonstrated a kind of frenzied drama of the wreck of the good-life fantasy when all of the economic promises and opportunities shatter. These protests commenced as a response to Greece's signing of the conditions for the first bailout package (officially referred to as the First Economic Adjustment Programme for Greece) put into motion by the grassroots Greek citizen organization Direct Democracy Now! The protests quickly metastasized into a broader national movement of anger among Greek citizens, often referred to as the Indignant Citizens Movement, or the "*Aganaktismenoi* [*polites*] movement," a term coined by the Greek media and adapted from the Spanish *Indignados*, movement of the "outraged" and the "infuriated." Greece and Spain were among the countries hit hardest by the eurozone crisis. Contained within the Greek and Spanish words is the notion of the angry citizen who is politically mobilized. The germ of expectation is enfolded in this identity. Are you a citizen? If you are, then you should be angry.[28] Addressing the youth of today in his short 2010 manifesto, Stéphane Hessel declares: "The basic motive of the Resistance was indignation. Here is our message: It's time to take over! It's time to get angry!"[29] The title of his manifesto is indeed an imperative: "Indignifiez-vous!" – that is, "Get angry! Get outraged!" For Hessel there is no other way to confront or respond to the crisis of the present and the extreme dispossession and precarity of citizens at the turn of the 2010s than with anger. With minor exception, this was not debilitating anger, or even a violent anger, but an attributed and mobilizing anger that sought change, a different future. It wanted to reclaim democracy from the clutches of neoliberal capitalism.[30]

In the context of protest movements, anger responds to something directly. It is also driven by a certain degree of hope. The indignant citizen or the raging revolutionary is always one who invests in futurity – and in the pursuit of change. Here it is the robust will to (re-)invigorate direct democracy. If dispossession is the object of anger, then anger itself is the motivating force for change. It is a force that responds and moves towards a lost or a desired equilibrium. In Greece, bodies took to the streets. They assembled, they shouted, they marched. They performed their anger as a struggle for social justice. In the context of the *Aganaktismenoi* movement, the struggle becomes the condition of citizenship itself. As Chantal Mouffe contends, "[p]eople struggle for equality not because of some ontological postulate, but because they have been constructed as subjects in a democratic tradition that puts those values at the center of social life."[31] I would further add that people can get angry for the same reasons. Anger becomes the recalcitrant response to the violation of political and social agreements between subjects in a democratic tradition. This simmering moment of politics and anger, which emerged as a result of the Greek debt crisis, returned to the theatre in numerous forms, inspiring two other plays, which also premiered in 2013: *I Want a Country* (directed by Andreas Flourakis), and *Kangaroo* (directed by Katsikonouris Vassilis). Azas and Tsinikoris even followed up their collaborative work on *Telemachos* with three other thematically related plays: *Utopia in Progress* (2014), *Geblieben um zu gehen* (*Stayed in Order to Go*, 2015), and *Clean City* (2016), which all explore the crisis from different perspectives and communities.

Back in Berlin: Raging politics of the street takes on new life when restaged in the theatre. Restaging is not only a mode of repetition or re-performance; it enacts a performance within a performance that permits a reshaping, a narrativizing, and a historicizing of the event or series of events in question. *Telemachos* restages history, politics, and culture, and in this way transports them into a new context of multiple encounters – theatre's standing charge. On one level, this encounter occurs within the dramaturgy of the play as the encounter between young and old, that is, between postwar Greek migrants to Germany and newer migrants to Germany in the crisis period.[32] The play brings forth these two generations of labour migration from Greece to Germany – their collective experiences and their distinctions – in this encounter. Among the first generation is the former political prisoner Chryssi Kyriakidou, who fled Greece for Germany in the 1960s both to escape the Greek military junta (1967–1974) and to look for new opportunities abroad. The other half of this first-generation duo is the labour migrant, Christos Sarafianos, who in the mid-1960s found himself in a car bound for Munich, where he eventually settled and opened his own restaurant. Bridging this first generation of labour migrants to the second is the Greek German citizen Prodromos Tsinikoris himself (the son of Greek labour migrants), who begins and frames *Telemachos* with a personal account of struggle with antagonistic attachments and transnational identity. His struggle plays out as a longer digital communication project, first through a Skype conversation with his mother, who has returned to Greece and wishes for him to also stay there with her, and then through video footage of him interviewing random people on the streets of Berlin (and then later in Athens) to ask their thoughts. Opinions vary; scripted or not, a mixture of humour, openness, and thinly veiled racism is revealed through this public performance. Prodromos appears to be none the wiser for his efforts. Similar in age to Prodromos are the recent migrants from Greece, Despina Bibika, Kostis Kallivretakis, and Giannis Tsoukalas, who all made the move to Germany in search of work in the immediate period of the post-2010 crisis and the resulting spike in unemployment in Greece. Finally, there is the young ethnically German Knut Berger, who ironically refers to himself as the "Gastgeber" or the "host" (no doubt alluding to the term "Gastarbeiter") of this theatrical event. Representing the embedded audience or even the chorus in the play, whose comportment results in critical reflection as well as conflict, Knut's role is theatrically instrumental and politically charged. His presence signals another kind of encounter important to theatre and performance: the encounter between performers and spectators. Yet his conceivable role as a (white German, heterosexual, cisgender male) spectator also mobilizes its own self-interrogation, precisely for its hegemonic cultural positioning and homogeneity. Knut's figure is the instrument of provocation, a point to which I will return. The relationships between the figures is, theatrically speaking, tangential. They are not bound by a clear-cut cause-and-effect dramatic narrative, only a historical loop of emigration. If there is dramatic conflict, the monologic structure of the play often directs this outward.

Personal stories of hardship, anger, migration, and hope are articulated and performed in a three-fold way in *Telemachos*, in what Martin calls "the tripartite structure of contemporary documentary theatre: technology, text, and body."[33] All three are critical components of *Telemachos*. Technology comes in myriad forms in the play. From digital videos to telecommunications (including a Skype call to Athens), film, music, photographs, factual reports and documents, and projection, technology allows the performers to revisit and re-present past events with authentic indexical and archival flourish. These props support and supplement the text and the stories shared by the performers. Each story is accompanied by the display of real documents, in one case an identification card, and in another, old bank statements, which are projected onto the large screen upstage. *Telemachos* is representative of Azas and Tsinikoris's broader corpus of work, which is heavily influenced by documentary and research theatre, an approach Azas describes in the following way: "When we start a project, we have 100–200 pages of interview transcripts, notes, etc. We first draw a map. We think of what we are interested in, what issues we want to explore, why we choose the protagonists we choose – because they have a problem, a conflict, because they are good performers – and instinctively, step by step."[34] As "real people," the performers are living witnesses of the events of history and of the politics of the present – *Aganaktismenoi* on the stage. In the spirit of "direct protest," document and body align to present an up-close perspective on reality to which the audience may otherwise not have access.[35] Theatre, and especially documentary theatre, provides this access, this direct encounter, with a drive to, in Martin's words, "stir up conflict" and "unsettle the present."[36]

Telemachos does not merely offer a dramatic relaying and resituating of Greek precarity both in Greece and as migrants to Germany; instead, it delivers a heterogeneous assemblage of narratives and experiences that unfold over a layered series of encounters by way of which the audience becomes implicated in the performance. According to Janelle

G. Reinelt, the spectator's experience of performance, determined to large degree by cultural positioning, is imperative for the sensemaking of the play. In the case of documentaries, "the meanings are produced relationally."[37] The abundant use of monologue in *Telemachos* offers a case in point. These monologues form the underpinning of the confrontational encounter of this theatre experience, for theatre performance emerges through an encounter, a confrontation, an interaction, as Erika Fischer-Lichte holds.[38] Individual verbal acts are performative in their assertion of identity and history, but also precarious in their performance of bodily enactment and vulnerability. Fischer-Lichte reminds us that theatre performance must reckon with the radical possibilities of bodily co-presence of performers and spectators in a given space.

In its direct display of bodies as spectacle, theatre (and especially the monologic act of self-narration onstage) enters this phenomenological sphere of the relational, and even the social. With bracing insight, each performer tells her or his story of forced migration. In *Telemachos*, Despina, a young college graduate, tells of her degrading work as a maid for a wealthy German family. "My German was not very good, so I had to work as a maid in a big fancy house. ... Why do I have to work as a maid?!?! I have education and skills." Kostis speaks of his father's inconceivable gambling debts in Greece, which not only resulted in the family's bankruptcy but also triggered his father's attempted suicide. "I came to Berlin two years ago to look for work. I was buried by my father's debts. The banks kept giving him credit cards and loans. He had twenty-five credit cards!!!" Giannis tells of how the dispossession of his beloved record store in Thessaloniki, his life and livelihood, led to his unemployment and his own eventual contemplation of suicide. "In Greece I had a legendary record store, but it went belly up in the crisis and I had to perform hourly jobs. ... I became so embarrassed and ashamed that I went into hiding. Finally, it was either suicide or emigration. I came to Berlin." These verbal performances of dispossession and anger transform into affective encounters. Their anger is manifested on their bodies. As she speaks, Despina's body trembles, Kostis flails around, and Giannis's body simmers under a veneer of composure. While distinct in their physical expressivity, these raging bodies offer a forceful and affective charge that assails the audience. Crisis is embodied; it becomes palpable. Anger becomes palpable. Judith Butler describes this spectacle of the body in the following way:

> The body implies mutability, vulnerability, agency: the skin and the flesh expose us to the gaze of others, but also to touch, violence, and bodies put us at risk of becoming the agency and instrument of all these as well.

> Although we struggle for rights over our own bodies, the very rights are not quite ever our own. The body has its invariably public dimension.[39]

Inasmuch as the phenomenological bodily co-presence of performers and spectators is distilled in these moments when the physicality of the performer demands the audience's attention, the affect of the angry body spreads itself out, shows itself, and inflames the nerves and muscles of other bodies like a contagion, an infectious twitch. Even in their differences, angry bodies in performance open up and expand affective fields of force.

In her illuminating dialogue with Athena Athanasiou in *Dispossession: The Performative in the Political* (2013), Butler asserts that the presence of protesting bodies, even in their individual performances, collectively "articulate a voice of the people from the singularity of the story and the obduracy of the body, a voice at once individual and social" and "is the reproduction of community or sociality itself as bodies congregate and 'live together' on the street."[40] This is instructive to the performances in *Telemachos*. These theatrical displays of the body are corporeal spectacles and enactments of power despite the overwhelming sense of powerlessness they experience. They are exposed and vulnerable. An emphasis on the display and exposure of bodies in performance forms a critical intersection between protest and theatre. Frequently discussed as acts of staging, the protests linked to the Indignant Citizens Movement have been likened to performance spectacles themselves. In Philip Hager's account, these protests are "dramaturgies ... synecdochic spectacles of politics that are indicative of the political and social relations and traditions in and through which performances of citizenship operate."[41] One might argue that the sheer assembling of bodies in a public space performatively asserts their place and rights as citizens. Within and beyond the theatre space, assembled bodies adopt what performance studies scholars and artists Bojana Cvejić and Ana Vujanović call the "affective virtuosity" of bodies in performance, which injects them with a reckonable force and a political operability.[42] Collective protest is performative insofar as it effects a politics of bodily action and reaction through the physical assertion of presence that demands attention and engagement.

But sometimes the encounter with angry bodies becomes too much to bear. Affect can cleave to angry bodies. Karl A.E. Enenkel and Anita Traninger refer to this as the psychophysical quality of anger for which they provide a grammar of body language that stretches the morphological possibilities of the Laocoön: "indignant posture[s], stern looks, impudent manners, grinding of teeth, and [wild] gestures of hands and feet."[43] The physicality of angry bodies can overwhelm, unsettle, and threaten to consume the spectator. Certainly not universal in their corporeal expressivity, as the different examples of Despina, Kostis, and Giannis also demonstrate, angry bodies are nonetheless not docile. The impulse to bring them under control, to discipline them (especially in the theatre), can be compelling. In public spaces, outraged, dissident bodies are disciplined through police intervention. Indeed, the riot police responded to the summer 2011 protests in Athens with excessive force, tear gas, and flash grenades. In *Telemachos*, the police violence is heatedly discussed, but actual intervention onstage takes another form. When the indignant body onstage overwhelms and unsettles through its pulsing rhythms and display of affect, it is disciplined, not by the police, but by Knut. Consider Despina's monologue, in which she concludes with an anecdote about her experience at the job centre in Berlin and the words of an employee there, who chauvinistically posed the rhetorical question: "Warum kommen alle hierher?" ("Why do they all come here?") Frontally positioned before the audience, Despina stamps her feet, raises her hands in fists, and repeatedly screams this defeating line of condemnation. Her body writhes in anger downstage, in threatening proximity to the audience. The overwhelming physicality of the angry body becomes too much to bear. Knut intervenes. He hoists Despina up over his shoulder and carries her to the side of the stage. This act of interception by Knut is troubling in its heavy-handed paternalism and is instrumental in its theatrical display of German aggression.

Knut is the condescending and didactic German figure who meddles, "mansplains," and moralizes. Unlike the others, he has no story of migration of his own to share. In place of narrating, he lectures on Adorno and punctuates the others' monologues with his own interpretation of events and narratives. For instance, in response to the historical continuum of labour migration from Greece to Germany, he remarks that it demonstrates the (unfortunate) repetition of history. "Ihr macht den gleichen Fehler nochmal. Wir zerstören euer Land und ihr kommt hierher and arbeitet für uns." ("You're making the same mistake again. We destroy your land and you come here and work for us.") This subtle locutionary inversion of (German) responsibility via a purporting of the (Greek) seizure of victimhood is shot through with an oversimplified and even troubling reading of history. By the same token, this declaration unearths a discourse of historical narrative of relationality that is not officially recognized, especially not in Germany. During the Second World War, Nazi Germany occupied Greece between 1941 and 1944, and maintained control of several Greek islands until 1945. This occupation was devastating for Greece. Not only did it lead to the decimation of the Jewish community as well as many other civilian deaths, it also destroyed Greece's infrastructure, economy, and resulted in widespread famine.[44] In the decades immediately following the Second World War, Greece's economy continued to suffer while West Germany's economy began to surge in the 1950s with the help of American monetary infusion. That Greece became an emigration country in the postwar period and Greek labourers poured into West Germany between 1960 and 1973, as a result of unemployment and economic hardship at home, certainly seems like a cruel twist of fate. To this day, Germany refuses to pay reparations for the damages wrought by its destructive occupation. Further, it comes as a harsh reminder of that earlier period, half a century later, that Greeks would be forced to seek work in Germany again after the Greek national economy collapsed, in part under the weight of the severe austerity measures imposed by its moneylenders within the eurozone, in particular Germany.

Knut's comment, while rhetorically problematic, does at least pay heed to this historical loop of injustice. Objectionable or not, Knut's character exemplifies in Brechtian fashion the underlying layer of criticism of Germany and the Greek-German entanglement mobilized in *Telemachos*. He invokes the audience's capacity for self-reflection. When Prodromos accuses Knut of being patronizing and retorts: "Ja klar, der Deutsche spricht und der Grieche ist still" ("Of course, the German speaks and the Greek is quiet"), his criticism comments both on the stage of geopolitical chauvinism and on the politics of the German stage, against which this play (and the theatre of anger) pushes back. Knut's figure is a kind of trope in postmigrant theatre more broadly. We see a similar figure in Yael Ronen's *Common Ground* (premiere 2014), *The Situation* (premiere 2015), and *Winterreise* (*Winter Journey*, premiere 2017). In the first play, Niels (Niels Bormann), a white German, accompanies a group of Yugoslavian-born Germans to the former Yugoslavia in order to explore their history, remember the damage of war, and address matters of trauma. As the play opens, Niels enters the stage to reprimand another performer for speaking English: "Dies ist ein deutsches Theater. Das Publikum erwartet Deutsch." ("This is a German theatre. The audience expects to hear German.") He follows up with a farcical definition of postmigrant theatre: "*Post*-migrantisch heißt 'danach': Zuerst lernst du Deutsch danach kannst du kommen und einen Monolog halten." ("*Post*-migrant means 'after.' First you learn German then *after* you can come and deliver your monologue.") While humorous and flippant, these self-identifying "German" figures, Knut and Niels, invite criticism of themselves through a process of alienation. As the purported voice of authority on the German stage, the white, first-language-speaking German represents and embodies this role, which theatre history and its tradition of ethnonational whiteness in Germany affirms, but here also remains detached from it.

At one point in *Telemachos*, Prodromos becomes so frustrated with Knut's unrelenting arrogance and meddling that he stomps off the stage in a fit of anger, offering a blow to the already shaky fourth wall. For a moment in the theatre, spectators looked around, unsure if this was scripted or not. This coup de théâtre, this evocation of what Martin has named "ontological theatre doubt,"[45] offers its own kind of protest. Prodromos refuses to participate in this theatre tradition of monoculturalism and German chauvinism. Staging protest in the theatre opens up as a protest against the institution of theatre itself. Even when Christos, the elder and "wiser" figure, who attempts to broker peace throughout the play, coaxes Prodromos back to the stage with the promise of a reconciliatory meal and the platitude "überall ist man fremd" ("one is a stranger everywhere"), Prodromos reminds the audience that this issue cannot be resolved so easily. In an earlier reading of *Telemachos*, I proposed that the play does in fact conclude on a conciliatory note with Christos and his stew serving as a kind of culinary feat of deus ex machina.[46] However, focusing on the other performers in the play, I failed to recognize that another narrative is at work and the play's overall more complex engagement with Homer's *Odyssey*, which itself does not conclude with the divine intervention of the gods, but with massacre and civil war. As the others begin to eat Christos's stew, Prodromos returns to the stage to recite from the close of the *Odyssey* a gruesome passage about torture and punishment. While he does later join the group for the communal meal, Prodromos leaves this final scene in a state of crisis with his literary gesture of the continued threat of violence and enmity. Theatre does not become a space for resolution or reconciliation, but one where protest endures and confronts. Finally, in its adherence to the documentary form it is also Brechtian in its open-endedness. The audience is not provided with easy answers; it is jolted into reflection and action. If nothing else, this is the work of the documentary of outrage. This work continues with Kiyak's *Aufstand*.

"Berlin Calling Istanbul via Diyarbakır," or *Aufstand*

On the small black box stage, clouds of smoke billow from a handheld smoke machine. The performer, Mehmet Yilmaz, a permanent ensemble member of the Maxim Gorki Theatre, begins to cough. Audience members also begin to cough. He sarcastically advises the audience not to cough just because he is coughing, as the smoke is supposed to mimic the experience of being in a tear gas attack, but really it is not that bad. With this opening, he offers further counsel: If you are caught in a tear gas attack, you should not use water to cleanse burning eyes and skin, but milk and, if you can withstand the sting, lemons. Upstage right is a table stacked with reserves: eight cartons of milk and piles of lemons. So begins *Aufstand*, with direct references to the tactics of street protesters, the recollection of the plethora of circulated images of the Gezi protestors in makeshift gas masks, and with the heady anticipation that there will be a use for this stockpile of milk and lemons. If there is a symbol for the Gezi Park protests, then it is the excessive use of tear gas employed by the police and the creative ways protesters practised self-preservation in the face of this violence.

As a journalist and columnist, an activist and artist, a Turkish Kurd and a German, Kiyak penned *Aufstand* through the authoritative labour of an eyewitness with transnational connections and experiences. I refer to *Aufstand* as a play, but as its descriptive subtitle indicates, it is the monologue of an angry artist, "*Monolog eines wütenden Künstlers*," that premiered one year after the Gezi Park protests erupted in Istanbul in the late spring of 2013. A long speech act that interjects with aggression, confrontation, and provocation, this entire play is indeed a raging monologue. Under the experimental vision of Hungarian theatre director, András Dömötör, *Aufstand* premiered at the Badisches Staatstheater Karlsruhe in June 2014. That same year, in November, it was performed at the Studio Я as part of the "Voicing Resistance" festival. Throughout, I will refer to this later performance, which remained part of the theatre's repertoire for four seasons until early 2018.

In its studio/black box setting, the performance is intimate, even cramped. Yilmaz plays Bênav and is the solo performer. As he informs the audience, "Bênav" is an adopted name, meaning "without name," taken in defiance of the Turkish authorities, who had forbidden his parents to give him a Kurdish name. In Turkey, the assignment of a name is a matter of the state. Parents are not permitted to give their children "non-Turkish" names, with minor exception for Armenian and Jewish names. Bênav is a Kurd from Diyarbakır, a city in northeastern Turkey, predominantly inhabited by Kurds. By day, Bênav teaches geography at a middle school there; in his free time he develops artistic performance videos about the repressed Kurdish history of expulsion, dispossession, and massacre in eastern Turkey, such as the Dersin Rebellion and the Zilan Massacre in the 1930s, the multiple evacuations in the 1980s and 1990s, and the more recent Roboski Massacre in 2011.

Despite its attunement to serious matters, *Aufstand* is wrapped in playfully dark humour and the partially fictive premise of the play is embedded in metaperformance: Benâv is an artist currently in Germany on a DAAD fellowship (German Academic Exchange Service fellowship) and seeks to present his art to a German audience. Similar to *Telemachos*, *Aufstand* is reflexively aware of its audience and its positioning in German theatre and in culture more broadly. Before launching into a narrative about oppression in Turkey, Benâv speaks to Germany's violent past in order to trouble the audience's potential pursuit of a cultural and moral high ground. He ironically thanks the audience for the fellowship and declares his love for this country. Remarking that the Germans are great in everything, especially art, Benâv reminds the audience of Hitler and the sustained importance of art under the Third Reich. "Ihr habt in aller Grausamkeit die Kunst nicht verloren" ("In a period of utter atrocity, you didn't lose sight of art.") The scathing sarcasm is evident.

Also, caught within a conditioning transnational entanglement, *Aufstand* provides another important example of how theatre expands on the performance and narrative possibilities of protest, insofar as it offers an individual point of view in the midst of the subjective vagaries common to protest movements, a single voice and words that became overpowered by more dominant and prolific ones. This is one of the generic qualities of documentary theatre in its historiographic function. It tells a story of an experience of an event from a perspective outside the fold of the commonly known and recognized. In its Berlin setting, a play about the Gezi Park protests from the point of view of a Turkish Kurd from Diyarbakır undertakes a unique transnational reach and dialogue.

Calling Istanbul: Initially mounted as a smaller-scale protest by environmentalists against the planned destruction of Gezi Park in Taksim, in central Istanbul, one of the city's few remaining green spaces, the Gezi Park protests began in late May 2013 as a peaceful sit-in. The park was to be converted into a replica of the Ottoman-era Taksim Military Barracks-cum-shopping centre. In an effort resonant with the words of David Harvey, following Henri Lefebvre, protesters sought "to reclaim the right to the city" and its public spaces from the clutches of neoliberal enterprise, by putting bodies in that space to literally block the bulldozers.[47] But like so many protests in the early part of the 2010s, these protests quickly intensified into a nationwide anti-government movement and civil revolt. The violence of the police against a peaceful group of sit-in protesters enraged onlookers and spurred them to join the protest. Such vivifies what Sara Ahmed refers to as the "promiscuity in rebellion: witnessing the blows we receive can create more disobedient parts."[48] In other words, we are motivated by anger to act in defence and care of others in the face of injustice. Through grand acts of anger and civil disobedience, protest proliferates. Distinct from the Syntagma Square protests in Greece, or the anti-austerity protests on the Puerta del Sol Square in Madrid, or throughout the major cities of the West with the Occupy Movement, the rise of the Gezi Park protests did not form into a movement expressly as a response to unlivable conditions as a result of imposed austerity, but rather against the attenuation of civil rights and freedoms under the current government. Since coming into power in 2002, the ruling party in Turkey, the Adalet ve Kalkinma Partisi (Justice and Development Party), or the AKP for short, led by Recep Tayyip Erdoğan, has gradually seized more authoritarian control over the country and its citizens via a platform of neoliberalism, populism, and Islamic conservatism. While the party's support base was and remains significant, the Gezi Park protests revealed to the world the massive extent of both the discontent among many citizens and the brutality of the government and police in their effort to quell the demonstration and the public performance of the discontent of the polity.

As Erdem Yörük reminds us, even in the years leading up to the Gezi Park protests (and the situation has significantly worsened since the alleged coup d'état during the summer of 2016), under the AKP, Turkey has chalked up an unprecedented record of anti-democratic policies. "Turkey alone accounts for one-third of all terror convictions in the world after 9/11 and has more journalists in jail than any other country, followed by Iran and China."[49] The AKP's impositions on women's rights and liberties also became increasingly alarming, including among other things a proposed ban on abortion. A spike in hate crime against women and LGBTQ+ people has also been documented. Overall, many different groups of mostly young people made up the crowds of protesters in the park, Taksim Square, and the streets of Istanbul and other major cities. The protest swelled far beyond the government's consistent and spurious claim that this was an insignificant group of "çapulcu" (looters). While no one would have guessed that this post-coup generation, which had not experienced the violence of previous generations, would have the courage and fortitude to initiate and sustain such a powerful protest movement, a revolution, as some have called it, they did.[50] They did because they were outraged. As Benâv declares: "Du stehst da, weil du nichts hast! ... Du bist voller Wut!" ("You stand there because you have nothing! ... You are full of anger!")

The fact that Gezi Park is adjacent to Taksim Square, the major central square in Istanbul, bore great significance in terms of visibility for the movement but also because of the square's spatially marked history. Similar to Syntagma Square, Taksim Square is considered the heart of the city, the cultural centre, and (previously) the hub for public transportation. For this reason, it has also long been an important venue for political protests. Myriad political and social groups try to demonstrate on Taksim Square because of its centrality and visibility. But it has also been a site of violence, where the government has demonstrated its authoritarian might against its citizens, and antagonistic groups have confronted each other in deadly clashes. Permanently positioned just on the peripheries of the square are the menacing TOMA (an abbreviation for Toplumsal Olaylara Müdahale Aracı, or in English "Intervention Vehicles for Social Incidents"), used by the police and gendarmerie for riot control. (Since the Gezi Park protests, the presence of these vehicles in Taksim has vastly increased.) It was inevitable that the Gezi Park protests quickly spilled over into the square and metastasized into the occupation of the entire Taksim Square. This wide-open space became an eminent terrain paced out by social and political movements and on which a provisional stage came to form for a grand spectacle of dissent and angry bodies to articulate this dissent, what Susan Leigh Foster calls the "choreographies of protest."[51]

Theatre and protest go hand in hand. Much like the Greek protests on Syntagma Square, the dramaturgy of the protests in Istanbul two summers later was also exemplary of Schechner's concept of "direct theatre." Theatrical and carnivalesque moments arose in the midst of political protest. Direct theatre does not detract from the political earnestness of the protest but undergirds it in an equally subversive manner. A number of scholars have remarked on the performance and even the theatrical quality of the Gezi Park protests, what Arzu Öztürkmen refers to as the layered "performances within performances," which included "carnivalesque fairs and festivals, dance, music, drama, and puppet shows."[52] Most famous among these performances was that of the "Standing Man" (*Duran Adam*). Over two weeks into the protests, after Taksim Square had been all but forcefully cleared and reoccupied by the police, on June 17 performance artist Erdem Gündüz positioned himself in the centre of the square, facing north, and remained static for eight hours. His performance act of civil disobedience, for the police had forbade further assembling on the square, quickly went viral and over 300 people joined him. Since these bodies were not actively protesting or causing a disturbance, authorities were not sure at first how to address this silent and still demonstration of individuals.[53] Judith

Butler surmises that the brilliant strategy of the Standing Man performance was that it presented an open act of defiance without technically breaking any laws.

> When the Turkish government in the summer of 2013 banned assemblies in Taksim Square, one man stood alone, facing the police, clearly "obeying" the law not to assemble. As he stood there, more individuals stood "alone" in proximity to him, but not exactly as a "crowd." They were standing as single individuals, but they were all standing, silent and motionless, as single individuals, evading the standard idea of an "assembly" yet producing another one in its place. They technically obeyed the law forbidding groups from assembling and moving by standing separately and saying nothing. This became an articulate yet wordless demonstration.[54]

A convergence of protest performance and theatre performance was also made visible through the Turkish play *Mi Minör* (*Minor Key*, 2012), which was inspired by the Arab Spring and dramatizes a democracy in which authoritarian rule has taken over. The play is thought to have influenced the Gezi Park protests. The conjuncture was so widely recognized that the director, Memet Ali Alabora, was forced to go into exile for fear of being arrested.[55] Theatre also left its mark on the protests through the on-site work of Jale Karabekir, the director of the feminist theatre company Boyalı Kuş and the pioneer of the "Theatre of the Oppressed" in Turkey, who cancelled all the performances in her theatre, Sahne Cihangir, and told everyone to go and join the protests, in the middle of which she apparently organized workshops using performance techniques.[56] But this crossover between theatre and protest is conceived and examined as a unilateral movement of political theatre that liberates itself into the public spaces of a city. In place of these tendencies, the return of these synecdochic spectacles of protest to the theatre is what drives the present study.

Kiyak began writing *Aufstand* in Istanbul in 2013 in the swell of the Gezi Park protests. Simultaneously writing for the German weekly *Die Zeit*, in a series titled *Türkische Tage* (Turkish Days), about the protests, Kiyak (re-)turns to art and theatre as witness. *Aufstand* is her first play. Not exclusively about the Gezi Park protests, *Aufstand* explores resistance through a broader scope of Kurdish-Turkish history and politics. It uses documentary theatre to create an additional account and thus also add complexity to existing ones, what Laureen Nussbaum has referred to as the stereoscopic view of the history of documentary theatre.[57] Some scholars and journalists have addressed the importance of Kurdish politics for Gezi, as Yörük writes, "The Kurdish peace process was critical for the Gezi uprising."[58] However, it remains peripheral to mainstream discourse on the protests. For over three decades the Kurdish political movement has been actively struggling with the state against violence, dispossession, and oppression. While this struggle has resulted in armed conflict, it has also witnessed the development of an active and vibrant Kurdish civil society and the formation of Kurdish political parties.[59] The years 2012 and 2013 marked a turning point in Kurdish-Turkish relations. A sixty-eight-day hunger strike among Kurdish political prisoners concluded with the promise of negotiations between the Turkish government and the leader of the Kurdistan Workers' Party (PKK), Abdullah Öcalan. According to Yörük, the prospect of a peace process began to fray public antagonism against Kurdish politics.[60] The Manichaeism that had so starkly shaped state rhetoric and procedure briefly halted. Yet *Aufstand* is not about a move toward reconciliation. It actually criticizes the taint of falsehood that arose amid the Gezi Park protests. Those who chanted "We are all Kurds" on Taksim Square in solidarity with the Kurdish cause are revealed to be naïve opportunists. Kiyak's play does not align itself with the protests the way *Telemachos* does; it observes with even more critical distance. In the spirit of documentary theatre, it invites ambivalence. Engaging with the affective politics of outrage, *Aufstand* stages its own resistance.

Kiyak's field research as an eyewitness to the events and her interviews form the basis of the play. Unlike *Telemachos*, a professional actor (Mehmet Yilmaz) plays the role of a Kurdish artist in Germany who tells his story about Gezi. What most spectators might not realize is that the figure for this artist is based on a real person, Şener Özmen, a Kurdish artist from Diyarbakır who Kiyak interviewed while on her extended research stay in Turkey, in an article titled "Auf einmal alle Kurden" ("All of a Sudden Everyone's a Kurd").[61] Kiyak's journalistic account of Özmen and his experience at Gezi bears much resemblance to her dramatic tale. Even the video material Benâv shows is modelled after a video installation by Özmen, titled *The Road to Tate Modern*, in which Özmen and his colleague Cengiz Tekin (called Django in the play and performed digitally by Mehmet Ateşçi) ride around the countryside on donkeys in the vicinity of Diyarbakır, apparently in search of the Tate Modern museum. In the play the digital performance is given the title "Lese ich die Karte falsch?" ("Am I Reading the Map Wrong?"), in which they search unavailingly for former Kurdish-named villages. Although the medial documents employed in the play are fictionalized instead of archival, they are based on real materials.

Documentary invites a negotiation between reality and interpretation, what Reinelt, drawing on Peter Weiss and Stella Bruzzi, refers to as "the dialectical relationship between raw material and the theatrical apparatus."[62] Emerging from and within this performative negotiation is an interrogation of events and practices that hold up certain histories and the establishment of truths. The project of documentary as described by Martin is also instructive here: "[T]hose who make documentary theatre interrogate specific events, systems of beliefs, and political affiliations precisely through the creation of their own versions of events, beliefs, and politics by exploiting technology that enables replication; video, film, tape recorders, radio, copy machines, and computers are the sometimes visible, sometimes invisible technological means of documentary theatre."[63] I thus refer to *Aufstand* as documentary theatre, which is at once invested in new historiographies and unsettling those in place.

Given its liveness, its forms of embodiment, and its sense of community and contingency, theatre presents itself as a galvanizing mode of representation of a complex network of events. Not only does Benâv's raging monologue draw connections between Germany and Turkey, Istanbul and Diyarbakır, politics and art, reality and fiction, it also brings the audience into the spectacle through direct address and participation. More than any other performance explored in this book, *Aufstand* repeatedly breaks with the convention of the fourth wall. At the beginning, Benâv reassures the audience that this is not a performance in which the audience has to do anything, only to later recant this proclamation. At various points during the performance, when Benâv raises his right arm, makes a revolutionary fist, and yells "Eine andere Welt, eine andere Ordnung soll her!" ("Bring me another world, another order!"), the audience is instructed to clap loudly and cheer. The performance of the revolutionary body and its theatrical call to action becomes a striking figure of anger and protest. Playful and ironic, *Aufstand* nonetheless commands a level of political radicalism with an aspiration to social justice that is brought forth in this theatrical reenactment and narration of the Gezi Park protests.

Roughly three quarters of the way into the play, Benâv declares that he will now begin the performance. He requests orange lighting that appears to effect the tinge of a summer of revolution: the fire and smoke, the street lights, the heat. The chromatic shift adds an air of mystery to the mise-en-scène and even formally conjures a fiery sense of anger that matches the pulsing electronic music that fills the theatre. In preparation for this scene, Benâv has strewn the cartons of milk and the lemons across the stage. He places a small potted tree centre stage and beside it an equally puny chainsaw. Pulling on a jacket and safety goggles, Benâv narrates his adventure: my wife gave me a ride to the

4.1 Performing the chants of the Gezi Park Protest in *Aufstand*. Image © Ute Langkafel MAIFOTO.

airport; when I arrived in Istanbul I went directly from the airport to the park. Standing behind the tiny tree, he energetically performs verbatim the shouts of the different groups he encounters among the congeries of protesters (figure 4.1):

> Eine Gruppe schrie, "Istifa! Istifa!" Also: "Rücktritt! Rücktritt!"
>
> Eine andere Gruppe schrie, wie besinnungslos, "Faschisma karşı, Omuz omuza!" Also: "Gegen Faschismus, Schulter an Schulter!"
>
> Eine andere Gruppe schrie, "Özgürlük! Özgürlük!" "Freiheit! Freiheit!"
>
> Ich ging weiter und eine andere Gruppe schrie, "Wir wollen saufen und knutschen so viel wie es uns gefällt!"
>
> ...
>
> Eine andere Gruppe schrie: "Wir sind alle Kurden! Wir sind alle Kurden!" Mein Herz klopfte... Zum ersten Mal dachte ich, vielleicht ändert sich unser Leben doch noch.

> One group was yelling, "Istifa! Istifa!" So, "Resignation! Resignation!"
>
> Another group was yelling, like crazy, "Against fascism, shoulder to shoulder!"
>
> Another group was yelling, "Freedom! Freedom!"

> I went further and another group was yelling, "We want to drink and make out as much as we like!"
>
> ...
>
> Another group was yelling: "We are all Kurds! We are all Kurds!" My heart raced. ... For the first time I thought that maybe our lives would actually change.

This verbal performance of mimesis reveals the multitude of voices comprising this assembly of resistance. But as we also discover, it reveals the disingenuous co-option of causes that needs to be brought under duress. Among those screaming "We are all Kurds" is a fellow artist who had signed a petition to ban Benâv from participating in a tour to Germany, ironically because his work was too political and provocative. Benâv is not only disappointed, he is outraged. When he confronts this fellow artist at Gezi with his anger about this injustice, he is silenced, told that he is getting in the way of *real* political work. He immediately returns to Diyarbakır. What does it mean then to proclaim that "We are all Kurds"? The much-cited axiom by Martin Luther King, Jr. in his celebrated 1963 "Letter from a Birmingham Jail," that "[i]njustice anywhere is a threat to justice everywhere," captures the transcendence of a declaration of "we" in the name of fighting injustice, which returns to each one of us. Yet some might also claim that this hackneyed phrase "We are all..." can make short shrift of a movement with false sympathies and the ruse of community. What Benâv's brief sojourn on Taksim Square reveals is the myopia of the protesters, who, according to him, do not realize that it is not solely the people in power who are responsible for the prevailing tyranny and injustice in Turkey, but the nescience and the intransigence of the people and their failure to recognize their civic divides. Through monologue, he utters in acid tones an account of this nearsightedness:

> Wir leben in einem Land, in dem mich deine Polizei und dein Militär und deine Fernsehsender und deine Zeitung als Feind betrachten. Und du hast das einfach so geglaubt. Jetzt wo ihr selber rebelliert, weil ihr die Schnauze voll habt von diesen ganzen Schweinereien, die um euch herum passieren, kommt ihr und sagt: „Ist das keine Schweinerei, wie sie mit uns umgehen?" Jetzt, wo ihr merkt, dass die Zeitungen Scheißdreck verbreiten, kommt ihr und fragt: „Sind diese Medien kein Skandal?" „Nein! Das sind keine Schweinereien, das ist kein Skandal! Das lief doch immer schon so."

> We live in a country in which your police and your military and your television networks and your newspaper regard me as the enemy. And you

> just simply believed it. Now that you yourselves are also rebelling because you've had enough of all this treachery that's going on around you, you come and say: "Isn't how they treat us treacherous?" Now that you notice that the newspapers spread shit, you come and ask: "Aren't these media scandalous?" "No! That's not treachery, that's not scandalous! That's always been that way."

The fact that Kurds in Turkey have been rebelling against the same treachery of the Turkish government for decades appears to be of scant relevance. That the multiple TOMA used by the police and gendarmerie against the protesters during Gezi were actually imported from Diyarbakır, where they had heretofore been almost fixtures on that urban landscape, is also not part of the dissenting discourse on Taksim Square in Istanbul. So, what does it mean to resist certain types of resistance? To refuse to be a mere subtext to this important moment of dissent? *Aufstand* does not simply celebrate the Gezi Park protests as a civic revolt against the will of a tyrant. It is in tune with the fact that "the politics of demonstrating are indeed messy," as Ahmed puts it.[64] Embracing this messiness, *Aufstand* reenacts protest and outrage with its own protest and outrage.

Back in Berlin: Never losing sight of the locative conceit of the performance, Benâv returns to the German context. In-yer-face, he declares that the reason the deportation and genocide of the Jews functioned so well under National Socialism is because there was precedent: Turkey did it first with the Armenians and then later with the Kurds. "Wir sind alle Armenier! Ja, klar, jetzt wo alle weg sind, sind sie alle Armenier, und Juden, und Kurden." ("We are all Armenians! Sure, now that they are all gone, they're all Armenians, and Jews, and Kurds.") Expulsion and genocide become not only confounding points of tangency but horrific entanglements of transnational synthesis between Turkey and Germany, which, as Benâv explains, is entombed in bodily memory by its survivors. In particular, theatre and performance are the modes by way of which, in Joseph Roach's words, "'counter-memories,' or the disparities between history as it is discursively transmitted and memory as it is publicly enacted by the bodies that bear its consequences," are exposed and drawn out.[65] The act of remembering itself becomes an important performance of resistance in *Aufstand*, insofar as the memory of genocide and deportation is, in the case of the Armenians, not only repressed, it is also punishable under Article 301 of the Turkish Penal Code as an insult against the Turkish nation. That memory would manifest itself through embodied modes of performance resonates with a rich tradition in anthropological performance studies, such as through the work of Roach and others. Paul Connerton and Diana Taylor have discussed the importance of the embodied transmission of social knowledge and memory, in what they refer to as "acts of transfer" in performance.[66] Recalling Necati Öziri's figure of the second-generation "migrant" Arda, the body not only becomes a kind of alternative archive of collective memory in the metaphysical sense, but also an agent of remembering in a manner that eludes historically tutored narratives and mimesis.

Division is physically collapsed in this theatrical performance when Benâv turns the video camera onstage towards the audience and projects an image of the house (now alit) onto the large screen upstage. Spectators become the spectacle and the scopic regime of theatre with its inveterately binary structures of stage and house, performance and spectators, spectacle and gaze, are confounded through the strategy of reflection. Benâv then enters the house himself. Standing amid the tightly seated spectators, he too is confronted with his own reflection and launches into a rousing monologue about solidarity. While an argument could certainly be made for the double sense of solidarity conjured in this scene through the physical blurring of boundaries and the sudden unity of spectator and performer, this fails to account for the speech genre of the monologue and its rhetorical tradition of self-reflection in theatre. Deborah R. Geis asserts that in its direct address, the monologue can be employed to play with the discomfort of the audience members. She cites Peter Handke's *Publikumsbeschimpfung* as a preeminent example of the power of the monologue to compel the audience into a state of disconcerting self-consciousness, something I also explore in chapter 1.[67]

Aufstand heightens the possibilities of the monologue and its demand on the audience famously asserted by the performers in Handke's play. States of self-consciousness are intensified. The projection of live video footage of the audience coerces even the visual confrontation with one's role as spectator, and part of a larger audience, in a theatre. Forced to engage in a spectacle of self, one is not only exposed to oneself but also to the gaze of others. This scene does what so much political theatre does, but in an altogether direct manner. The audience members are not only invited to contemplate their role in these events, but are forced to ask themselves: "How are *you* responsible for this?" In this live group image that haunts the stage screen in its spectral mix of liveness and mediation, collective responsibility and even guilt seem to loom. The spectators are interpellated into the mise-en-scène and into a digital documentation of presence. The meta-theatricality prompted by the use of the screen is, as Martin observes, ever more common in contemporary theatre, and in its recent iteration seems to get at political and social questions.[68] In Reinelt's formulation, "[t]he documentary theatre calls the public sphere into being by presupposing it exists, and constructs its audience to be part of a temporary sociality to attend to the matters portrayed."[69] The interpellation of a "German" audience, or at least a "Germany-situated" audience, into the history and politics of Turkey is by no means arbitrary. Even beyond the murky global entanglements that bind us all, the transnational fold of Turkey and Germany from the First World War all the way to the present is clear, complex, and marked by violence, as explored throughout *Theatre of Anger*.

Despite its criticism of the potential for false sociality in resistance movements, and in Gezi in particular, *Aufstand* is by no means a play against protest. It too pays witness to the political practice of injustice and the intensified scenes of dissent that emerged as a result. Even as a monologue and solo performance, which might suggest a concerted turning away from the assembly and alliance so telling of the power of protest, *Aufstand* seeks connectivity and coalition of earnest solidarity. This is performed through mediation and projection in which, for instance, the audience becomes the spectacle. Another example is when Benâv joins his colleague and friend Django in Istanbul onscreen. Throughout the play, Benâv apparently prepares an interactive and intermedial performance between Berlin and Istanbul, which never materializes due to various transmission glitches. I am interested in how these apparent glitches in technology might echo the story being staged. Lauren Berlant discusses the glitches of the moment, which reveal infrastructural failure such as financial crisis and force us to pause and reevaluate our current direction.[70] This resonates here. On the other end of the digital image is his colleague and friend, Django. When Benâv finally enters the digital realm and meets his friend "on the other side," two worlds are symbolically converged in this spatial crossover. They embrace. But this is not the final image. Parting ways with Benâv, Django goes offscreen. Benâv is left alone to continue to observe the screen, which contains an image of the performance space in the Berlin theatre. In its closing, *Aufstand* does not offer a passageway through the straits of political and infrastructural glitches. It also problematizes an ethos of reconciliation as an act that might point to more bearable conditions of life. Ambivalence pervades to the very end.

Like no other form, documentary has the capacity to catalyze public engagement. To this I add that documentary theatre has the rare capacity to also capture the spirit of outrage of a moment, in which a sense of redress for injustice is ignited and united. Documentary theatre as it is examined here returns the politics of the streets to the theatre, but not through displacement or substitution. Theatre that addresses social justice is nothing new, yet the documentary of outrage is a radical interplay of politics, art, and affect. If Augusto Boal notably imagined a theatre that is the rehearsal of resistance and protest,[71] then *Telemachos* and *Aufstand* are representations of a theatre that brings revolution to a new audience in a transnational proliferation of experiences, ideas, and affects. These plays yell into the noise of revolution. Created in the clamour of protest movements, and performed in the breath-catching moment of their ebb but not their end, both plays not only mimetically but also poietically explore and expand on the possibilities of anger and political protest and their important intersections with art and performance. Resistance movements find new audiences, new groups to be engaged, to be yelled at, to be riled up. Anger is not cathartically released in these theatre events; instead, it is energetically fueled as an affective motor that exposes the presence of violence and incites response. In a more direct manner than in previous chapters, this chapter demonstrates the adamant new ways in which political protest and theatre intersect through the theatre of anger. The political effectiveness and the participatory relational aesthetics of the theatre of anger is brought forth through these plays in particular. Here the stakes of the theatre of anger are raised. The present chapter demonstrates theatrical anger's capacity not only to interrupt and intervene but also to assert change in global political matters. Staying with politics, Sasha Marianna Salzmann's views, examined in the final chapter, continue to expose the violence of hate, especially systemic violence, but with a focus on youth plays; the chapter looks towards the future and directly asks what comes next.

Chapter Five

Salzmann's Angry Youths

– Nächste Frage. Was macht dich wütend? ...
– Wenn ich arme Menschen sehe.
– Weiβt du, dieses Interview macht wirklich nur Sinn, wenn du dich darauf einlässt. Wenn du ehrlich bist.[1]

– Next question: What makes you angry? ...
– When I see poor people.
– You know, this interview only really makes sense if you are engaged. If you are honest.

Sasha Marianna Salzmann, *Verstehen Sie den Dschihadismus in acht Schritten! (Zucken)*

A scene, entitled "Würde" ("Dignity"), in Sasha Marianna Salzmann's dramatic text *Verstehen Sie den Dschihadismus in acht Schritten! (Zucken)* (*Understanding Jihadism in Eight Steps! [Twitching]*, 2017) is composed of what appears to be an interview led by a white German woman talking with a refugee living in Germany. While the nationality of this person is unclear, he is young, male, and Muslim. Throughout, the interviewer makes no attempt to conceal her own prejudices about Muslim males as angry, violent, and sexist, and she employs an aggressive mode and line of questioning with the intention of drawing out these presumed qualities. Unable to achieve the results she seeks, the interviewer herself becomes angry and adopts increasingly injurious language. To propose that others are angry, to attach anger to certain bodies, is always a deleterious act not unlike the ideological act of interpellation, of calling one into an identity that can be harmful. The assignment of anger is often about creating a fantasy figure marked by culture, race, and/or religion. The fantasy figure of the angry Muslim male, explored at various points in this book, produces its own effects.[2] For if one is presumed an angry person based on cultural or racial prejudice, then, as Sara Ahmed writes, "[r]easonable, thoughtful arguments are dismissed as anger (which of course empties anger of its own reason), which makes you angry, such that your response becomes read as the confirmation of evidence that you are not only angry but also unreasonable!"[3] The theatre of anger is not about producing fantasy figures and narratives consumable for a white German audience. It works against this and simultaneously recuperates and reworks anger as a powerful affect that produces important political effects. This is, inter alia, also the performance of Salzmann's dramatic writing.

In many ways this book about theatre and anger began with Salzmann and their declaration of indebtedness to the work of British playwright Sarah Kane, in comments that arose in a public discussion I facilitated at Stanford University in the fall of 2016. It seems thus appropriate that this final chapter should focus expressly on Salzmann's work. Throughout *Theatre of Anger*, I have sought to draw parallels between British in-yer-face theatre of the 1990s and the theatre of anger in Germany of the early twenty-first century. This comparison is helpful because in-yer-face theatre provides a recognizable and established example of a movement reliant on themes and forms of anger. Perhaps no contributor to the theatre of anger more convincingly and consistently brings its qualities to presence in their work than Salzmann. While the theatre of anger is not explicitly a movement of playwrights in the way that in-yer-face theatre was, as the former has an equal (or possibly greater) number of celebrated directors, it has introduced a handful of playwrights whose work presents something groundbreakingly new to the German stage. (Consider also the plays of Necati Öziri and Mely Kiyak.) Compared to Germany's other recent turns in the conceptualization of theatre, specifically performative, post-Brechtian, and postdramatic, the theatre of anger revives and expands on the art of playwriting in its effort to provide new narratives for the stage as well as to introduce new dramatic categories and a new theatrical grammar. As the only (now former) permanent writer-in-residence and playwright at the Maxim Gorki Theatre, Salzmann is the most distinguished among this new group of playwrights, and their theatrical texts are published and commercially available. They are also involved in the productions and performances of their plays, not to mention engaged in theatre, cultural, and political work, in Germany and abroad.

Reckoned the most provocative playwright to emerge as part of the in-yer-face generation and labelled "an angry young woman" by theatre critics, Kane was arguably the generation's most controversial and influential figure.[4] Such a qualification, while tinged with criticism, might be redeemed as the killjoy attitude she demonstrated with a minor corrective variation: "an angry young playwright." This duly applies to Salzmann as well. Salzmann is also a kind of killjoy. They aim to unsettle the audience in a way that might spoil their fun, make them feel ill at ease. That is not to say that Salzmann's plays are analogous with those of Kane, who was more interested in the shocking truth at the heart of graphic dramatizations of sex and violence, such as portrayed in her plays *Blasted* (1995) and *Cleansed* (1998), and what these revealed about society, and especially class.[5] (It might be noted, though, that Salzmann's chamber play *Die Aristokraten* [*The Aristocrats*, premiere 2016] bears direct elements of Kane's style.) By comparison, many of Salzmann's earlier plays – (*Weißbrotmusik* [*White Bread Music*, 2010], *Satt* [*Full*, 2011], *Beg Your Pardon*, 2012, *Muttersprache Mameloschn* [*Mameloschn Mother Tongue*, 2012]) – are much more naturalistic and even authentic portrayals, which explore personal relationships and the affective weight of the political on these relationships. Salzmann's dramatic narratives are often inspired by contemporaneous news events and the impulse, incited by anger because of the way these events are represented, to probe them through theatre. At a moment of crisis in the media, Salzmann's work might be aligned with that of their theatre contemporaries intent on creating a space in which public discourse around world events and politics may be pursued.[6] But unlike some of their contemporaries, Salzmann's dramatic mode is not documentary; instead, they are driven by the potential stories behind the event, the unequivocal entanglements of the personal and political. They draw them out with fictional flourish. Yet Salzmann's portrayals always contain the feel of relevance, even authenticity. They never cease to ask what it means to live in our present with the politics of race and identity that shape it. Much like their in-yer-face predecessor, Salzmann maintains a firm belief in the capacity and potency of theatre to shift perspectives and even society.[7] Both playwrights bring into relief scenes of contemporary society in Britain of the 1990s and Germany of the 2010s, respectively, which are new to the stage. If class was the pressing issue of 1990s Britain, then, according to Salzmann, migration is its equivalent in Germany today. To cite Sierz's diagnosis of in-yer-face theatre, both playwrights "tell us all we need to know about what a culture is embarrassed by, afraid of, or resentful of."[8]

Still at an early stage in their career, Salzmann has nonetheless become a prominent and influential voice in the Berlin (and German) theatre and literature scene. To date, they have written more than sixteen plays, numerous essays, and a novel. For half a decade the permanent playwright at the Maxim Gorki Theatre, Salzmann's dramatic work is at once representational of and foundational to postmigrant theatre more broadly, and in particular its later, intersectional directions. Consider, for instance, their pieces *Schwimmen lernen* (*Learning to Swim*, 2013), *Wir Zöpfe* (*We Braids*, 2015), and *Meteoriten* (*Meteorites*, 2016), all part of the repertoire at the Maxim Gorki Theatre and all concerned with cultural diversity and LGBTQ+ identities and narratives. Next to their writing, they have also directed Sivan Ben Yishai's play *Die Geschichte vom Leben und Sterben des neuen Juppi Ja Jey Juden* (*The History of the Life and Death of the New Juppi Ja Jey Jews*, premiere 2017) and numerous performance pieces when they headed the Studio Я between 2013 and 2015. They are also the co-founder of the cultural and social journal *FREITEXT* and the New Institute for Dramatic Writing (NIDS), initiated in 2015. Finally, they also co-initiated *Desintegration: A Congress on Jewish Contemporary Positions* in 2016 with Max Czollek, discussed at greater length in the introduction of this book, which continues annually as *Radikale jüdische Kulturtage* (*Radical Jewish Culture Days*) at the Studio Я.

Much of Salzmann's theatre work could speak to the scope of this book, but I will focus on two plays, which engage and address anger, its attributions and its attachments in direct ways. These include their first play, *Weißbrotmusik* (*White Bread Music*, 2010) and one of their more recent plays, *Zucken*. Both are youth plays, which speak to and expand the theatrical possibilities this book explores in earlier chapters. Distinct in style, *Weißbrotmusik* contains a linear narrative and clear-cut characters, whereas *Zucken* is a blast of noncohesive vignettes and no explicitly named characters. Yet Salzmann's two plays dialogue in their treatment of anger through acts of bodily aggression and violent language in a manner that further connects them to other plays explored throughout *Theatre of Anger*. Parallels can be drawn between the plays' themes and affective registers. This chapter explores these plays through their treatment of contemporary discourses about the ostensibly deleterious nature of anger and the teleology of violence, even terrorism, that is routinely thought to arise from an excess of anger as *ressentiment*. Rather than giving into these popular claims about anger, these plays invite contemplation about anger as an important, radical theatrical and affective form, as well as a site of political and social protest.

More consistently than any other artist associated with the theatre of anger, Salzmann engages the energy, action, and collective force of anger rooted in Black feminist discourse. In this tradition, anger arises in response to injustice and its attendant pain. But it is not simply a response or even an outlet; it is also an action, a forward movement, a future. If chapter 4 teaches us how to use anger as a form of protest, then this chapter asks what comes next. A return to Audre Lorde's take on anger sets us on this forward-moving track. Lorde writes:

> My response to racism is anger. I have lived with that anger, ignoring it, feeding upon it, learning to use it before it laid my vision to waste, for most of my life. Once I did it in silence, afraid of the weight. My fear of anger taught me nothing ... [A]nger expressed and translated into action in the service of our vision and our future is a liberating and strengthening act of clarification ... Anger is loaded with information and energy.[9]

What is striking here is the word "future." Anger not only responds to injustice, it also fights for justice. It does not simply look back to acts committed but also forward to new possibilities. This is what moves it beyond *ressentiment*. Reading this same quote, Ahmed observes that anger is not merely a reaction to a past event, it also engages a futurity. "Anger does not necessarily become 'stuck' on its object... Being against something is also being for something."[10] But according to Ahmed this "for something" has yet to be articulated and determined.[11] I propose that the elements of being-against and being-for of anger (its refusal and its ambition) are captured in the work of Salzmann's youth plays, which always contain a germ of futurity, even hope. Anger bears out both through words and embodiment, through text and performance. Its "energy" is exhortatively and palpably brought forth on the stage.

This chapter's more focused treatment of the work of a playwright does not indicate a concurrent turn to the text and away from performance. Much has been written on the role of dramatic theatre in what Diana Taylor has famously referred to as the archive and repertoire divide.[12] Frequently placed in the former category, dramatic theatre, and especially playwriting, has a strained relationship with performance. Like the plays of Kane, Salzmann's texts also contain elements of the postdramatic in their open and writerly style. Their work smooths out the prohibitive fault lines ever undercutting theatre and performance – that of the regulatory role of the text and the irruptive force of performance. In conversation, Salzmann has noted the distinct nature of dramatic writing juxtaposed with the descriptive and representative modes of prose writing. Dramatic writing is always performative, interactive, and infused with an awareness of what W.B. Worthen calls dramatic language's "alterity to embodiment and subjection into the location and temporality of enactment."[13] Worthen also observes that political theatre from the 1970s through the 1990s witnessed this important both/and sequence of text-to-performance.[14] In Salzmann's plays, anger and its affective politics become an interface between text and performance, which emphasizes both the text's plasticity and dynamism as well as performance's reliance on language and form. Words, and especially emotional language, seek expression through bodies. Notwithstanding the risk of objectifying bodies by linking them to emotions, it might be said that "angry bodies" are also a new way of thinking about the "heavy bodies" central to much contemporary political theatre, what Stanton B. Garner Jr. might refer to as contemporary theatre's phenomenology of the political. Indeed, if the early political theatre of Brecht sought to objectify everything onstage as potentially agonistic symbols of a society, including of course the bodies of actors, then late and post-Brechtian theatre returns us to the lived body, to the embodied subject. Salzmann's theatre recasts this convergence of the political and the sentient body as one that is also culturally and politically marked.

This chapter's analyses of Salzmann's *Weißbrotmusik* and *Zucken* are concerned with anger's forms both in language and what I call language-to-embodiment. Written and performed nearly a decade apart, these plays frame the multiscalar evolution of Salzmann's work and possibly also an evolution of the plays associated with the theatre of anger. Juxtaposing *Weißbrotmusik* and *Zucken* proffers (or, at the very least, speculates on) a promise of anger's expressive and dramatized expansion. The chapter moves from the emotionally affective to the phenomenologically affective, from politics of emotion to politics of form as they run through these plays.

Speaking and Acting Out in Anger: *Weißbrotmusik*

Weißbrotmusik is not only an angry play, it is also a violent play. But on offer here is not a threadbare tale of an anger that turns to violence. This play explores instead the violent connections between the local and the minor and the structural and the major, which often remain invisible. As Tom Sellar indicates, with its physical proximity and generally unmediated nature, "[t]heater is uniquely positioned to say something on the subject [of violence]. No other art form can suggest connections between small, everyday behavior and larger forces as palpably."[15] That there is a link between violence that physically shows itself and violence that is systemic and often concealed, is nothing new. In this play anger becomes the contact zone between the two. A play that premiered in 2010, *Weißbrotmusik* tackles popular discourses of violence among youth of colour and migrant youth so dominant at the time. Absent from much of this debate were discussions about institutionalized and police violence against youths of colour. The play was inspired by the real case of the physical injury of an elderly man on a Munich subway train in 2007, after he reprimanded two young men for smoking. In response, the young men verbally abused the man, followed him off the subway train, and beat him up. Without condoning such acts of violence, it bears noting that the case renewed widespread conjecture about the imbrication of violence and migrant youth. In conversation, Salzmann reveals that the play was inspired by their own anger at how the story was misaddressed in mainstream news and its rash degeneration into a hate campaign against Muslim youth. It stoked what Fatima El-Tayeb describes as "a moral panic discourse around male migrant and Muslim youths as delinquent" in existence in Germany since the 1990s.[16] Throughout the West, the criminalization of young men of colour is an ineluctable reality. The nefarious phenomenon of the "Cradle to Prison Pipeline" is not altogether unique to the US context.[17]

Marginal to the debate about the so-called criminal nature of male Muslim youth, which emerged anew in the aftermath of the Munich subway incident, were discussions about the sources of anger especially among second- and third-generation "migrant" youth and the realities of marginalization and disenfranchisement. Without moralizing, Salzmann's play seeks to examine other sides of the debate and to redramatize the story with a broader context and complexity. They introduce three young people, Sedat, Aron, and Nurit, who find themselves in a world that not only overwhelms but also seems to have predetermined their future failure. The play's title, "white bread music," is treated, on the one hand, as a motif of the inescapable conservatism and rigidity of white German society that weighs on the characters, as a reminder of their differences, their nonconformism. On the other hand, it also marks whiteness in a manner that suggests it is not altogether silent and impenetrable.[18] "White bread music" is not dissimilar to what José Esteban Muñoz calls the "white noise;" that is, "the official national affect, the beat of a majoritarian drum that defies a minoritarian sense of rhythm,"[19] against which those who do not fall into rhythm must struggle. Salzmann proposes that the play could in fact be a rap song, that musical genre that is deliberately out of sync, designed to intervene, interject, and *to talk back*.

The dramatic text contains ten distinct scenes, separated by descriptive titles in lieu of numbered acts or scenes. Nurit, who is pregnant with Sedat's child, spends the play trying to find Sedat, while Sedat is busy dodging Nurit and the authorities, and Aron is somehow always caught in the middle. The play begins with a focus on Sedat, a young, self-identified Turkish German and a Muslim, who has apparently lost his national identification card, an event that aptly frames a play about marginalization. For a young man of colour and a Muslim in Germany, being without an ID can only mean trouble. Salzmann titles the scene in French, "Carte d'identité," with a nod both to the sans-papiers movement against the deportation of undocumented residents in France and to the French Riots of 2005 as well as the ongoing problem of police harassment against young men of colour.[20] A scene of violence breaks out as performance within performance when Sedat decides to demonstrate (or possibly reenact) an encounter with the German police when caught without an ID. His unsuspecting friend, Aron, is forced into the role of Sedat himself and the whole scene ends in an act of play violence when Sedat, as a German policeman, pins Aron to the wall and, according to Salzmann's stage instructions, "boxt voller Wucht gegen die Wand, tritt, boxt, tritt, tritt" ("vehemently boxes against the wall, kicks, boxes, kicks, kicks").[21] Framing *Weißbrotmusik*, this first scene is a performance of surveilling violence that appears to be so omnipresent in contemporary Germany that it has become internalized by minoritized Germans. Anger as a reaction to the injustice of such policing of bodies of colour is manifested in this performative act of violence. Here citizenship itself becomes a dramatic scene of contestation, in which the one routinely placed outside of national participatory boundaries, because of an apparent inability to *look* and *act* within majoritarian scripts and scenarios, internalizes externalization and repeats the injury.

Weißbrotmusik Staged

Similar to much of Salzmann's work, *Weißbrotmusik* is an intimate play with few characters (consider for instance: *Satt* [*Full*, premiere 2011]; *Beg Your Pardon*, premiere 2012; *Muttersprache Mameloschn* [*Mameloschn Mother Tongue*, premiere 2013]; *Schwimmen lernen* [*Learning to Swim*, 2013]; *Die Aristokraten* [*The Aristocrats*, premiere 2016], and *Ich, ein Anfang* [*I, A Beginning*, premiere 2017]). In *Weißbrotmusik* there are only three main characters: Sedat, Aron, and Nurit. The cast is rounded off with mothers of the three main characters, all of whom are played by the same actress. Then there is a drunken bar patron and an elderly man (in the staged version I refer to there is an audience member in lieu of the elderly man).[22] *Weißbrotmusik* had its world premiere in 2010 at the Berliner Arbeiter Theater associated with the Ernst Busch Academy of Dramatic Arts, and then at the Theater Strahl, in a production directed by Nick Hartnagel. This production had re-performances at the Theater Strahl between 2012–2013. The following analysis will focus on this later series of performances. In these performances, physical proximity between actors and spectators is architecturally underscored with the presence of a thrust stage in the shape of a narrow rectangular runway and flanked by the audience on three sides. The purpose of the thrust stage is to facilitate intimacy and dialogue between actors and spectators in such a way that is not possible with the traditional proscenium experience. This spatial strategy aims to draw the spectators into the performance by creating flexibility and flow for performer-spectator interaction. Resonant with Richard Schechner's concept of environmental theatre and the living space of theatre, the stage creates a literal pathway that cuts through the house so that performers can (uncomfortably) encroach on the space of the audience and interact with individual spectators, which becomes the case in this production. Further, the physical crossing of boundaries sets up the breakdown of what Schechner refers to as "the usual agreements between performer and spectator."[23] The spectators – by choice or not – become implicated in the actions of the play, insofar as the audience's presence is made present. For Schechner, the entire theatre space is performance space. Performance is not isolated to the stage; it is everywhere. Such is the living space of theatre and its entirety.[24] The staging of *Weißbrotmusik* structurally gives shape to this perception of the theatre. There are also no props, which might distract attention away from the actors, and the set and stage are painted entirely in white. Although the play does not consist primarily of monologues, the structure of the thrust stage, the intimacy of the smaller theatre, and the starkly minimalist mise-en-scène, makes it seem as though much of the speech is actually in monologue as these staging elements establish performer-spectator interaction further. Even in dialogue, performers speak outward towards the audience and rarely (physically) to each other. The borders of the diegetic world of the play are repeatedly loosened, even compromised. For the audience, *Weißbrotmusik* is a heightened experiential theatrical event.

The play proceeds in a similar rhythm to which it begins. Sedat and Aron, his Jewish German friend, seem to spend most of their time smoking, getting high, shirking responsibility, and dreaming of a better Germany – of a better future. Nurit is pregnant. For all three characters, the child she is carrying is the embodiment of this better future. A dialogue between Sedat and Aron as they repose in their boxers reveals as much:

SEDAT: Hey – mein Sohn wird der erste Kanakenpräsident von Deutschland.
ARON: Na, dann kann er doch jüdische Familienangehörige gut gebrauchen. Wir haben unsere Finger in allem.
Sie lachen, kiffen, lachen.

SEDAT: Mein Sohn wird so schön, der wird sich vor Weibern gar nicht retten können.
ARON: Und ein Auto haben, mit dem er die abholt.
SEDAT: Mercy.[25] Ganz klar.
ARON: Und Abi machen.
SEDAT: Und jede Menge Kohle.
ARON: Und stark wird er, täglich Fitnessbudentraining.
SEDAT: Ich will, dass er studieren geht.
ARON: Und irgendwo anders aufwächst.
SEDAT: Ich könnte ja. Weiβ nicht. In ein anderes Stadtteil oder so. Was Besseres.
ARON: Was Ruhigeres.[26]

SEDAT: Hey – my son will be the first Kanake president of Germany.
ARON: See, then he could use some Jewish relatives. We have our hands in everything.
They laugh, toke, laugh.
SEDAT: My son will be so handsome, he won't be able to get the women off of him.
ARON: And he'll have a car, to pick them up.
SEDAT: Definitely. Of course.
ARON: And he'll finish high school.
SEDAT: And have lots of money.
ARON: And be strong, he'll go to the gym daily.
SEDAT: I want him to study.
ARON: And grow up somewhere else.
SEDAT: I could. I don't know. In another part of the city or something. Somewhere better.
ARON: Somewhere quieter.

Over a joint, Sedat and Aron both express their dreams for Sedat's unborn child, who in their estimation will be male, strong, smart, handsome, and rich. Only indirectly articulated is the wish that he will, most importantly, be different from them both and will pursue all the goals they did not or could not. That Sedat is unwilling to take any responsibility for the child speaks to a fear of failure and repetition, and an anger that arises as a result of this fear, reminiscent of Necati Öziri's *Get Deutsch or Die Tryin'*. In a later scene, Sedat gives a startlingly vulnerable monologue bound up with the pervasiveness of history and social violence by way of which even second- and third-generation migrants are made to feel stuck, unworthy of hope for a better life – always just "migrants."

> SEDAT: Ich kann nicht das hier ist nicht meins das bin ich nicht nicht mein Leben ich habe das Gefühl das hat mir jetzt einer in die Akte geschrieben aber ich habe nichts damit zu tun was soll ich mit einer mit einem Mädchen was noch zu Schule geht ich will das niemandem antun mein Kind wird mir nie Respekt geben können ich werde wie mein Groβvater hier die Straβen putzen und es wird mich anschauen und sagen so will ich nie werden und gehe weg aus diesem Land wenn ich groβ bin also mache ich das schon mal komme allen Enttäuschungen zuvor und gehe.[27]

> SEDAT: I can't do that here it isn't my place that's not me not my life I have this feeling someone wrote that in my file but I have nothing to do with it what am I supposed to do with a girl who still goes to school I don't want to do that to anyone my child will never be able to respect me I will clean the streets like my grandfather and it will look at me and say I never want to be like that I will leave this country when I'm old so I've done this before I anticipate all the disappointments and go.

The lack of punctuation in Salzmann's text here is meant to indicate delivery without regard to the rules of grammar. The effect is language that flows from thought to speech in stream-of-consciousness fashion. Inherent to the monologic form, this speech performatively and affectively expresses feelings in an unbidden flow of words. The grandson of a migrant worker, Sedat perceives his fate as weighed down by the past. The optimism of the earlier scene is crushed by a sobering recognition of an inescapable cyclic reality.

Anger shows itself especially in the final two scenes of the play, in which performance takes over. The events of the news story from Munich that inspired the play are taken up in the penultimate scene, titled "Ausmachen" (to put out). Sedat and Aron are on the subway train. According to Salzmann's stage instructions, they are listening to Alpa Gun's 2007 song "Ausländer" ("Foreigner"), a song by a Turkish German rapper about Turks in Germany and their struggles to be accepted as citizens. The sonic register of this song and its content are all too evocative of the scene itself. Turkish German rap is an important hybrid and politicized genre of hip-hop music, which has had a similar cultural/social development (albeit slightly later) in Germany as (predominantly) African American rap in the United States.[28] Sedat and Aron rap along for several lines. Attempting to find one's own groove, or even a collective one that is different and open, relies heavily on riffing on the sonic anger of hip-hop artists who offer a roiling voice of discordance. They sing: "Nicht jeder von uns würde mit Koks und Hero dealen" ("Not all of us would deal cocaine and heroin").[29] The conversation then turns to

Nurit and things become heated. Aron sympathizes with her and Sedat feels betrayed. They argue and smoke. An elderly man abruptly intervenes and tells them to put out their cigarettes. Aron gets defensive, yells, spits at the man's feet, and eventually chases after him, Sedat in pursuit. In Salzmann's text, the brutality that ensues in this scene, an outburst of violence on which the entire play seems to hinge, is left out, rendered absent like a dramatic ellipsis. Instead, Salzmann adds a final scene and long monologue by Nurit, who relates the events of the subway incident and its resulting consequences – Sedat's arrest and possible deportation to Turkey. In her monologue, Nurit also recalls a dream in which she confronts the old man from the subway in the hospital and brutally attacks him further, stepping on him, stomping on his head until his stitches tear open. "Drauf! Drauf! Drauf!" ("Take that and that!") she yells.[30] In an "in-yer-face" charge, Nurit describes how blood spurts everywhere and she slips around in the old man's seeping brains.

The Theater Strahl production, directed by Hartnagel, however, does stage the physical attack on the old man in the subway. The scene unravels when Sedat and Aron begin to argue while seated at the edge of the stage. The argument turns physically aggressive. An audience member in the first row stands up and tries to intervene; instead, Sedat and Aron go after him. They push him to the ground and begin kicking him. Blood streams over his face. The audience is perplexed. Is this man a plant, part of the play the whole time? Or have they just beaten up a spectator? A glance at the program, in which under "Darsteller*innen" Bernd Ocker Hölters is identified as the "Zuschauer" (spectator), allays concerns, but the realism of the scene and its violence still disturbs. Early in the performance, the same man opens up the feedback loop when he makes loud, racist comments about the play being "too aggressive," even provoking a reprimand from a young audience member in the back row: "Nazi!" The reactions from the audience during this scene are mixed to the extreme. During some performances, spectators observe with shock but do not intervene. Could the audience members also be thinking that this man got what he deserved and this is why they do not intervene?[31] This question powerfully invokes the opening of Erika Fischer-Lichte's study on performative theatre, *The Transformative Power of Performance*, in which she analyses the audience's protracted incapacity to physically intervene during Marina Abramović's infamous self-torture performance *The Lips of Thomas* and refusal (at first) to be drawn into the performance as physical players themselves.[32] Perhaps the fourth wall of theatre is still too inhibiting. Yet other performances of this scene were met with physical aggression from individual spectators, who took it upon themselves to defend the man and attack the two actors. Real violence thus was periodically introduced but could not be predicted.[33] Whatever the outcome, violence quite literally marked the stage in *Weißbrotmusik*. Once the assault comes to an end and Sedat and Aron flee the stage, the bloodied body of the man remains prostrate onstage. Bloodied handprints and trails of red have also left visible traces on the pristine white stage. While praised and even honoured with the Wiener Wortstaetten Prize in 2010, *Weißbrotmusik* has also been criticized for its excessive dramatized violence and injurious language. It was one of the first plays, if not *the* first, to stage "migrant" youth violence without bias and in such an unforgiving way. The play closes with Nurit's own personal, monologic declaration of revenge against a white Christian German society with the choice to name her unborn daughter Rehan, an explicitly Muslim Turkish name. In particular, the play's imbrication of religions and cultures (Sedat as Muslim Turkish, Aron as Jewish, Nurit as half German, half Turkish, but apparently raised Christian) in a portrayal about reckless youths, anger, and violence compels pause in the face of mainstream sensibility. For a German audience, possibly anticipating something more along the lines of the reconciliatory narrative of Lessing's famous Enlightenment play *Nathan the Wise* (1779), with its "Ring Parable" aimed at offering a lesson in religious multiplicity and mutual respect, *Weißbrotmusik* shocks.[34] Suffice to say, the public discussions that routinely followed performances of the play were frequently set in this direction with certain preconceived expectations and interpretations. In their essay, "Natürlich ist es ein Mohammed. Eine Provokation" ("Of Course It's a Mohammed: A Provocation"), Salzmann reflects on these experiences and the typical questions posed during post-performance discussions by teachers who brought their classes to see the play. For instance, one teacher asked: "Sie zeigen eine Freundschaft zwischen einem Juden und einem Türken. Ist das eine Provokation?" ("You show a friendship between a Jew and a Turk. Is that a provocation?") Or, "In Ihrem Stück sagt der Türke, 'man sollte sie alle vergasen.' Da hat's mich durchgezückt. Sagen das die Türken?" ("In your play, the Turk says, 'They should all be gassed.' That made me wince. Do Turks say that?") According to Salzmann, Sedat's comment to Aron in the play that all dogs, along with their owners, should be "gassed," also routinely seemed to unsettle the adults in the audience and often elicited the question of whether Turks truly say such things, as though to suggest that such a comment is altogether "non-German" or against the politically correct rhetoric of German society. Salzmann's response has always been along the lines of the following: "[S]ince when do the Germans need Turks in order to be anti-Semitic?" At one discussion, Salzmann responded with a rhetorical counterquestion to the high school students in the audience. They asked them if "Jude" ("Jew") had not once again become an insult on the playgrounds at schools, and to the surprise of their teachers the (overwhelmingly white German) students present in the audience all nodded in the affirmative.[35]

Salzmann has argued against the narrowly construed views of mainstream society that Muslims have brought anti-Semitism back to Germany, and Europe more broadly. It is early May 2018: As I write this chapter the German news is flooded with reports and comments about the violent incident involving a young Syrian refugee in Berlin who attacked two men with kippahs on the street with his belt.[36] Almost simultaneously, the scandal over the anti-Semitic lyrics of rappers Kollegah and Farid Bang arose when the two received the prestigious German music Echo award.[37] No doubt, anti-Semitic acts are again on the rise in Europe (and around the world).[38] However, this is not a result of an increased number of migrants and immigrants from predominantly Muslim countries, as many in Germany are wont to believe, that is, with the rise and expansion of so-called Muslim Anti-Semitism in Europe. As the reactions of the young audience members at the performance of *Weißbrotmusik* attest, there is evidence to support the fact that anti-Semitic discrimination and crimes are most frequently committed by white Germans.[39] Instrumentalizing anti-Semitism as a threshold of permissibility for Islamophobic thinking and politics (with the purported intent to discipline a group of people) is of course nothing new and has long deflected the reality of the continued presence of anti-Semitism and its counterpart in unquestioned philo-Semitism in majoritarian society in Germany. As the teachers' comments during the post-performance discussion demonstrate, white (or majority) Germans routinely position Jews and Muslims in an antagonistic relationship so that they may act as righteous mediators, conveniently neutralized. El-Tayeb indicates that this act removes the issue of racialization of non-Christian religious groups from a central focus and renders it unimportant and irrelevant.[40] The truth of the matter is, acts of anti-Semitism, Islamophobia, and racism are all on the rise in Europe.

Weißbrotmusik recasts and localizes these issues and prompts the audience to consider the religious and racial entanglements and intricacies of German society brought to our attention by Leslie A. Adelson's concept of "touching tales," which proposes that the histories of different cultural groups cannot be considered as discrete objects of analysis, for they are narratives that critically intersect.[41] Along these lines, Michael Rothberg has further articulated the importance of collective memory that is not competitive but "multidirectional" – that is "as subject to ongoing negotiation, cross-referencing, and borrowing, as productive and not private."[42] The interfaith friendships in *Weißbrotmusik* expose this connectivity and empathy, but in its theatrical directness, proximity, and intimacy, the play and its premise are also unsettling. That seems to be the point. It refuses, like so much of Salzmann's work, to partake in the reification of ideological structures of white European culture and logic, not to mention its narrative worldmaking. Anger bears out this refusal. It shows itself not as the problem but as a response to the problem. And it energizes our ability to respond.

Weißbrotmusik gives a stage to the speech act of anger, so often blocked by others out of defensiveness (such as displayed by the audience member that later gets beat up during the performance). It forces the audience to listen to voices long silenced. It demands that the anger of others be heard. This resonates with Ahmed's incisive charge that we must "learn to hear the anger of others, without blocking the anger through a defence of one's own position."[43] Given the liveness of theatre performance, the setting of the theatre becomes an ideal place to provoke, shock, and unsettle because it is out in the open and not in individual seclusion. The spectators might be able to intervene but they cannot easily stop or pause the performance. They can leave the theatre, though not without attracting public attention. On offer here are the conditions of possibility for anger to get a just hearing. While cushioned in the context of art and aesthetics, anger finds fertile ground in theatre's formidable ability to slide into a social event at a moment's notice by way of which spectators also become performers. The fictional universe of the theatre play is perhaps more fragile than in any other art form. By the same token, it is that much more rife with potential. Expanding the limits of the theatre experience, *Weißbrotmusik*'s almost programmatic post-performance discussions frequently turn to the political. These discussions heighten awareness and adjure reflection in a way that aims to make us uncomfortable insofar as our positions are exposed to the critique of others. Since Brecht this has been the ambition of theatre, one that also speaks to the politics of Black feminist anger – to the outrage against injustice. It brings people into proximity. It opens up dialogue and keeps it open. To paraphrase Hans-Thies Lehmann, theatre is a process and not a finished result; it is the activity of production and action instead of a product, an active force (energeia) and not a work (ergon).[44] Anger and theatre thus converge formally by way of their particular processual qualities, which direct them towards a futurity. The focus on angry youths pushes this thematically further.

As a variation of late or post-Brechtian theatre that maintains the province of the political and yet (re-)introduces the centrality of the body, the conventions of Lehmann's notion of postdramatic theatre are also perceptible in Salzmann's plays, in particular as their style has evolved. From *Weißbrotmusik* to *Zucken*, transformations in the structure of the dramatic text alone can be observed. The Aristotelian dramatic categories placed under duress in their earlier play are exploded to the point of unrecognizability in their later play, which does not even contain a narrative cohesion of scenes and characters but instead consists of a literary compilation of vignettes. Dialogue is frequently replaced by prose, interior monologue, and conversation via text messaging. In the balance of this chapter, I take up aspects of theatrical anger when the stakes of bodily form and themes are radicalized both in the direction of the postdramatic and in episodes of terrorism.

The Energetic Forms of Anger: *Zucken*[45]

If anger is the affect that keeps on shaking, then it is also the affect that keeps on twitching. It is a twitch that begins in your eye, like a persistent blinking. Moving to other regions of the face, micromovements transform into muscular shifts. The head and shoulders begin to vibrate in a vertical manner. The upper body stretches into a pulsating heave. The hips rock on quaking legs. Anger's twitch catches a corporeal drift that sets the whole body into a violent spasm. For Antonin Artaud, the agonism of theatre, the dramatic conflict, is itself "*un spasme*" (a spasm), which violently and physically unsettles.[46] Unlike any other play considered in this book, Salzmann's *Zucken* revisceralizes theatre's bodily intuition.[47] Anger thus assumes a corporeal form in this play. Maintaining its affective force, anger takes shape in performance, a performance of movement and agitation. It is what one might call a high frequency affect.

In addition to the lengthy interview scene entitled "Würde" ("Dignity"), with which I open this chapter, *Zucken* presents four distinct stories about marginalization, violence, and radicalization. In Sebastian Nübling's dramatic version, four stories become three and narrative gives way to form. Put another way, both corporeal (even haptic) and sonic registers of "Zucken," as an action, take over. Violent twitching, shuddering, and spasming become the embodiment of anger onstage – an anger that seems to know no physical bounds. The second half of this chapter explores *Zucken* in its performance at the Maxim Gorki Theatre in Berlin, which had its premiere in 2017. This is a wildly energetic engagement with contemporary discourses on anger and its alleged teleology of violence, even terrorism. The abbreviated title, while a form of censorship, speaks to the performative function and energy of the play.[48] Instead of giving into these popular claims about anger, *Zucken* invites contemplation about this affect as an important, radical theatrical form as well as the site of political and social protest, which manifests itself through a relentless force of energy performed by young bodies.

A focus on form and performance in the theatre of anger opens up a reading with Lehmann's concept of postdramatic theatre. While there are myriad points of tangency with postdramatic theatre, which I address at various moments throughout these chapters, I engage more fully with Lehmann's work here. As a conceptual model of theatre that postulates, among other things, a dialectical relationship between content and form, postdramatic theatre is particularly concerned with the drama of the mise-en-scène, and the "heavy" bodies on the stage.[49] For as Lehmann contends, "the dynamic that used to maintain the drama as a form of development has moved into the body."[50] In other words, postdramatic theatre asks what stories the gestures and movements of the body, its legible form, tell the audience. Postdramatic theatre does not simply imply a moving away from the dramatic text to a "beyond" or an "afterness" of drama. The prefix "post-" should be understood instead as a break and a fissure. Postdramatic theatre is a demand to rethink dramatic theatre beyond the authority of a single text, a single author, a single voice. Indeed, if "post-" indicates, on the one hand, a treading in the moment, an embeddedness in a thick historical present, a temporality conditioned by an event in the past, then it is, on the other hand, also interruptive, insofar as it distinguishes itself from a moment in the past. It says this is something different. Indeed, Salzmann's play is something quite different.

The most recent play by Salzmann to be staged (excluding the adaptation of their novel, *Außer sich* [*Beside Myself*]), *Zucken* is also one of their more aggressive and critical works. It responds to Europe's discursive preoccupation with the radicalization of youths compelled into battle in Syria and Iraq, particularly with ISIS. Taking an altogether different approach from the mainstream, *Zucken* condemns Europe for its tragic failure to examine its own role in the cultural, social, and political marginalization of minoritized groups. It is a play that cuts with indictment. This ethos framed the premiere of the play. In a video introduction featured on YouTube and linked to the Maxim Gorki website, entitled *5 Fragen (5 Questions)*, Salzmann poses five questions to the viewer about discrimination, including racism, homophobia, and transphobia:

> (1) Gehst du jedes Wochenende in den Club und weißt, du kommst wieder nicht rein?; (2) Durchsucht man immer deine Tasche, wenn du aus dem Supermarkt rausgehst?; (3) Packen Fremde ungefragt in deine Haare?; (4) Bist du Schwul? Ich meine, es ist mir egal; ich wollte es nur wissen; (5) Aber was bist du denn?

> (1) Do you go to the club every weekend and know that again you won't be allowed in?; (2) Is your bag always subject to search when you leave the supermarket?; (3) Do strangers touch your hair without asking?; (4) Are you gay? I mean, I don't care; I just wanted to know; (5) But what are you, then?

These rhetorical questions evoke the grim reality of the pervasiveness of discrimination in German and European society and the daily adversity and injustice experienced by minoritized Germans. As an introduction to the premise of the play, the video also reawakens and reframes thoughtfulness.

Zucken Staged

Sebastian Nübling directs a number of plays in the Maxim Gorki Theatre's repertoire. In addition to Necati Öziri's *Get Deutsch or Die Tryin'*, some of these include Sibylle Berg's *Es sagt mir nichts, das sogenannte Draußen* (*The So-Called Outside Means Nothing to Me*, premiere 2013), *Und dann kam Mirna* (*Along Came Mirna*, premiere 2015), and *Nach Uns das All – Das innere Team kennt keine Pause* (*The Universe after Us – The Inner Team Knows No Break*, premiere 2017). (Nübling also adapted Salzmann's novel *Außer sich* for the stage, premiere 2018). His proclivity for athletic theatre, as established in chapter 2, shows itself again here in even fuller form. Nübling often works with young actors and is active at the Junges Theater Basel, where *Zucken* has also been performed. Nübling's staging of *Zucken* significantly departs from Salzmann's original text. It converts a 100-page play into an accelerated seventy-five-minute performance, in which dance and movement frequently take over. Nübling creates what the daily *Berliner Zeitung* refers to as a "rhythmisch sportliches Kampf-Tanz-Theater" ("rhythmic athletic fighting-dance-theatre").[51] Yet Salzmann's text is not a conventional one to begin with. Structurally exceptional and experimental, the play is also devoid of a true dramatic narrative. The text does not have clear-cut characters and contains more prose than theatrical dialogue or monologue. Four stories about radicalization coincide but intersect only thematically. Nübling applies just three of the narratives from the text, which he also modifies, as well as an extended chorus scene. One could summarize the stories as follows: (1): Girl becomes radicalized and tries to go to Syria; (2) Boy becomes radicalized and decides to go to eastern Ukraine; (3) Girl had become radicalized, has already gone to Kurdistan, and sends a video report of her experience there. Overall, the dearth of text, not to mention dramatic content and development, has been a source of criticism of Nübling's production of the play.[52] However, such criticism not only fails to recognize the significance of form in the play as more than just auxiliary to the text, but also Salzmann's own nod to bodily form with the application of the subtitle *Zucken*. A corporeal twitch stands in place of dramatic feelings and verbal expression as an articulation of complexity. How contemporary young people become radicalized is a question whose answer is anything but simple. And this theatre does not provide answers. But the punch of Salzmann's political ethos is not lost in Nübling's production; rather, it is accelerated and distilled into rhythmic form.

The play begins: seven performers climb upon a stage occupied by four large black leather couches, the cumbersome but not completely immobile fixtures of the performance space designed by Magda Willi. The performers are young and dressed casually. All seven are non- or semiprofessional actors and actresses. They tightly clutch smartphones, whose blue screens glow in the semidarkness of the theatre. The area lights remain lit (a general directorial preference). Clustered at first stage left atop two of the couches and ignoring the audience, the performers begin to play the sentimentally slow Pachelbel's *Canon in D* on their phones, a song often played at weddings. The repetitive harmony and conventional tonality of the piece juxtaposed with the atonality and speed of the rest of the soundscape of the play creates (certainly in retrospect) an amusing and perplexing effect. Finally, one performer stands up, plugs his phone into an amp, intentionally creating a loud jolt of beam noise, and the word "Zucken" appears across the back wall upstage. Pachelbel ends, "Zucken" begins. Considered intertextually, as an example of Western classical kitsch, Pachelbel's *Canon in D* might be described as the "white bread music" that is promptly silenced so that "Zucken" may begin. If *Weißbrotmusik* is a struggle to be heard over the "white bread music," *Zucken* is already there – it immediately asserts itself and takes over.

Throughout the performance, music and speech, like movement, come in spurts and stutters through unexpected outbreaks. Music and movement are always synchronized. Just as these performers treat their phones as prostheses to their own bodies, their bodies seem to move at the will of the music. The first sequence of *Zucken* contains four punctuated, collective dance routines to hip-hop music with sound effects. Each time, these routines abruptly end with flailing agitation as though the performers' bodies were being pumped full of bullets from an assault rifle, or tasered. It should be noted that the promotional poster for the performance of *Zucken* at the Junges Theater Basel in fact featured an image of a taser in disrepair.

The heart of *Zucken* is its pulsing nerve centre. As Salzmann writes in the original text, "[d]u erwartest etwas, du erwartest etwas von der Welt, und diese Erwartung ist ein Nerv, der zuckt." ("You expect something, you expect something from the world, and this expectation is a nerve that twitches.")[53] The play's dramaturgy takes the act of "Zucken" literally and affectively. It is composed of a choreography of almost relentless movement but it is also full of hiccupping sequences. Movement can erupt and then quickly stop again. This kinesthetic stuttering in dance has been conceptualized as the manifestation of anxiety about its own ontology as a form. André Lepecki describes this phenomenon of contemporary dance in the following way: "Perception of a hiccupping in choreographed movement produces critical anxiety; it is dance's very future that appears menaced by the eruption of kinesthetic stuttering."[54] Extended to theatre, this ontological anxiety manifested in movement is likewise a concern of postdramatic forms, which similarly attend to dynamic formations and energies that not only create hiccups and breaks in movement, but also extend these to dramatic narratives. In theatre, these kinesthetic breaks bring forth the presence of the bodies of the performers. According to Lehmann, "[i]n postdramatic theatre, breath, rhythm and the present actuality of the body's visceral presence take precedence over the logos."[55] Postdramatic theatre is a form of "energetic theatre," which employs movement and corporeal intensities that elide representation. In lieu of metaphysics of presence and transcendental meaning, postdramatic theatre evokes real "forces, intensities, [and] present affects."[56] Circling back to the affects of bodies in movement in *Zucken*, if anxiety can take the form of hiccupping in dance, then anger can also be displayed through corporeal spasming and twitching. As affects, anxiety and anger are distinct. The former often has no definite end or object; anxiety is thought to be the affect that has to do with nothing.[57] Anger, as I have argued throughout this book, by contrast responds to something and leads us somewhere. It can be the appropriate response to injustice and thus useful in the pursuit of justice. On the surface, the physical manifestations of anxiety and anger do intersect. However, when dancing, jumping, and sputtering transform into fighting in a scene in which the stage is converted into a makeshift boxing club and the couches are turned upwards to serve as punching bags, anxiety effectively gives way to anger.

Nübling's version contains three separate stories of radicalization, but the performance of the second one is most kinesthetically galvanized with anger's sparking circuits. Here anger assumes its most explicit form: fighting. There is no direct description of fighting in Salzmann's text, but Pawlik, a student of Russian Ukrainian parentage, who gets caught between emotional nationalist debates at the height of the war in Donbass and struggles within himself, when his father demands that he make a choice between being Russian or Ukrainian. "Bist du Russe oder Ukrainer?" ("Are you a Russian or a Ukrainian?") is a question posed only twice in Salzmann's text, but it heaves with such paternal force as it pathetically yet threateningly spills from the lips of Pawlik's blubbering and drunken father that its assault feels relentless. The same question is posed in the performance in chorus multiple times. All the while, the performer playing Pawlik moves back and forth, sparring atop a semiraised platform centre stage. Pawlik performs his inexhaustible anger as an inescapable circular pattern of physical aggression. That Pawlik decides to travel to eastern Ukraine to fight in the war may be a somewhat predictable outcome of his struggle. However, the fact that it remains unclear for which side he will fight belies his (if any) nationalist ideologies and attests rather to a more personal battle with the pressures of identity and belonging. This is a battle that lies much closer to home – in Germany. Before making the decision to set off for Ukraine, he also has a sexual encounter with his friend turned lover, Rüzgar. In Salzmann's text, interiority conveys Pawlik's struggle with the encounter, which on the one hand he violently contests and on the other hand he cannot resist for overpowering desire. Again, Nübling relies on kinetic force. At first, Pawlik challenges Rüzgar to a fight. They both remove their shirts. Rüzgar prepares by exuberantly applying body spray. The action elicited chuckles from the audience. The two playfight, then Rüzgar lights a joint and the tempo of the music changes from fast to more mellow. They smoke and the scene becomes playful. Physical intimacy swells during this energetic scene of foreplay and ends with the two on top of each other on one of the couches, turned away from the audience.

Playfulness, as well as moments of comedy, in Nübling's production pare down some of the anger and the gravity of the central turn to violence and radicalism of the play. The roles of Rüzgar and another character (who remains nameless) are performed in Swiss German, such that their speech requires translation and is subtitled and projected onto the back wall upstage. This performance flourish marks difference and potential miscommunication even within "nativist" concepts of community. Many spectators responded with laughter during these scenes. In the first story adopted in Nübling's production, a girl falls for a young man she meets online in a chat room. He is supposedly a jihadist and is in Syria. They text each other and the performers speak their text messages aloud, including the emojis, applied by the girl with amusing exuberance. Immediately and naïvely ready to take up his ideologies as her own, the girl tries to join him in Syria. When this fails, she instead packs up all the kitchen knives in her backpack and takes them to school, then on her way she stabs someone in the train station. What is so striking, even comically entertaining, about this spectacle is, however, not the absurdity of the narrative so much as the way in which it is performed. That this maladroit girl in an oversized purple sweatshirt and athletic pants, with her Swiss German and her childishly angry bursts of energetic stomping around and screaming that she hates her mother, would become radicalized, seems ridiculous. The brief narrative itself ends in a coup de théâtre when another performer abruptly calls an end to the story. "Cut! Das ist zu einfach! Viel zu unkompliziert! Es ist wie eine Liebesgeschichte." ("Cut! That's too easy! Much too uncomplicated! It's like a love story.")[58] He assures the audience that the remainder of the play will be different. "Wir brauchen mehr Beat," he says, "viel mehr Beat" ("We need more beat, much more beat"). Despite their potential irony, moments such as these open up a reading with postdramatic theatre. A refusal to rest with rote and predictable structures, particularly as mandated by the logics of genre, is critical. Rupturing the generic structures of drama and rendering them obsolete, or at least nonrepresentational, is the crux of postdramatic theatre. This nonmimetic principle turns into improvisation without plot or specific roles and emphasizes the intensive physical presence of the performers.[59] Suffice to say, a call for more "beat" signals the drive for corporeal intensity, experience, and performance. In *Zucken,* and in the theatre of anger more generally, performers do not physically alight to the auditorium, but the space of the theatre is a shared space of co-presence, in which frequent outbreaks of direct address (particularly in the choral scenes, to be examined more fully in the next section) strike a blow to the fourth wall. The energy of the performance is so powerful and fervent that it becomes contagious. Palpable twitching among spectators as the performance progressed displayed this. Yet the convulsive twitching of the collective body onstage does not mirror that of the house or vice versa. If anything, *Zucken,* as much of the theatre of anger, takes on an antagonistic position vis-à-vis the audience – this European social body.

The Body's Kinetic Form of Anger

If, according to Peter Sloterdijk, modernity ushered in a kinetic excess that hinged on a subjectivity of mobilization, what he refers to as "being-unto-movement,"[60] then it was, in Lepecki's analysis, one of complete fantasy, unburdened by history and the politics of repression.

Lepecki describes the nearsightedness of the kinesthetic in the following way: "The kinetic spectacle of modernity erases from the picture of movement all the ecological catastrophes, personal tragedies, and communal disruptions brought about by colonial plundering of resources, bodies, and subjectivities."[61] Some postmodern and postcolonial thought has recuperated movement in productive ways, but not without maintaining a degree of scepticism. Rethinking movement and the kinetic force of the body as a potential site of recognition, resistance, and antagonism against oppression has, for instance, been critical to Black studies discourse, in particular with the work of Fred Moten, Daphne A. Brooks, and C. Riley Snorton, who have all argued for the emancipatory possibilities achievable in radical acts of fugitivity through movement.[62] More recent studies on utopia, such as José Esteban Muñoz's *Cruising Utopia,* also explore the potential to be found in movement, because the body in motion "rapidly deploys the signs, the gestures, of queer communication, survival, and self-making."[63] Salzmann's play similarly recasts movement through affective politics to communicate something new and declarative.

"Zucken" (as "twitching," "shuddering," or "spasming"), in my contention, is an exterior form that presents an affective state of collective anger in the play. It incites and is incited by the physical stomping and the roiling that fills, even overwhelms, this particular theatre experience. Such is the anger that also threatens and admonishes the audience directly with the words from Salzmann's text in the chorus section, entitled "Wir" ("We") (figure 5.1):

> Du hast eine Geschichte. Sie steht fest. In die vertraust du.
> Du hast Pyramide auf uns gebaut.
> Wir sind der Grund deiner Geschichte.
> Du hast Angst, aber nicht wirklich.
> Weil du glaubst, wenn du die Polizei rufst, dann kommt
> sie und rettet dich,
> und danach gibt es ein faires Verfahren, ein Gericht,
> Krankenhausaufenthalt, Entscheidungen, Entschädigung
> sogar und die Ordnung ist wiederhergestellt.
> Wenn einer mit Kalaschnikow im Kinosaal auftaucht.[64]

> You have a history. It is certain. In which you trust.
> You have built pyramids on our backs.
> We are the foundation of your history.
> You are afraid, but not really.
> Because you believe that when you call the police, then

5.1 The Angry Chorus in *Zucken*. Image © Uwe Heinrich.

they will come and rescue you,
and after that there will be due process, a court of law,
a stay at the hospital, decisions reached, compensation
even and order will be reestablished.
When someone appears in the cinema with a Kalashnikov.

Even with its experimental structure and lack of clearly demarcated roles, *Zucken* is a play definitively directed at a European public that perceives itself as the innocent victim of terrorism, a terrorism that ostensibly hails from elsewhere. This ruse of innocence is anchored to a blind spot. It presents an emphatic refusal to bear the burden of the reality of global entanglements, conflict, terrorism, and war, perpetuated by centuries of Western colonialism and neocolonialism. *Zucken* does not defend radicalization and especially not terrorism, but it brings into relief the duplicity of the dominant European position. Anger does not allow majoritarian society to simply forget and move on; with anger there is no getting off easy. Ahmed once more offers insight about the function of anger in this direction: "If anger is a form of 'against-ness,' then it is precisely about the impossibility of moving beyond the history of injuries to a pure or innocent position."[65]

Choral interludes of monologue – indeed, the chorus can also deliver raging monologues – and movement also resonate with postdramatic forms. A collective "Wir" onstage is both political and performative. Salzmann's text and the performance of it are a reminder of the important practice of "talking back," discussed in chapter 3.[66] From Aristotle to Audre Lorde and bell hooks, the long discursive history of anger is linked to talking back as political struggle and strategy for social justice.[67] This is the exhortative ethos of the chorus in *Zucken*. In the theatre, "talking back" is also structurally disintegrative insofar as it shifts the theatricality from stage to house in its verbal assault on the audience.

Despite its narrative link to the radicalization of young people in this play, anger should not be interpreted as pathological. These youths are not simply angry misfits. Anger becomes attributed to the injustices of the social and political present. Its manifestation is brought forth in the labile movements of dance, fighting, marching, jumping, and gymnastics performed onstage. The extended chorus sequence concludes with the performers donning black balaclavas, which have become iconic symbols of both terrorism and collective protest (consider, for instance, the radical feminist protest group Pussy Riot and its outgrowths),[68] and a kinetic outburst when several performers use the assembled couches as a tumbling mat for leapfrog and somersaults. At every moment, the body is a spectacle of its own dynamism, a figure of its own possibilities for physical expression. *Zucken* galvanizes the potential of the theatrical body, that heavy body, that angry body. Anger's forms cleave to the corporeal refusal to remain still and stay put. It is a form generated by body and motion. Sharp, aggressive, and heavy movements, which elicit loud thuds and bangs, create this physical choreography and topography of anger.

To propose that the young bodies onstage in *Zucken* are merely representational of an ethos of anger and radicalization would be an oversimplification. The present analysis does not follow a narrowly construed semiotic reading of the spasming bodies onstage. The impulse of postdramatic theatre continues in a different direction. To quote Lehmann:

> The dramatic process occurred *between* the bodies; the postdramatic process occurs *with/on/to* the body. The mental duel, which the physical murder on stage and the stage duel only translate metaphorically, is replaced by the physical motor activity or its handicap, shape or shapelessness,

> wholeness or fragmentation. While the dramatic body was the carrier of the agon, the postdramatic body offers the image of its *agony*.[69]

Postdramatic theatre is the theatre of the body, whose drama is the drama of the body. The body in agony is the spasm, the *agonism* of theatre embodied. Gesture becomes a radical expression of energy, movement, and performance. This is not gesture in the Brechtian sense of *Gestus*, which signifies estrangement; it is gesture that opens itself up to affective form, which, to borrow Muñoz's words, "atomizes movement."[70] Put another way, gesture brings bodies and movement into sharp focus, in which every turn, twitch, and shrug can be scrutinized as performance and expression. Dance, as the emphatic outburst of gestures, especially has the capacity to put bodies on display in a way that heeds such scrutiny.

Much of the dance in *Zucken* is reminiscent of contemporary breakout dance with hip-hop influence. The style of dance of one performer in particular, Elif Karcı, stuns and provokes the audience with its sharp angular movements that violently pierce the space around her upper body. Maintaining a rigid and steady frame, her arms and hands whip around her head and body. Through these vogueing moves, hands are altogether expressive; they shade and highlight the body and the face. There is something combatively angry about Karcı's dancing that easily slides into fighting when she dons boxing gloves midperformance and begins using everyone and everything as a punching bag. That each performer dances in a different way, and with varying levels of ability and flair, underscores the freestyle nature of dance in *Zucken* as it liberates the body. (Indeed, Nübling did not work with a choreographer on this play.) The performers were likely instructed to dance as they normally would to such beats. Variation of movements can be detected between performances as well. What becomes foregrounded is the pure presence of the body as body.

The theatre of anger and postdramatic theatre are keenly concerned with bodies. Postdramatic theatre is hailed as the return of the centrality of the body with its emphasis on presence over representation. For postmigrant theatre, the return of the body brings into relief the reality of institutional discrimination in German theatres, which must be subverted and dismantled. The vast majority of the performers in the theatre of anger, and in this *Zucken* is certainly exemplary, are performers of colour, who assert and embody their place onstage – and in the theatre. At one point during the performance all seven performers assemble on a single couch as though in preparation for a group photo and from a standing position yell in chorus "Wir" multiple times to the pounding beat of a drum. Each "Wir" is accompanied by a physical jolt of this hostile mass, akin to a verbal bullet.[71] The in-yer-face impulse of this scene declares the presence of these performers – this raging collective of bodies – that must be reckoned with. This act of antagonizing the audience is reminiscent of Nurkan Erpulat's opening prelude in *Verrücktes Blut*. Whereas *Verrücktes Blut* addresses the problematic phenomenon that anger regularly becomes attached to certain bodies – in this case to young, male, Muslim bodies – *Zucken* looks for the sources of anger and displays its energetic potential in the struggle against social injustice in and beyond the theatre space.

At a time when Europe perceives itself in a state of security and cultural crisis – even in a war against terror, as former French president François Hollande was eager to declare in the wake of the Charlie Hebdo tragedy in 2015 – a play such as *Zucken* is an exhortation of protest against not only this myopia but also the resulting panic, territorial hedging, social marginalizing, and new nativism in Europe and around the world. It works to undo the audience's assumption that radicalization is cultural (not least religious) and particular rather than political and universal, and that it is something happening to Europe (and the rest of the West) and not *because of* Europe. *Zucken* does not apply the phenomenon of jihadism exclusively to the pursuit of holy war within the Islamic context, a connection many in the West are wont to make. Neither Salzmann's text nor Nübling's production offer conclusions about how and why young people are drawn to jihadism, despite the promissory directive of Salzmann's ironically suggestive longer title. This play does not provide an explanation of jihadism in eight steps. Instead, *Zucken* revels in a state of (out)rage predicated not on hate per se but on protest against the unjust conditions of the present.

With a focus on both text and performance, *Zucken* can be viewed as a manifestation of theatrical anger through an excess of bodily movement and presence. In its confluence of postdramatic and angry practices, *Zucken* wrests theatrical performance from its aesthetic and structural rules of logic and takes it in the direction of an event of diversity, politics, and collective activism that resonates even beyond the theatre space. Reading anger as a physical and energetic performance of recalcitrant intervention into dominant forms and narratives of theatre reestablishes its potential as a productive instrument for social justice. Finally, the concluding question posed in chorus to the audience – "Wohin? Ihr wisst es nicht, was nach uns kommen könnte." ("Where to? You don't know what could come after us.") – articulates this outward swerve in *Zucken* and so much of the theatre of anger, this concluding turn to the audience, which always sounds like a demand and threat rather than a simple question. The same can be argued for the final (speech) acts in *Get Deutsch or Die Tryin'*, *Schwarze Jungfrauen*, and *Verrücktes Blut*. In particular, the radically violent act of shooting into the audience at the close of *Verrücktes Blut* is the angry peripeteia that refuses reconciliation and closure. *Zucken* also ends with pugnacious denunciation and warning that swells with the exhilarating experience of anger and a heady promise of more to come, albeit in yet unknown form.[72] The final act of the performance rebounds in a not-yet-realized act from the world (off-stage).

Similarly characterized as Nurit's declaration at the end of *Weißbrotmusik* that her daughter would be given a Muslim name, Salzmann's plays habitually conclude with a provocation. There is a repeated reinforcement of the aleatory nature of theatre in these transitional final moments, which never offer closure and always threaten to spill over into the real world like a simmering reservoir of anger. The rhythms of refusal, youth resilience, and retaliation draw through lines from *Weißbrotmusik* to *Zucken*, from the beginning of the theatre of anger to its present directions and future progressions. Anger is the affect that defies both the deafening "white bread music" and the "white noise" and responds with violent bodily spasms. But even more than an affective groove, anger fights back with the energetic pulse of temerity – a boxer's punch. Salzmann theatricalizes this mode of anger as a feeling that reverberates across the performance and bends it towards the vociferousness of in-yer-face theatre for a new era, a theatre for the future, what they call a theatre for the twenty-first century. These are youth plays, which inescapably push towards a future. That is not to say that they are sentimentally optimistic or utopian; this would be an obvious misreading. Rather, these plays present a youthful will that refuses defeat. They stage the energy to persist and to flourish. This is the final turn *Theatre of Anger* makes, and it is a turn towards the then and there, because the present is just not enough.

Chapter Six

"Theatre of the Twenty-First Century": An Interview with Sasha Marianna Salzmann

One sunny afternoon in Berlin, in June 2018, I sat down with the playwright and novelist Sasha Marianna Salzmann. Over coffee and baklava, they generously, evocatively, and eloquently shared their experiences, feelings, and thoughts on their connection and contributions to contemporary theatre, the role of anger in their work, and the future of postmigrant theatre, in particular with its turn to *Desintegration*.

I would like to begin by asking you to describe what "postmigrant theatre" means to you.

I have been answering this question so much over the last few years, and you know what is beautiful is that the answer is transforming with time. I remember entering a space, which was Ballhaus Naunynstraβe, an alternative theatre in Kreuzberg, Berlin, not knowing that it is a political space, not knowing anything about a postmigrant agenda. I wanted to party, basically. It seems ridiculous, but it was not easy for me, even in Berlin in 2008, to find a place where I would feel welcome. I rarely felt like an addressee in theatre spaces or cultural spaces in general. Exclusion always works on different levels; it could have been the way the events were advertised, could have been the bodies on the posters, or simply the price of a ticket that would make me stay away. Yet, although I was afraid that I do not belong in the art world, I somehow always wanted to be in theatre. I remember the feeling of entering the Ballhaus Naunynstraβe for their opening, and for this party, and it felt so different. The bodies onstage were different. The main character was an Armenian Turkish doorman – I had never seen that kind of character at the centre of a story. The DJ at the after-show party was playing different music than minimalist. And there was this other woman who started to smoke with me by the bar, meaning inside of the building, which is of course forbidden, and we had an amazing conversation and I thought she was beautiful, and then she left. Someone told me later: "She's the new artistic director of this place, by the way; that was Shermin Langhoff." I started to think about what it means to feel welcome in a space and how to create these spaces.

I guess that postmigrant means for me today that everybody is welcome. This sounds a bit like these refugee centre slogans, but I mean it as a policy about how to create social spaces. The definition offered by Shermin Langhoff was: postmigrants are those who are Germans, who were born and raised here, but are being called and treated as migrants when it comes to accessing theatre schools, cultural institutions, et cetera. So, they must carry the migrant or postmigrant label in their bones until Germany collapses. The movement started with a big population of Turkish, Greek, and Armenian artists, who didn't have access to the art world, so they started to create their own productions, write their own plays. They were no longer willing to play the dealer, the pimp, the sex worker. They started telling their own stories; another canon was developed, where topics like the Armenian genocide, for instance, found their way onto German stages.

I thought it was extremely interesting and even more effective than the protests I was attending at that time, so I decided to stay at the Ballhaus Naunynstraβe to try to understand how the movement works. I became part of their team. I remember how my understanding of what a theatre can do started to change. Before that, I didn't know that art could be a productive tool for rewriting the national myth. And I didn't know that I as a migrant could be part of the German cultural scene, for I was told at school that I would never be. You always need someone who encourages you. The postmigrant agenda encouraged me a lot. I can pass for so many things and I am othered in completely different ways. I somehow was the "good Jew" before I came to Ballhaus Naunynstraβe. I was the "welcomed other," while my colleagues with Turkish or Greek backgrounds, Black Germans of course, as well, would not even be considered as protagonists of any kind of story. A Jew has a story in the German national myth, a tragic one. But you don't know all these things when you grow up, you don't know that you've been seen as the victim. That you are being used. I understood it later in my exchange with all these people at the Ballhaus Naunynstraβe. They were producing all kinds of very fun and very aggressive plays; they were working on a counternarrative. I connected this to the postmigrant approach. A counternarrative in a German Jewish context would be, for example, to be the "bad Jew," the aggressive Jew, who wants revenge.

Postmigrant theatre brought forth stories, which a national audience had never heard before. The whole history of the so-called Gastarbeiter [guest workers] was so silenced before. It was there, it was obvious, there were historical facts, and many books, but who reads books? In the Ballhaus those stories found their way onstage in a very sexy, provocative way. And people came to see. Because you hear something or someone writes something. The hype hit us with *Verrücktes Blut*.

I was friends with the director, Nurkan [Erpulat], even before Ballhaus Naunynstraβe, and I loved his aesthetics and his *Frechheit* [effrontery], his very "I-don't-give-a-fuck" attitude. He was a role model in a way, but when I saw *Verrücktes Blut*, I didn't think it was so groundbreaking. I thought that other works by him are so much more breakthrough, fun, and important for our discourses. It is a play about racism and discrimination of the third generation of postmigrant kids in school. A comedy. I observed that our audience started to change. You would suddenly have all these white people in nice dresses at the Ballhaus Naunynstraβe, complaining about our wine at the canteen bar not being good enough. I realized that this audience laughed at different things. They applauded certain things the racist characters said. They applauded when a girl, a character of the piece [*Verrücktes Blut*], was forced by the antagonist to take off her veil. I started to conduct a study because I wanted to figure out how things were changing in our space. I started to interview audience members after the show. I would ask them what they thought was so great about the piece. I also wrote an essay entitled "What Are You Laughing About?"[1] I felt like it was a very obvious take-over, but sometimes you see it and can't really stop it. It was clear to Shermin what was going on. But at the same time, that was the starting point for postmigrant theatre to become a mainstream discourse, and every theatre in Germany started to feel challenged and provoked. Some other spaces started to put on productions of *Verrücktes Blut* with white actors and white actresses. It was horrible. They should have been ashamed, really. But at the same time people started to reflect on their own ensembles and realize that they actually don't have bodies to fill the roles for an alternative canon.

I remember how becoming mainstream terrified me a lot, because I thought part of our agenda was to be subversive, not to sell ourselves, but to be in-yer-face. When we became "Theatre of the Year" [2014] at Gorki I was confused. What does it mean to be honoured by those who you criticize? It was so interesting. We became big when we had actually already left the postmigrant concept; we were trying to push it to another step. When we went to Maxim Gorki Theatre as an artistic crew, we claimed that we are not postmigrants anymore, but the theatre of the twenty-first century. We said: We are a state theatre, so we address the issues of the state – including gender identities and sexual identities. We tried and are still trying to be more complex, to speak about intersectionality. But, I guess, if you were to ask a stereotypical Berliner who knows a bit about the theatre scene in town what we do and who we are, he or she would simply say: Maxim Gorki is a Turkish theatre. Because Shermin Langhoff's background is Turkish, because our ensemble is diverse, too. People here are not used to nonwhite faces in state-funded institutions. It was a small sensation when we were invited to curate Gorki.

I became the artistic director of the small stage. We called it Studio Я. We entered as a network of artists from all kinds of places – from Detroit to Tel Aviv. There was a big difference between us and the main stage. The Studio Я was actually not a state theatre. It's in the same building, but we got zero money from the state. That's what made everything that happened possible; we were independent. We opened up our formats, which were not common in theatres before. Shermin gave us space and had faith in my belief that a theatre should be open to all kinds of discourses. Shermin brought me back from Istanbul, where I was living back then. She said, "You constantly say that Berlin needs a queer diverse space for marginalized people. Go and do it."

In what ways does your work contribute to this theatre movement? In other words, how has your work been shaped by and how does it shape postmigrant theatre?

In 2008, when I wrote my first play, *Weißbrotmusik*, I remember being afraid that they were going to kick me out of university [University of the Arts in Berlin] for it. It was before I met Shermin and the crew. We had only white male mentors. And my play was about two angry young men with Turkish and Jewish backgrounds, respectively, who beat an old white German man nearly to death at the end of the play. With *Weißbrotmusik* I didn't claim that the guys were right, but I did propose that the story is more complex than the crime they committed. It's a piece on racism and exclusion. It is written in a hip-hop manner. That I made one of the characters Jewish was perceived as a huge provocation. I had serious discussions because Jews are not to be touched when it comes to the stereotype of angry, criminal migrants in Germany. When I started to write, there were only a few actors and directors of colour, and nearly no playwrights. It was not common to see protagonists like that onstage at all. The university didn't know what to do with me. But then I received my first acknowledgments; I received prizes and the show started to run well. Now it [*Weißbrotmusik*] has been running for ten years and it is mainstream, I guess. That is somehow a relief.

I was inspired by the aggressive way of the postmigrant theatre. That really shaped my language. I started to think a lot about shame, such as migrant shame. What does shame do to us? Why are we silent in the face of the dominant culture? In my first novel *Außer sich* (*Beside Myself*, 2017), the first German word the main protagonist Ali tries to say is "sorry." I was thinking a lot about what it does to a body to be raised to be ashamed and modest. It obviously puts your body in a certain position in which you try to be especially nice and be the "good Other," and not be visible. Ballhaus Naunynstraße did the opposite. This is what the postmigrant movement gave me: confidence, strength, inspiration. My own direct contribution, I remember, was when we were already at Gorki and I brought queer discourse into the discussions, which they didn't applaud in the beginning at all. I de-gendered the bathrooms of the Studio Я and had awkward arguments with the rest of artistic team about it. It's funny that now they are proud of it, showing them to journalists, talking about the queer agenda.

I think my work always focused on intersectionality. I could never participate "just" in feminist discourse, the Jewish discourse, the queer discourse, all of that. It comes from what I am. I was always curious about the connection between the communities – the contradictions, the similarities. We tend to live separately but I don't really see that. Just go to a *Gayhane* in Kreuzberg [gay dance party with Arabic-themed music and entertainment popular in Berlin] and you see how complex bodies are and how we badly need spaces where we can be what we are.

Where do you see intersections between postmigrant theatre and other theatrical forms? Such as post-Brechtian theatre? Or postdramatic theatre?

It's very interesting that you mention Brecht. I used to be anti-Brecht. But that has changed. I came into to a postdramatic theatre world, where it was clear that there was to be no story, no dialogue, and no emotions, and that is due to Brecht's theories. We were taught at university that since our ancestors were Nazis, or people who made the Holocaust possible, we have no right to trigger the emotions of the masses anymore. We will not march and salute to one opinion. In the case of theatre, this one opinion-giver would be the playwright. And so, the classic drama, written by one individual, had to end. I agree that we have to reinvent the dynamics of how we interact with each other in theatre. I am not against kicking the playwright off their throne. But I disagree that we are all descendants of Nazis. Sorry, that is a white German problem. Yes, *Publikumsbeschimpfung* (*Offending the Audience*, 1966) was extremely important because there were actual Nazis sitting in the audience you could offend, but that was in the sixties. Now we have a diverse audience: Germany's population is also made up of marginalized people, so why yell at them? What kind of audience are you anticipating? Are you are making plays for descendants of Nazis?

So, coming back to Brecht, I was critical because his ideas were used for an old-fashioned fantasy of how Germany might be today, not representing voices outside of the dominant culture. I started very consciously to write classic dialogues in the style of Ibsen and others, epic stories. I wanted to learn how to create emotions. I wanted people like my mother and her friends to come the theatre, I wanted them to understand; I wanted them to feel. They don't have to be yelled at. I wanted to use an aesthetic language that is not for a certain elite clique.

Recently, I was part of a panel called "*Glotzt nicht so romantisch*" ("Don't gawk so romantically") during the *Theatertreffen*. It is a quote from Brecht. I think that this panel made me understand how I am suddenly becoming more Brechtian. That was weird. But times change and I was sitting onstage with young, shooting-star artists of the theatre scene in Germany, and all of them were so unpolitical, cared mainly about their aesthetics. They use masks and digital performances to challenge the boundaries of art today. Yes, of course, why not? But what else? What is behind the form? Where is your pain? Why do you do art, just because you can? All of these people I debated with didn't care about Brechtian theatre anymore and I started to defend it somehow. To defend the need to bring clear vision and political statements back onstage.

This is, obviously, what postmigrant theatre is doing today. For me the theatre of the twenty-first century can't be unpolitical. For that we have too many burning issues. Maybe postmigrant is, in a way, thinking about Brecht further, a very in-yer-face way.

If postmigrant theatre were to have a manifesto, what might be some critical formulaic points?

In my opinion it starts with the structural makeup of institutions: you need someone with experience of migration on top. The people who make decisions must come from minority positions. I have seen so many theatres try to jump on this train of postmigrant theatre, and of course it didn't work because they simply hired a Turk for one play and thought that this solved the problem of injustice. They don't "feel" what the problem is. You need people who have real empathy. The content onstage changes, if marginalized people are part of the structure. If there are, for example, transgender people as part of the crew, then of course things will change. Not only bathroom politics, but also the way an advertisement looks, whom it addresses, et cetera.

More recently, postmigrant theatre has been termed a "theatre of Desintegration," which was also the theme of the Third Herbstsalon in the fall of 2017. Can you speak about this and elaborate on your own significant contribution to this turn?

Desintegration is my new favourite resistance practice. This is basically what I teach most, when I teach. I don't teach playwrights how to write a scene anymore. Let me give you an example of a pedagogical exercise. I start with: "Hello, it's great that you're here. I'm Sasha and I would like for us to introduce ourselves." So, it would go something like: "Hi, I'm Sasha. I'm from Russia. I'm thirty-two. I'm..." After everyone is done, I would instruct them to take a sheet of paper and write down everything they didn't say about themselves. What it provokes in people is an encounter with personal identity and the person they sell themselves as. We are used to selling our labels in official introductions: you sell your nation; you sell your age; you sell your gender; and so forth. When people start to reflect on what they are ready to give in order to gain power and recognition, this is where the work starts.

Practically speaking, Max Czollek and I have been talking for ages about the fact that we are always the "Jewish writers." No matter what you do, you have this adjective on your forehead, which of course in Germany is a very particular experience. Max's and my experiences were exceedingly different because he's German Jewish and I am Russian Jewish, or Ukrainian Jewish, in any case, a Soviet Jew: I come from this feeling of being part of the partisans, the Red Army – we opened up the concentration camps. That kind of pride. For him, on the one hand, it was a feeling that his family was erased. On the other hand, as a German, he also feels responsible for the fact that so few of us are sitting at the table now. Different stories, different perspectives. It was very enriching to exchange and to see what is happening to our art and to our bodies in interaction with so-called state authorities. Being proud, being ashamed. Then came the question: what do we want to do with this? To reach conclusions about what it could mean for our generation of Jews we needed more colleagues for the exchange, so we decided to organize a congress. We thought it would be good to bring different Jewish positions together and speak. We announced it as a "Congress on Contemporary Jewish Positions" and said that everyone is invited, even Germans. You can imagine – "even Germans!" To advertise the event, we had postcards made with slogans such as: "Keine Juden mehr für Deutsche" ("No more Jews for Germans"), et cetera. People reacted very strongly. Normally in the German context there is this automatic love for Jews and everything they do. If you're radical, they'll love that you're radical. They love that you're "so different." They would love your gayness, et cetera. But what we started with the *Desintegration* congress was going too far for a lot of people. So in a way, that was our in-yer-face theatre or theatre of the twenty-first century.

To de-integrate from the dominant culture is to say: "I don't need your recognition anymore." It was incredibly fun to think this through. How are we going to do this? How far can we go? To create an alternative narrative of a Jew, we felt that we needed to push all clichés to the limits. We presented ourselves with axes and a globe while speaking about the global conspiracy of the *Elders of Zion* with the proclamation: "Of course we exist, look at us!"

We had a very clear approach of revenge: "You destroyed our culture and we are going to make you pay for it." And it hits you. This was the self-presentation of the new Jews of the twenty-first century. It was a bit frightening; we were risking our careers. We were in the media, saying that we are not going to play along with the German culture anymore and at the same time claiming that they owe us money. It sounds fun, but in the end, we didn't know if we would ever get funding to do any of our projects again. We had rules for interviews and media: we do not speak about Israel, about our biographies, or about anti-Semitism. We would repeat these like puppets. It became a performance. We would always say: "We are de-integrated Jews; you cannot use us for your purposes." Because, really, the only thing that the German dominant culture needs a Jew for is to speak about this "tree thing" [menorah] and then to be happy that we are "protected from Muslims." We needed to first de-integrate from this. Then we looked for alliances, other marginalized groups to join in the *Desintegration* movement – the queers, the Muslims, all kind of intersectional groups. We were strongly supported by so many to create the de-integrated space. It was a pre-enacting of a network we wanted to have. Now we have it.

I think that one of the central projects of *Desintegration* is to look for alliances. What does it mean to be in solidarity against the dominant culture? To not play the "good Turk," the "good Jew," the "good gay," and so forth. What happens if we refuse these roles? I think it doesn't work if there is only one community. This is very much connected to what bell hooks has been working on her whole life, James Baldwin, as well. Malcolm X, too. They are all on our walls [in the Studio Я].

One thing, though, that was regrettable to me was that there were mainly white Jews involved in the event. We had difficulty getting Mizrahi Jews to come,[2] for instance. But it spoke to the asylum politics of Germany in the years following unification that when Germans invited Jews to come [especially from the former Soviet Union], these were

6.1 Some of the walls in the foyer of the Studio Я, June 2018. Photo by Olivia Landry.

white Jews. Today, there are certain Jews still not wanted in this country. And that is due to their othered appearances.

The event of *Desintegration* was so powerful that Shermin decided to make it the theme of the Herbstsalon, which is a huge art festival at the Gorki that takes place every two years. After that, the concept exploded. It went beyond Germany's borders and was adopted by other minority groups. This was important to Max and me, because it is not a Jewish concept at all. It broadly asked: How can we not play along with the dominant culture? We gave workshops on *Desintegration* at the *Theatertreffen*, and one of the most encouraging things to realize is that people who think like us are everywhere. The workshops included participants from all over the world, every continent, over thirty countries, and our concept was not that crazy to them; they adopted it very playfully for their own environments.

To follow up on the previous question, the concept of a theatre of anger, which forms the scope of this book, was partly inspired by the discourses which arose from the 2016 event "Desintegration: A Congress on Contemporary Jewish Positions." In particular, I was interested in the expression of anger as a counterposition to victimhood. Is this a correct interpretation and could you possibly say more about this?

Absolutely, that's why we posed with axes and the globe for the cameras. Of course, it is different for every minority, but in the German Jewish context the stereotypes for us to play with are very clear. Germans know that they killed us, but little else. They see us as victims that need to be protected like animals in a zoo. This is how I grew up in this country, that is what I experienced. I have witnessed with my parents what it means to always be ashamed of what you are, to look down, to never raise your voice. They were proud of being Jewish in private but they didn't tell anyone. So I felt provoked to scream. The generation before mine wanted to live without discrimination, and they thought that being invisible would help. They wanted the German Jewish friendship. They wanted a quiet life. But quiet does not mean peaceful.

The fact that Hitler took power at the peak of the assimilation of Jews is telling; that he reminded people of being Jews meant something very clear to me – the opposite of "be silent." If you do not perform Jewish culture, it is dead. It does not exist for people. They think, they will find us in museums, that's it. But already as a teenager I was furious: "What do you mean, the case is closed?" "What do you mean with *Vergangenheitsbewältigung* [working through the past]?" "It is not the past but the present that we're dealing with." You see, I experienced anti-Semitism in Germany from a young age, and people forbade me to speak about it, because they claimed that "we are over this problem." And now we have [Alternative for Germany] AfD in the parliament and six million Germans voted for them.

In our *Desintegration* congress, which took place soon after the elections, Max and I performed with a very aggressive attitude to make it clear that we will not be the good Jews, who don't create noise around having fascists in the parliament. How can we be expected to react? Instead, we screened movie-collages called "Punching Nazis" and talked about our fantasies to torture parliament members from the extreme right-wing party. We were and are a permanent performance of the counterposition to the good, dead victim.

In this book, I argue that anger needs to be recuperated as an affect that is energizing and politically forceful. I follow the Aristotelian tradition, which perceives anger as attributed insofar as it responds to

an action of injustice; therefore, it is both acceptable and justifiable. I trace this tradition through feminist scholars of colour, in particular Audre Lorde, bell hooks, and Sara Ahmed, who powerfully propose that anger is both an attributed affect and one that points us towards the future, towards a new future. Would you agree that anger has this power? Can you say more about anger in your plays?

I entered the theatre scene as young person without much of a concept of what it was going to be like, but I was always an angry child. I still remember beating up boys in the bathroom at school in Moscow. Anger was always part of my identity. I was never auto-aggressive, but boxing was clearly a way for me to physically vent my anger. This was before I started writing, before I knew I could be a writer in the German language. When I went to university, I went through an identity crisis because it felt like a betrayal of everything that I am and what I come from, namely, working-class, and just my lifestyle up until then, which was mostly boxing and drugs. What happened when I started to study was that all the anger that I was releasing on the streets started to come out in my writing. Today I would be more elaborate, but back then when journalists asked me what my inspiration for writing was I would always say "*Wut*" ["anger"]. Maybe it still is, but now there are also other feelings like love or the will to understand an unknown perspective.

I remember that my first play, *Weißbrotmusik*, was very clearly a result of my outrage at what I read about the case in the newspapers at the time. Reporting on the crime and on the two young men who committed it, German newspapers spoke directly and openly about "criminal blood." For me back then in my twenties I was furious. I could not accept that German journalists were using and publishing these words. I was very young, I didn't know how to put my feelings into a theatrical form, so I listened to hip-hop, smoked pot, and wrote and wrote. I was fortunate enough to have a direct connection to the stage through my studies at the University of the Arts [in Berlin], where everyone's first play is staged as a tryout and you get feedback. This was so important. The director of *Weißbrotmusik*, Nick Hartnagel, liked the play, but also said that the audience will feel too safe, because everyone could get behind the criticism of racism. He suggested that we make it more provocative. He planted the actor, who played the "old man," who will be beaten up at the end of the show, in the first row in the audience "undercover." So the impression the audience had was that these two boys, the protagonists of the story, with whom we identified throughout the whole play, jumped down from the stage and beat up an innocent old fellow spectator. When the actors started attacking the "old man," people from the audience would run to the stage and fight with the actors, and among themselves. Well, they would never forget that experience. None of us would. As my first theatre piece, this has had a great impact on my work, even today. I had to learn to always think about my audience. They should not feel comfortable, and as a playwright I should also not be too secure.

When I write, even if it's prose, I think about who it provokes and how. I believe that to trigger people's emotions is necessary to change their minds. They anticipate that they would do or feel something and then you surprise them with their own feelings of anger. I think I learned how (or at least I am getting better at) achieving this onstage, even at the Gorki, which generally attracts an audience not so easily shocked or deterred.

I can share an anecdote. My mom came to a performance of my play *Meteoriten* (*Meteorites*, 2016) and was sitting in the third row beside a man. When the male gay sex scene started, the man said aloud, "Why do I have to watch this?" He then started to talk to my mom about it. Despite the fact that the scene is so abstract, the man was furious; he didn't want to see gay love. But when my mom asked him what he was upset about, he wasn't able to provide a response. He was surprised at his reaction himself.

So, I think this is how I write. I figure out what I want to write about and then how to de-integrate from the expectations – mine and the others. From the "good side," from the "please-like-me side." To challenge my own beliefs, to surprise myself, too. In the best-case scenario, my works are controversial but you will still tell your mother to go see the play.

Of course, anger also gets a bad rap. There is the widespread perception that anger is a negative affect, which is frequently linked to hate and violence. By calling postmigrant theatre a "theatre of anger," I must be cautious not to negatively code the work of this theatre movement and its artists, especially considering that anger is often attached to communities and bodies of colour, for instance, young Muslim men and young Black men. This is a topic you treat in **Weißbrotmusik.** ***How would you (or do you) recuperate anger in a productive way in this play, when some might be intent on reading anger as pathological because it seems to lead to violence?***

Violence and anger do not have to go together. Both have consequences and we have to be aware of that. I never wanted to justify what the real guys did, namely, nearly kill a man. It was clear to me that it was a crime and needed to be brought to trial. I reacted with anger to the racist media.

I did it without violence, but through art. It reached a lot of people. I also questioned the stereotypes of "the angry Turkish man" and "the always good Jew." Bringing that together created the scandal. I think my contribution was the counterposition. Would I be spoken about in the same way? Would they dare to speak about "criminal blood" in my case?

I think that anger is something very complex, and for me something very relieving because I can deal with it in a productive way. I am lucky to have this outlet. If I didn't have my writing, perhaps I would have become a boxer. I don't know how it is for people who do not have an outlet for anger. But I want the audience to deal with their suppressed feelings. If there is something suppressed – and their feelings about postmigrants surely are – then we need to speak about it. Theatre is the right place for that. We need to learn to live and deal with our anger. This is where the actual dialogue starts. It's really exhausting, but I don't see that happening without bringing out our emotions.

In the book, I examine* Weißbrotmusik *and* Verstehen Sie den Dschihadismus in acht Schritten! (Zucken). *The former is your first play and the latter is one of your most recent plays. How would you describe how your style and overall approach to playwriting has developed and changed from one play to the other?

Something I learned while writing *Außer sich* is that I never think in a linear manner. As my best friend, Sivan Ben Yishai, who is a gifted writer, said, "The only form I can identify with is a spiral." Speaking about postmigrant theatre now and coming back to all these topics in a different way, this is important. I think that *Zucken*, my last piece, and *Weißbrotmusik*, the first one, are not very far from each other, while some of my other plays would be considered completely different in terms of genre. *Weißbrotmusik* was written on an impulse. There was no concept. I really thought that they would kick me out of university. Then I wrote *Muttermale Fenster blau* [premiere 2012], which was the opposite; it's a poem, it's about incest in a German family. It takes a different form and pursues a different political topic – though, perhaps not even political – with a very provocative happy ending. There is the father and his daughter and their child, the outcome of their love. This is what got the Kleist prize [for up-and-coming playwrights] back then. I thought it was interesting that *Weißbrotmusik*, which was also in the running, did not win. Then I wrote *Schwimmen lernen* [premiere 2013], which was another example of experimenting with forms; it was my first love song, a full-length poem. I was trying to challenge the question of how, with time, we rewrite our past. After these, I started to politicize my work more. As I said, I wanted to write more psychological plays. I wanted to write with depth and a psychoanalytical approach to our status quo today. I didn't want the audience to necessarily like me, but I wanted them to see my view on the political situation. For that I felt I had to be very straightforward. No experiments with form anymore, just good dialogue. I have always been a huge fan of US American and North American playwriting. I learned a lot from Tony Kushner and Tracy Letts. I did exercises with *August: Osage County* because I thought it was so brilliant and I really wanted to learn this [art of playwriting].

When I wrote *Muttersprache Mameloschn* [premiere 2012] on contemporary Jewish life in Germany, I felt that I was getting the audience's attention; this was an audience which had never cared about Jewish life in Germany before. I never thought that the reactions would be that big. I thought only a small community would care. It's a Jewish story with three women onstage. Hello, boring! I guess it became my blockbuster, people say, my breakthrough as an artist. I was sceptical; I felt like leaving these clear narratives behind again.

Then in 2016, Sebastian Nübling asked me to do something with him on the topic of anger. I've known Sebastian for about fifteen years. I was his assistant when I was sixteen, after I left school. I didn't have a high school diploma. I was literally hanging around, doing nothing. Then I got a Hospitanz [unpaid internship] at the theatre and I would make coffee for Sebastian Nübling. He influenced me so much. When he approached me about doing something together, it was really exciting. But then he asked me to do something on ISIS and my first response was: "No way! I will not do anything about Jihadism." I thought, this is a trap, that they ask a white Jewish voice to write something about these topics. He was also the fifth person to ask me; dramaturgs from different theatres found this topic fashionable: Jihad and young people, especially young women ... I thought that this was insane. It is pornography. But then I thought, "OK, it is Sebastian and I can improvise on the topic of anger. I don't have to write about things I don't know about." In fact, it was the opposite: I actually wanted to go back to my feelings as a young person. *Zucken* became this hit for a young audience. *Weißbrotmusik* is also a play for young people, which I didn't even realize at the time because I was a young person myself. So, yes, I'm going in spirals.

In an earlier conversation, you mentioned that Sarah Kane's dramatic work has been an inspiration for your own. Can you elaborate on this? How might you position the in-yer-face theatre movement, with which Kane was affiliated, in relationship to postmigrant theatre?

I think, in the end, it's the same, in-yer-face theatre and postmigrant theatre. I am really happy that you bring up this connection. It's the same idea but in different centuries, different contexts. I think that in the nineties the question of class, especially in Great Britain, or let's say shopping addictions or the Royals, were burning issues. Sarah Kane could not have been more provocative, even as the white body she was; she was clearly queer and different, marginalized in many ways. She worked on particular topics, which were the wound of the society she lived in. She didn't just write to provoke. Because if you are just trying to provoke, it doesn't have that much of an effect. You don't get recognized beyond the borders of your own country. But everyone I meet in the theatre world knows who Sarah Kane is; she influenced my generation.

I think the burning issue of our century is migration, not that this is a new thing, but let's say that now everything we discuss – in media, politics, and art – is somehow connected to migration. The postmigrant movement is dealing with it by giving migrant voices opportunities to speak. That they actually have access to what has been hitherto only available to a certain white elite is amazing. I think this is in-yer-face. When Shermin Langhoff became the artistic director of the Maxim Gorki Theatre in Berlin, this was also an in-yer-face act.

Recently, I was telling a friend about a panel I sat on; we discussed how to give more space to marginalized voices. And I mentioned that I quoted Frantz Fanon onstage. She then asked what would be not quoting, but doing. For me, not quoting but doing would be ousting all the white people from powerful positions in institutions – onstage and in the artistic team. That would be in-yer-face as a political act. After that, what happens onstage will come naturally. It can even be Heinrich von Kleist. It would be a great Kleist. It could also be stories which no one in the audience has ever heard before.

Something that Sarah Kane also worked on was her ambiguity about being in the body she was born in and somehow, for me, that is connected to the contemporary discourse of gender. Being part of the queer community in Berlin, I learned that we can speak also about migration through bodies or genders. People migrate from what people told them they are to what they actually feel they are.

In your opinion, what is the future of postmigrant theatre? What is also the future of your work as a playwright?

I guess there are two directions for the theatre, and we need both of them: *Desintegration* and *the postmigrant concept*. So one strategy is to not play along with dominant culture and to create our own independent networks with alliances. The other is to create platforms for people who migrated or are still migrating and need to share their stories with an audience. They need space to speak.

The situation in Germany today is very serious. Many Germans voted for AfD. Their first target is to attack the culture departments. Of course! Because culture is what defines identity. National identity in that case. It was not by accident that the first thing the AfD tried to do was close the Maxim Gorki Theatre. They don't want us as part of the German identity. But we are here, we are not leaving, and more and more are coming. I wish everybody would come. If we are many, we can rewrite the national identity of this country.

When it comes to my work, I feel like I should shut up and listen for a while. I was part of so many panels and discussions in the last few years; I was publishing a magazine; I was an artistic director of a space. I love to curate festivals and I started to direct pieces, too. The different forms of artistic expression are part of the toolbox; I use them depending on the challenges I face. But I really wish I could unlearn everything I think I know in order to become more sensitive to what is happening in the actual moment. The writer who always helps me when I feel empty or I feel as though I am losing perspective is James Baldwin. He knew about hard times, and he says that the role of artists is to be witnesses of their time. To write everything down, to put their feelings into words. I will try to do this, but for that I need to observe more, to stop my output for a while.

My first novel was a portrait of a time during the Gezi Park protests in Istanbul and before AfD in the German parliament. Let's see where the material of my second novel leads me. As a playwright, I am taking a break. There are so many amazing voices out there right now – it's beautiful to hear them speak.

Conclusion

Anger in the Future Sense

In Sibylle Berg's *Nach Uns das All – Das Innere Team kennt keine Pause* (*The Universe after Us – The Inner Team Knows No Break*, premiere 2017), Europe in the not-too-distant future has succumbed to the nightmare of fascism and nationalism. A group of young women, best described as a chorus of kinetic force, wants to leave and join an expedition to start a colony-cum-reality show on Mars. Trouble ensues when these women must find male partners to accompany them to ensure propagation on the Red Planet and secure the future of this alternative colony. Men and patriarchy, in particular, are precisely what these women are trying to escape. The young women encounter a group of young men eager to join them. This chorus of men describes itself as emerging from the anger movement: "Wir kommen aus der Wiege der Wutbewegung" ("We come from the cradle of the anger movement"). Through this declaration, these young men willfully position themselves at the centre of this Trump-Putin-Orban-AfD nightmarish reality – a reality of hate-filled politics. The women are not amused. Rhetorically, anger is presented as tantamount to patriarchy, entitlement, even fascism. But through the aggressive choreography of their own collective movement, including kicks and jumps, the women also perform anger that intervenes and resists.

The play indirectly raises the question of who has purchase over anger. In 2010 the German media coined the term *Wutbürger* (literally, enraged citizen or citizens), which immediately became a buzzword and was even named "Wort des Jahres" (Word of the Year). The *Wutbürger*, while coinciding temporally with Spanish *Indignados* or the Greek *Aganaktismenoi* movements, were different. These were often older, white, middle-class, German men, who felt disaffected with and powerless in the face of the political process in Germany and gathered to articulate this frustration in loud and angry ways. Germany's authoritative dictionary *Duden* defines *Wutbürger* in much more general terms. It is "Zeitungsjargon" (newspaper jargon) to describe "aus Enttäuschung über bestimmte politische Entscheidungen sehr heftig öffentlich protestierende und demonstrierende Bürger" (a citizen or citizens who are disappointed by certain political decisions and very violently and publicly protest and demonstrate against them). The unmarkedness of this definition and the absence of the important contextual emergence are noteworthy. If white men protest in anger in Germany, they are "citizens," subjects entitled to certain rights and privileges. Why is this necessarily the case? The phenomenon of the *Wutbürger* exemplifies the discursive presence of anger in the current age as insidious but also often culturally specific.

I evoke this cultural tide as a means of garnering attention to the role of anger in today's world with the intent of providing an alternative to the pervasive narrative that states that anger is in the possession of disaffected (white) male "citizens." But anger's sociopolitical meaning is highly complex. It runs the risk of being taken up for the wrong (unattributive) reasons by irascible types. As a result, anger is perceived negatively as inappropriate, weak, useless, and even destructive – a disease of social ethics and moral life, to paraphrase Martha C. Nussbaum.[1] In the context of the *Wutbürger*, this estimation of anger is not entirely incorrect. At the same time, when anger is expressed by minoritized individuals or groups, the effect is often doubly negated. They are not heard as angry subjects, speaking out in anger against injustice, but as angry objects, whose speech acts are perceived as motivated by anger alone. Sara Ahmed explains this in the following way: as a minoritized subject, it becomes "harder to separate yourself from your object of anger" in the eyes and ears of others.[2] When anger gets stuck on certain bodies, such as for instance the bodies of Muslim men, it can reproduce them simply as angry objects, and not subjects entitled to specific rights and freedoms. These are negating effects of anger I have sought to go beyond in *Theatre of Anger*.

Anger here is not untenable; it is quite clearly a response to a wrong. Throughout this book I make a case for an anger that not only addresses social injustice through art but one that is also self-determining and future building. *Theatre of Anger* is a call to think about and recuperate the affirmation of anger as a powerful political and aesthetic tool, as part of an affective politics that can at once respond and transport. Accused of getting stuck in the past, getting hung up on a wrong and ultimately for not being forward thinking, anger is all too often trivialized and pathologized. The account offered in these pages is that anger does not produce an impasse to thought and action. Instead, it energizes and clarifies; it directs us towards a future. With this I return again to the wisdom of Audre Lorde, who most powerfully articulates the futurity of anger, its emancipatory and creative force with the words "[A]nger expressed and translated into action in the service of our vision and our future is a liberating and strengthening act."[3] This "future" is by no means a temporary change for Lorde, "a simple switch of positions or a temporary lessening of tensions, nor the ability to smile and feel good." Oh no, this is what she refers to as "a basic and radical alteration in those assumptions underlining our lives."[4] Insofar as it responds to something, anger does look back at the past. However, it also encourages creation and action in the pursuit of radical change towards a new future.

Thinking about anger and theatre provides new paths to both political theatre and a theatre invested in social justice. The theatre of anger directly raises minoritized subjects' main object of anger: social injustice manifested through racism, anti-Semitism, Islamophobia, and other modes of hate. As a form of vehement rejection, anger attacks these structures of hate and violence. As a speech act with performative power, it opens up a space for social justice. Such is the political substance of the theatre of anger. But this is not simply a case of politics shaping art. Theatre too gives new guises to anger and to the political purport it carries. Theatre provides new aesthetic forms of resistance as it also reaches new audiences. Like all art, it is capable of consciousness raising and of inciting strong emotions. Suffice to say, the intersection of anger and theatre is nothing if not radical and provocative. At a moment in which there are renewed efforts and interest in the revitalization of political art and theatre, it is the conviction of this book that the theatre of anger serves in the movement towards social change.

Both study and conceptualization of this theatre phenomenon, *Theatre of Anger* takes up a profound task. Individual plays have been hitherto described as containing anger, yet a discussion of these plays as forming a theatre of anger is altogether new. Further, there is no previously existing design for the theatre of anger. While influenced and shaped by other theatre aesthetics and forms, it too is original. This book is in many ways an introduction of something new, a classification of a new type of theatre. What does the theatre of anger look like? What are its aesthetic and political properties? These are questions taken up in large part in the first chapter of the book and then are substantiated through the analysis of examples in subsequent chapters. Framing and informing my analysis of the plays with an interdisciplinary history of anger as an affect grounded in protest, justice, and care, chapter 1 is concerned with establishing the foundation for the theatre of anger. On offer here is a rejuvenating history of philosophy and social thought which begins with Aristotle, who notably defends anger as a tenable response to injustice against oneself and others. From there the chapter moves forward to the eighteenth-, twentieth-, and twenty-first centuries, finally to the tremendous work of Audre Lorde, bell hooks, and Sara Ahmed and the influence of the extant civil rights movement and Black feminism. Anger is a source of energy, clarity, and creativity for these feminist thinkers. It provides an effective means of expressing opposition towards social injustice, racism and antifeminism in particular. It is the groundbreaking insight of these thinkers, which truly gives heft to this study and demonstrates the value of anger.

If the long history of humanity is in part a history of anger, then so is the history of theatre. The first chapter also provides a parallel history of the theatre and its stealth relationship with anger beginning with the startling bodily form of the Laocoön. The unlikely model of physical anger in this theatre, the Laocoön, read against the grain, is a morphological model of the enraged body. Anger must not tout court assume a physical form and this form is by no means universal, but the body is central to the theatre of anger. In the theatre of anger, this body is always political as well as phenomenological. Although the history of anger in the theatre begins and concludes within Western traditions, it also draws on non-Western performance influences resonating from Turkey and Argentina. Explicit impulses are garnered from twentieth- and early twenty-first-century theatre theories and forms. The radical theatrical insights of Antonin Artaud, Bertolt Brecht, "in-yer-face" theatre, and postdramatic theatre set the broad formal parameters of the theatre of anger.

An implicit question unfolds throughout *Theatre of Anger*: What does it mean to make political theatre after Brecht? In the context of German theatre, this question is especially poignant. Is there also a politics of claiming political theatre? Must political theatre always be measured against Brechtian theatre? These questions are by no means new, but they are particularly resonant here. Curious is the fact that the Maxim Gorki Theatre, under the direction of Shermin Langhoff and Jens Hillje, has only reproduced one lesser known play by Brecht. In 2017, Sebastian Baumgarten directed *Dickicht* (adopted from Brecht's early work *Im Dickicht der Städte* [*In the Jungle of the Cities*, 1921–1924]). This is despite the fact that the Maxim Gorki's repertoire consists of more than a nominal number of reproductions of canonical works by Maxim Gorki, Heiner Müller, Georg Büchner, Heinrich von Kleist, and others. I have argued throughout that the theatre of anger at once draws on and distinguishes itself from Brechtian and post-Brechtian political theatre, in particular in its address and treatment of transnational and affective politics, something which is quite novel to political theatre in the German space.

Technique also offers a distinction. The raging monologue is a device critical to this theatre. If anger brings people closer, as Lorde contends, insofar as it demands that we listen to each other, then the raging monologue is anger's modus operandi.[5] Activating the flow of anger in the theatre, the raging dramatic monologue transports the scene from stage to house. It is quite literally a speech act that asserts a presence and talks back in a manner both formally and politically charged. A reliance on both the aggressively expressive body of the performer, its often-agitated physicality, and rebarbative language, which can take the form of verbal artillery, is crucial to the forms of the theatre of anger. This line of fire hurtles forward with robust force through the investigation of the more categorical monologue plays, such as Necati Öziri's *Get Deutsch or Die Tryin'* and Feridun Zaimoğlu and Günter Senkel's *Schwarze Jungfrauen*. But in the more dialogue-driven plays, such as Nurkan Erpulat and Jens Hillje's *Verrücktes Blut* and Sasha Marianna Salzmann's *Weißbrotmusik*, monologues appear perhaps all the more formidable as a rupturing device.

One long monologue of rage, *Get Deutsch or Die Tryin'* initiates my performance analysis of this set of plays. A young Turkish man struggles with and responds in anger to a history and inheritance of marginalization and social violence as he attempts to obtain German citizenship at the age of eighteen. While he is shuffled through discriminatory German bureaucracy, he recalls his family history. The play's thematic treatment of migration history invites the occasion to examine the theatre of anger's important kinships with the late-1990s political performance network Kanak Attak and the contemporary postmigrant theatre movement, from within which the theatre of anger has developed. If migration history and its vicissitudes have been decisive impulses for both Kanak Attak and posmigrant theatre, then Islamophobia, which at once focalized and generalized hate in Germany and in much of the West following 9/11, is an oppressive force that also suddenly emerged and called for deconstruction and denunciation. Two of postmigrant theatre's most notable plays, which are also early representatives of the theatre of anger, *Schwarze Jungfrauen* and *Verrücktes Blut*, track and reproach Islamophobia in theatrically disparate yet effectively condemning ways. These plays are the objects of study in chapter 3. Here anger assumes a critically reflexive mode. When it comes to Muslims, many non-Muslims have strong, pathologizing opinions about what is what. These opinions are also irrevocably gendered in binary terms. If the female Muslim is perceived as a victim in need of saving, then the male Muslim is the angry, irrational, violent, misogynist – or worse, terrorist. Each play respectively undoes these stereotypes by facing Western projections head-on and performing in-yer-face anger that exposes and subverts Islamophobic expectations. *Schwarze Jungfrauen* shocks in its portrayal of five radical female Muslims who speak openly and directly (explicitly in monologue) about religion, desire, and sexuality. Anger provides tone and self-determining assertion. With a focus on young male Muslims in *Verrücktes Blut*, anger circulates within this much more conventionally naturalist play. However, here too, anger exposes social violence and debilitating structures of Islamophobia within society and the theatre.

Creative anger can be performative; it can be a speech act that also enacts what it utters; it can, for instance, erupt in blazing protests. Anger takes a slightly different turn in chapter 4 when it encounters the political protests on the urban streets and squares of Athens, Greece and Istanbul, Turkey. Explicitly trans-European and transnational in their scope and orientation, the plays *Telemachos* and *Aufstand* reach across borders and are connected both through thematic links to contemporary protests and the documentary forms of their productions. As such, the anger performed on stage is an extension of the politicized anger performed in the public spaces of the city. Anger is presented not only as attributive but also as politically efficacious. Our anger is our demand for change, inasmuch as anger performs politics. Contemporary in their politics, these plays also hark back to adamant exchanges between events on the street and in the theatre in West Germany during the revolutionary period of late 1960s and the intersecting documentary plays of Peter Weiss, as well as the promises of more recent incarnations of direct theatre – that is, political performance on the street – as theorized by Richard Schechner. Above all, these examples adopt movement-based political practice as artistic practice.

As the chapters of this book are distinct in their modes of pursuit of transnational and affective politics, it would be misleading to suggest that there is a sharply defined trajectory to the final portions of the book, which a focus on the playwright Sasha Marianna Salzmann. Yet the influence and inspiration of Salzmann's work can be felt throughout *Theatre of Anger*, and certainly this becomes more firmly articulated closer to the end. In formally distinctive ways, their plays *Weißbrotmusik* and *Zucken* bring into relief the corporeal hecticness of anger, in particular through a reading with postdramatic forms in the balance of the final chapter. Indeed, the theatre of anger is physical, and Salzmann's plays reflect this best. The spasming of the theatre of anger, like an Artaudian rupture, intervenes in and even violently overthrows German and European conceits of dominance and innocence, all the while assaulting the sensoria of the spectators through a radical subjection of often implacable forms and words. Systemic violence and its irreducible grasp on the lives of young migrants and Germans of colour are themes that run through both of Salzmann's plays. Violence becomes the consequence – violence begets violence. Yet these are not melodramatic tales of entrapment and circularity, universalized into neat generic parameters. By way of anger's disturbance and its denial of reconciliation, these plays once again introduce politics and resistance and conclude with provocation.

In the book's arc of anger, a culminating discussion of Salzmann's youth plays must also take into consideration their inherent quality of futurity; the youths who populate their two plays want to survive and flourish in a more just world. Embracing anger does not mean an unbidden descent into negativity, hate, and violence. Quite the contrary, embracing anger offers a powerful sense of both response and assertion of presence in otherwise exclusionary zones – theatre and mainstream society in Germany. All of these plays are concerned with how anger gets at what matters, gets at what makes us angry in the first place. The theatre of anger teaches us that to get things moving sometimes it is necessary to fly off the handle. This motivating force is the force of a new kind of theatre whose resonance and relevance today cannot be understated.

As I conclude this book, the question arises about where one lands after flying off the handle. That is, what is not only the future of the theatre of anger but what is the future of anger? Salzmann remarks in the interview that while anger serves as the spark and fuel for their theatre, sustaining oneself on anger alone is neither possible nor particularly productive. If the essay I lean on throughout this book is Lorde's "Uses of Anger" (1981), then Salzmann's words partly echo another, slightly later essay on anger by Lorde, "Eye to Eye" (1983), in which she recants her earlier position and posits that anger cannot actually create a future.

> And true, sometimes it seems that anger alone keeps me alive; it burns with a bright and undiminished flame. Yet anger, like guilt, is an incomplete form of human knowledge. More useful than hatred, but still limited. Anger is useful to help clarify our differences, but in the long run, strength that is bred by anger alone is a blind force which cannot create a future. It can only demolish the past.[6]

Anger, she proposes, is incomplete, and cannot be maintained in the long run. It is true that anger is not utopian. As I have shown here, anger is not the goal of this theatre; it is its mode. But inasmuch as anger is not *a* future, it is part of what will get us there – that is, to a more just future. Anger takes to task the injustice of the past and the present so that we may carry on into a different destiny. The message of this future sense in the theatre of anger is always a tangle of provocation, hope, and the unknown, often posed at the close of these plays in the form of a question to the audience. The final line of *Zucken*, for instance, illuminates this with an admonitory subjunctive: "Where to? You don't know what could come after us." This gesture toward the future in the theatre of anger is always tied to a demand for attunement to the reality of the past and present first. Anger is this demand for and practice of an extended temporality that includes historical reflection. Homing in on the force of anger in contemporary transnational theatre in Germany provides the means to locate the political as a rich engagement with past and present injustice. By the same token, this theatre's refusal to partake in the dominant narratives of the past and present is not a politics of eking out space on the margins, but of cutting right down the middle of that difficulty as it charts a path to more inclusive futures invested in social justice. Such is the world-changing possibility of anger pursued in this book.

In a study by Georg Baselitz and Alexander Kluge, recently translated into English, entitled *World-Changing Rage: News of the Antipodeans*, the history of anger is explored through the creative connectivity of Japanese ink and watercolor painting and European history and philosophy. This is an exploration of the human condition, which offers brief yet poignant commentary on the revolutionary potential of rage. Near the close of their book, Baselitz and Kluge leave us with the following words formidably presented in uppercase:

> THE RAGE OF ALL OPPRESSED AND BETRAYED
> HOUSES OUGHT TO SUFFICE TO OVERTURN
> ALL PREVIOUS REALITY IN ONE BLOW AND
> TO CREATE THE NEW MAN. RAGE SPEAKS:
> I AM, I WAS, I SHALL BE.[7]

The sweeping spirit of rage, its redress of injustice, addresses a temporal continuity and a recognition of the past, a being in the present, and a position towards the future. In condensed form, this passage is a narrative of the theatre of anger and the stakes of its roaring vigour. It is a narrative of anger that responds, incites, and revolutionizes.

On a final reflexive note, the future of the theatre of anger is more difficult to surmise. While cause for anger in Germany and elsewhere persists and will continue to compel response, it is difficult to determine if anger will continue to inspire the work of playwrights and directors in Berlin in the way that it has been over the past decades and expand its repertoire. Anger will certainly not disappear as a creative force. If I may transpose this future sense also in the direction of scholarship, there is still much to be learned from contemporary transnational theatre in Germany. *Theatre of Anger* provides more nuanced readings of this tremendous theatre work in Berlin via the possibilities of anger as both a politics and an aesthetic form. The contribution of the present study is modest in its scope but radical in its claim, and, I hope, in its gain. That the theatre of anger is a new paradigm of theatre in Germany, I can attest with conviction. But much scholarly work still needs to be done as we try to understand these perplexing plays and others like them. The ambition of this book is to inspire new conversations and studies in the formation of a salient and expansive archive of scholarship on transnational theatre in Berlin and beyond.

Notes

Introduction

1 Epigraph: © Bertolt Brecht, John Willet, *Brecht on Theatre*, 2015, Methuen Drama, an imprint of Bloomsbury Publishing Plc.
2 This is a variation of the powerful rallying call pronounced by Sara Ahmed, "do not adjust to an unjust world!" in *Living a Feminist Life* (Durham, NC: Duke University Press, 2017), 84.
3 Max Czollek and Sasha Marianna Salzmann, *Desintegration: A Congress on Contemporary Jewish Positions* (Bielefeld: Kerber, 2017), 12.
4 Czollek and Salzmann, *Desintegration*, 101.
(All translations from German to English are my own unless otherwise indicated.)
5 Max Czollek, *Desintegriert euch!* (München: Carl Hanser Verlag, 2018), 45.
6 A note should be added about *Desintegration*, which can also be translated as "disintegration," as the process of coming apart. This definition is not entirely irrelevant in this context, insofar as Czollek does indirectly call for a *disintegration* of hegemonic culture. But the heretofore use of the term "disintegration" in theatre studies should be avoided. For instance, in her study of contemporary Latin American theatre trends, Gail A. Bulman employs the name "theater of disintegration" to denote a theatre that "is profoundly pessimistic" in its demonstration of "familial miscommunication, ferocious consumerism, gratuitous violence, the absence of love" (154). Further, she positions "theater of disintegration" against "theater of resistance" (ibid.). See Gail A. Bulman, *Staging Words, Performing Worlds: Intertextuality and Nation in Contemporary Latin American Theater* (Lewisburg, PA: Bucknell University Press, 2007), 153–4.
7 See Shermin Langhoff, "Die Herkunft spielt keine Rolle: 'Postmigrantisches' Theater im Ballhaus Naunynstraβe," interviewed by Katharina Donath, *Bundeszentrale für politische Bildung*, March 10, 2011, http://

www.bpb.de/gesellschaft/bildung/kulturelle-bildung/60135/interview-mit-shermin-langhoff?p=all.

8 Ela E. Gezen, *Brecht, Turkish Theater, and Turkish-German Literatur* (Rochester: Camden House, 2018), 8–9.

9 Shermin Langhoff, "Nachwort," in *Postmigrantische Perspektiven: Ordnungssysteme, Repräsentationen, Kritik*, ed. Naika Foroutan, Juliane Karakayali, and Riem Spielhaus (Frankfurt am Main: Campus, 2018), 306.

10 Naika Foroutan, Juliane Karakayali, and Riem Spielhaus, eds. *Postmigrantische Perspektiven*, 9.

11 Citing Tom Mustroph, Maha El Hissy offers an illuminating explanation of this title, as "migrants to the power of two." She writes: "Auf den Namen *Migranten hoch zwei* wird eine Minderheit getauft, die sich sowohl von der Generation der Eltern sowie von der deutschen Gesellschaft abgrenzt. *Migranten hoch zwei* bezeichnet die Migranten, 'die die eigenen Wanderungsbewegungen und die der Eltern und Großeltern reflektieren und analysieren und dabei oft zu *anderen* Schlussfolgerungen als den im offiziellen politischen Diskurs favorisierten Schlagworten wie Multikulturalität und Integration gelangen.'" Maha El Hissy, *Getürkte Türken: Karnevaleske Stilmittel im Theater, Kabarett und Film deutsch-türkischer Künstlerinnen und Künstler* (Bielefeld: Transcript, 2012), 118. A rough translation of this quote would go as follows: "Under the name *migrants to the power of two* a new minority is established, one that both demarcates itself from the generation of its parents and from German society. *Migrants to the power of two* describes migrants, who reflect on and analyse their own migration paths and those of their parents and grandparents and often reach their own conclusions *distinct* from those favoured by official political discourse, such as multiculturalism and integration."

12 El Hissy, *Getürkte Türken*, 117.

13 Cited in Azadeh Sharifi, "Theatre and Migration," in *Independent Theatre in Contemporary Europe: Structures – Aesthetics – Cultural Policy*, ed. Manfred Brauneck and ITI Germany (Bielefeld: Transcript, 2017), 339.

14 Lizzie Stewart explores the emergence of the term "postmigrant" in her article "Postmigrant theatre: the Ballhaus Naunynstraße takes on sexual nationalism," *Journal of Aesthetics & Culture* 9, no. 2 (2017): 56–68. Already in 1995 Gerd Baumann and Thijl Sunier authored a book titled *Post-Migration Ethnicity: Cohesion, Commitments, Comparison* with Het Spinhuis Press. In an interview, Langhoff claims that she first learned of the term from an Anglophone academic conference. While Langhoff does not indicate specifically what conference this may have been, Stewart speculates that it could have been "Postmigrant Turkish-German Culture: Transnationalism, Translation, Politics of Representation," organized by Tom Cheesman in Swansea in the United Kingdom in 1998. See 58.

15 Stewart, "Postmigrant theatre: the Ballhaus Naunynstraβe takes on sexual nationalism," 57.

16 One should note that Brown's definition of "post" is drawn from the historical notion of post-Westphalianism (or globalization) and in conversation with political theories of sovereignty from Thomas Hobbes to Carl Schmitt. Despite this distinct context, the definition is rhetorically applicable here. Wendy Brown, *Walled States, Waning Sovereignty* (New York: Zone Books, 2010), 33.

17 Marianne Hirsch, *The Generation of Postmemory: Writing and Visual Culture After the Holocaust* (New York: Columbia University Press, 2012), 6.

18 Fatima El-Tayeb, *Undeutsch: Die Konstruktion des Anderen in der postmigrantischen Gesellschaft* (Bielefeld: Transcript, 2016), 12. For El-Tayeb, it is critical to note that while the term "postracial" in the United States certainly does not portray reality and that structural racism is still very much present, at least in the US context there have been and continue to be serious movements for change, whereas the "postmigrant" assertion in the German context remains unanchored to any kind of social or political movement that would aspire to its injunction.

19 Erika Fischer-Lichte, "Introduction," in *The Politics of Interweaving Performance Cultures: Beyond Postcolonialism*, ed. Erika Fischer-Lichte, Torsten Jost, and Saskya Iris Jain (New York: Routledge, 2014): 1–24.

20 Rüdiger Schaper, "Nach dem Theatercoup: Wie Langhoff und Hillje das Gorki leiten wollen," *Tagesspiegel*, May 23, 2012, http://www.tagesspiegel.de/kultur/nach-dem-theatercoup-wie-langhoff-und-hillje-das-gorki-leiten-wollen/6661782.html.

21 See Onur Suzan Kömürcü Nobrega, "'We bark from the third row': The position of the *Ballhaus Naunynstrasse* in Berlin's cultural landscape and the funding of cultural diversity work." *Türkisch-deutsch Studien Jahrbuch* (2011): 91–112.

22 See Manfred Brauneck, "Preface," in *Independent Theater in Contemporary Europe*, 13–41.

23 Henning Fülle has written extensively on the topic of free-scene theatre. For a comprehensive perspective, see *Freies Theater* (Berlin: Theater der Zeit, 2016).

24 Erol Boran, "A History of Turkish-German Theater and Cabaret" (PhD diss., Ohio State University, 2004).

25 See Lizzie Stewart, "Countermemory and the (Turkish-)German Theatrical Archive: Reading the Documentary Remains of Emine Sevgi Özdamar's *Karagöz in Alamania* (1986)." *TRANSIT: A Journal of Travel, Migration, and Multiculturalism in the German-speaking World* 8, no. 2 (2013), http://transit.berkeley.edu/2013/stewart/.

26 Katrin Sieg, *Ethnic Drag: Performing Race, Nation, Sexuality in West Germany* (Ann Arbor: University of Michigan Press, 2002), 234.

27 Gezen, *Brecht, Turkish Theater, and Turkish-German Literature.*
28 Azadeh Sharifi, *Theater für alle? Partizipation von Postmigranten am Beispiel der Bühnen der Stadt Köln* (Frankfurt am Main: Peter Lang, 2011).
29 Langhoff, "Nachwort," 306.
30 Claudia Breger, *An Aesthetics of Narrative Performance: Transnational Theater, Literature, and Film in Contemporary Germany* (Columbus: Ohio State University Press, 2012); and Matt Cornish, *Performing Unification: History and Nation in German Theater after 1989* (Ann Arbor: University of Michigan, 2017).
31 It bears noting that both Nora Haakh and Lizzie Stewart have forthcoming monographs, which explore different aspects of postmigrant theatre more comprehensively. These are *Muslimisierte Körper auf der Bühne: Die Islamdebatte im postmigrantischen Theater* and *Staging New German Realities: Turkish-German Scripts of Postmigration*, respectively.
32 Olivia Landry, "German Youth Against Sarrazin: Nurkan Erpulat's *Verrücktes Blut* and *Clash* as Political Theatre of Experience." *Jahrbuch Türkisch-deutsche Studien* 3 (2012): 105–21.
33 Sharifi offers a comprehensive overview of theaters across Western Europe, which have actively produced and performed transnational and postmigration theatre. See "Theatre and Migration," 321–407.
34 Gotthold Ephraim Lessing, *Laocoön: An Essay on the Limits of Painting and Poetry*, trans. Edward Allen McCormick (Baltimore, MD: Johns Hopkins University Press, [1766] 1984).
35 Aleks Sierz, *In-Yer-Face Theatre: British Drama Today* (London: Faber and Faber, 2001), xiii.
36 David Barnett, "Toward a Definition of Post-Brechtian Performance: The Example of *In the Jungle of the Cities* at the Berliner Ensemble, 1971." *Modern Drama* 54, no. 3 (2011): 333.
37 Janelle G. Reinelt, *After Brecht: British Epic Theater* (Ann Arbor: University of Michigan, 1996); Elin Diamond, "Brechtian Theory/Feminist Theory: Toward a Gestic Feminist Criticism." *TDR* 32, no. 1 (1988): 82–94; Augusto Boal, *Theatre of the Oppressed*, trans. Charles A. McBride and Maria-Odilia Leal McBride (New York: Theatre Communications Group, [1974] 1985).
38 Cited in Stanton B. Garner Jr., *Bodied Spaces: Phenomenology and Performance in Contemporary Drama* (Ithaca, NY: Cornell University Press, 1994), 160.
39 Garner Jr., *Bodied Spaces*, 160.
40 Others have resisted this qualification, for instance Barnett in "Toward a Definition of Post-Brechtian Performance," but I defer to Lehmann's study here. See Hans-Thies Lehmann, *Postdramatic Theatre*, trans. Karen Jürs-Munby (London: Routledge, [1999] 2006).
41 Lehmann, *Postdramatic Theatre*, 33.
42 See Cornish, *Performing Unification.*
43 Hasibe Kalkan Kocabay, "Searching for Identity," *Glimpse* 13 (2011): 82.

44 Richard Schechner, *Environmental Theater* (New York: Applause, [1973] 1994); Erika Fischer-Lichte, *The Transformative Power of Performance: A New Aesthetics*, trans. Saskya Iris Jain (London: Routledge, [2004] 2008).
45 José Esteban Muñoz, *Disidentifications: Queers of Color and the Performance of Politics* (Minneapolis: University of Minnesota Press, 1999); André Lepecki, *Exhausting Dance: Performance and the Politics of Movement* (New York: Routledge, 2006).
46 Marvin Carlson, "Introduction," in Fischer-Lichte, *The Transformative Power of Performance*, 4.
47 Aristotle, *Nicomachean Ethics*, trans. Roger Crisp (Cambridge: Cambridge University Press, 2004). See Book IV and V.
48 Johannes F. Lehmann, *Im Abgrund der Wut: Zur Kultur- und Literaturgeschichte des Zorns* (Freiburg: Rombach, 2012), 153.
49 Silvan S. Tomkins, *Affect Imagery Consciousness: Vol. 2: The Negative Affects* (New York: Springer, 1963), 52.
50 Martha C. Nussbaum, *Anger and Forgiveness: Resentment, Generosity, Justice* (New York: Oxford University Press, 2017); Carolin Emcke, *Gegen den Hass* (Frankfurt am Main: Fischer, 2016); Pankaj Mishra, *The Age of Anger: A History of the Present* (New York: Farrar, Straus and Giroux, 2017).
51 Audre Lorde, "The Uses of Anger: Women Responding to Racism," in *Sister Outsider* (Berkeley: Crossing Press, [1984] 2007), 127.
52 Fischer-Lichte, *The Transformative Power of Performance*, 58.
53 Sierz, *In-Yer-Face Theatre*, 29.
54 Antonin Artaud, *The Theatre and Its Double*, trans. Mary Caroline Richards (New York: Grove Press, [1938] 1958), 76.
55 Artaud, *The Theatre and Its Double*, 92.
56 A transcript of this discussion was made available by *Deutschlandfunk Kultur* and titled "Revolte und Kunst der Verantwortung." The panel was moderated by Susanne Burkhardt. May 19, 2018, https://www.deutschlandfunkkultur.de/berliner-theatertreffen-revolte-und-die-kunst-der.2159.de.html?dram:article_id=418304.

1 In Defence of Anger

1 Pankaj Mishra, *The Age of Anger: A History of the Present* (New York: Farrar, Straus and Giroux, 2017).
2 Johannes F. Lehmann, *Im Abgrund der Wut: Zur Kultur- und Literaturgeschichte des Zorns* (Freiburg: Rombach, 2012), 9.
3 Silvan S. Tomkins, *Affect Imagery Consciousness: Vol. 2: The Negative Affects* (New York: Springer, 1963), 64.
4 Sara Ahmed, *The Promise of Happiness* (Durham, NC: Duke University Press, 2010), 68.

5 Audre Lorde, *Sister Outsider* (Berkeley: Crossing Press, [1984] 2007), 132.
6 Brittany Cooper, *Eloquent Rage: A Black Feminist Discovers Her Superpower* (New York: St. Martins Press, 2018), 2.
7 Sara Ahmed, *The Cultural Politics of Emotion* (New York: Routledge, [2004] 2015), 174.
8 Aristotle, *Nicomachean Ethics*, trans. Roger Crisp (Cambridge: Cambridge University Press, 2004), 73.
9 Philip Fisher, *The Vehement Passions* (Princeton, NJ: Princeton University Press, 2002), 173. See also Sianne Ngai, *Ugly Feelings* (Cambridge, MA: Harvard University Press, 2005), 182.
10 Aristotle, *Nicomachean Ethics*, 73.
11 Aristotle, *Nicomachean Ethics*, 96.
12 Aristotle, *Nicomachean Ethics*, 73.
13 Fisher, *The Vehement Passions*, 174.
14 Karl A. E. Enenkel and Anita Traninger, eds. *Discourses of Anger in the Early Modern Period* (Leiden: Brill, 2015), 2.
15 Lucius Annaeus Seneca, *Anger, Mercy, Revenge*, trans. Robert A. Caster and Martha C. Nussbaum (Chicago, IL: University of Chicago Press, 2010), 14.
16 Peter Sloterdijk, *Rage and Time: A Psychopolitical Investigation*, trans. Mario Wenning (New York: Columbia University Press, 2012), 1.
17 There is minor exception to this claim. Thomas Aquinas famously attempted to reconcile Aristotelian philosophy with Christian theology, including the former's thoughts on anger. As Robert Miner explains in his study, *Thomas Aquinas on the Passions: A Study on Summa Theologiae Iazae* (Cambridge: Cambridge University Press, 2009), for Aquinas, anger was not a sin but a complex affect that merits exploration.
18 Immanuel Kant, *Anthropology from a Pragmatic Point of View*, trans. Robert B. Louden (Cambridge: Cambridge University Press, [1798] 2006), 159.
19 Lehmann, *Im Abgrund der Wut*, 153.
20 Lehmann, *Im Abgrund der Wut*, 14; 155.
21 Ngai, *Ugly Feelings*, 182.
22 In the age of decolonialism, Said's argument that the movement of theories is an enabling condition has been challenged. This is frequently because Eurocentric and US-American theories are solely those, which seem to circulate, and this creates an imbalance of knowledge and influence. However, the notion that cultural and intellectual life is fostered through the exchange of ideas across borders is something to which I fully subscribe. See Edward Said, *The World, the Text and the Critic* (London: Vintage, 1991), 226–47.
23 Fatima El-Tayeb, *Undeutsch: Die Konstruktion des Anderen in der postmigrantischen Gesellschaft* (Bielefeld: Transcript, 2016), 11.
24 In this context, the scholarship of Naika Foroutan and Erol Yıldız is particularly relevant.

25 James Baldwin, *Notes of a Native Son* (Boston: Beacon Press, [1955] 2012), 178; Stuart Hall, "Europe's Other Self," *Marxism Today* (1991): 18; Fatima El-Tayeb, *European Others: Queering Ethnicity in Postnational Europe* (Minneapolis: University of Minnesota Press, 2011), xxiv.
26 El-Tayeb, *Undeutsch*, 12.
27 It should be noted that many African American women have also been victims of police brutality. The movement #SayHerName, which was a response to #BlackLivesMatter, alerted us to the prevalence of police violence against women, which often goes unspoken.
28 Opal Tometi, "Celebrating MLK Day: Reclaiming Our Movement Legacy," *Huffington Post*, March 20, 2015, http://www.huffingtonpost.com/opal-tometi/reclaiming-our-movement-l_b_6498400.html.
29 The release of the documentary film, *I Am Not Your Negro* (dir. Raoul Peck 2016), based on Baldwin's final, unfinished work *Remember This House* about the assassinations of three leaders of the civil rights movement and friends of Baldwin, chronologically from Medgar Evers to Malcolm X and Martin Luther King, Jr. solidified this renaissance of Baldwin's work and his reception as a significant historical figure.
30 In a public statement in support of the Black Lives Matter movement, the former state senator of Ohio, Nina Turner, paraphrases Baldwin's words: "It's the perfect summation of the outrage that has been built up among African Americans who have been battling systemic oppression by speaking out against the constant killings of Black people by police." See Lilly Workneh, "Nina Turner quotes James Baldwin to sum up the Anger among Black Protestors," *The Huffington Post*, August 23, 2016, http://www.huffingtonpost.com/entry/nina-turner-quotes-james-baldwin-to-sum-up-the-anger-among-black-protesters_us_57e420d1e4b0e28b2b52cf14.
31 Baldwin, *Notes of a Native Son*, 96.
32 Lorde, *Sister Outsider*, 124.
33 Toni Morrison, *The Bluest Eye* (New York: Alfred A. Knopf, [1970] 2010), 50.
34 Ahmed, *The Cultural Politics of Emotion*, 177.
35 Cited in Ahmed, *The Cultural Politics of Emotion*, 177.
36 While effectually synonyms, "anger" and "rage" do pose a semantic fork. Rage is frequently described as anger intensified, or the latter's more violent (but not necessarily excessive and therefore depleted) form. However, some thinkers might apply "anger" and others "rage" to speak about a similar affective and political phenomenon. For instance, Audre Lorde employs "anger," whereas bell hooks uses "rage." For the purposes of the present study, I predominantly employ "anger" but will also use the two words interchangeably.
37 bell hooks, *Killing Rage: Ending Racism* (New York: Henry Holt & Co., 1995), 14.

38 hooks, *Killing Rage*, 14.
39 hooks, *Killing Rage*, 13.
40 hooks, *Killing Rage*, 13.
41 It may be noted that during the 2018 spring and summer theater season in the experimental black box Studio Я several portraits of Malcolm X, James Baldwin, and many others adorned the walls of the lobby. I offer an image in the book's interview with Sasha Marianna Salzmann.
42 Ahmed, *The Cultural Politics of Emotion*, 176.
43 Sara Ahmed, *Living a Feminist Life* (Durham, NC: Duke University, 2017), 3.
44 Raymond Williams, *Marxism and Literature* (Oxford: Oxford University Press, 1977), 130.
45 Williams, *Marxism and Literature*, 133.
46 Richard Hoggart, *Speaking to Each Other*, Vol. II (New York: Oxford University Press, 1970), 11–18.
47 I discuss this again in later pages with reference to Brecht's "A Short Organum for Theater."
48 Aristotle, *Poetics*, trans. Stephen Halliwell (Cambridge, MA: Harvard University Press, 1995), 47.
49 Gotthold Ephraim Lessing, *Laocoön: An Essay on the Limits of Painting and Poetry*, trans. Edward Allen McCormick (Baltimore, MD: Johns Hopkins University Press, [1766] 1984); Eugenie Brinkema, *The Forms of the Affects* (Durham, NC: Duke University Press, 2014).
50 David Wellbery, *Lessing's Laocoon: Semiotics and Aesthetics in the Age of Reason* (Cambridge: University of Cambridge Press, [1984] 2009).
51 Lessing, *Laocoön*, 17.
52 Lessing, *Laocoön*, 37.
53 Lessing, *Laocoön*, 36.
54 Compare, for instance, the facializing capacity of the close-up in cinema by way of which objects and body parts other than the face are bequeathed the signifying and subjectifying qualities of the face as famously conceptualized in Gilles Deleuze's important study on cinema, Gilles Deleuze, *Cinema 1: The Movement-Image*, trans. Hugh Tomlinson and Barbara Habberjam (Minneapolis: University of Minnesota Press, [1983] 2006), 85.
55 Simon Richter, *Laocoon's Body and the Aesthetics of Pain: Winckelmann, Lessing, Herder, Moritz, Goethe* (Detroit, MI: Wayne State University Press, 1992), 66–7.
56 Nico H. Frijda, *The Emotions* (Cambridge: Cambridge University Press, 1986), 199.
57 Antonin Artaud, *The Theatre and Its Double*, trans. Mary Caroline Richards (New York: Grove Press, [1938] 1958).
58 Bertolt Brecht, *Brecht on Theatre*, trans. Jack Davis, Romy Fursland, Steve Giles, Victoria Hill, Kristopher Imbrigotta, Marc Silberman, and John

Willett, ed. Marc Silberman, Steven Giles, and Tom Kuhn (London: Bloomsbury, [1957] 2015), 282.

59 For a brief but informative study on shadow puppet theater in Turkey and Greece, see James Smith, "Karagöz and Hacivat: Projections of Subversion and Conformance," *Asian Theatre Journal* 21, no. 2 (2004): 187–93.

60 A wonderfully in-depth analysis of the play and its history can be found in Lizzie Stewart, "Countermemory and the (Turkish-)German Theatrical Archive: Reading the Documentary Remains of Emine Sevgi Özdamar's *Karagöz in Alamania* (1986)," *TRANSIT* 8, no. 2 (2013 online).

61 Cited in Aleks Sierz, *In-Yer-Face Theatre: British Drama Today* (London: Faber and Faber, 2001), 16.

62 Sarah Hemming, "Look forward in Anger," *Financial Times*, November 18, 1995.

63 Hemming, "Look forward in Anger." Cited in Sierz, *In-Yer-Face Theatre*, 64.

64 Published as a theater manifesto in French in 1938, *Le Théâtre et son Double*," Artaud's concept of the "theatre of cruelty" as a praxis was first seriously taken up by British director Peter Brook in the mid-1960s with his 1964 season "Theatre of Cruelty" at the Royal Shakespeare Company Theatre.

65 Cited in Sierz, *In-Yer-Face Theatre*, 4.

66 Sierz, *In-Yer-Face Theatre*, 2.

67 Richard Schechner, "Invasions Friendly and Unfriendly: The Dramaturgy of Direct Theater," in *Critical Theory and Performance*, ed. Janelle G. Reinelt and Joseph Roach (Ann Arbor: University of Michigan Press, [1992] 2007), 477.

68 For an informed study on the Mothers of the Plaza de Mayo movement see Karen A. Foss and Kathy L. Domenici, "Haunting Argentina: Synecdoche in the Protests of the Mothers of the Plaza de Mayo," *Quarterly Journal of Speech* 87, no. 3 (2001): 237–58.

69 Gülsüm Baydar and Berfin Ivegen discuss the philosophical significance of this movement and its relationship to space, in particular as this space became marked by the violent presence of the police, which in a way staged its own counterprotest. See Gülsüm Baydar and Berfin Ivegen, "Territories, Identities, and Thresholds: The Saturday Mothers Phenomenon in Istanbul," *Signs* 31, no. 3 (2006): 689–715.

70 Diana Taylor, *The Archive and the Repertoire: Performing Cultural Memory in the Americas* (Durham, NC: Duke University Press, 2003), 165, 167.

71 Judith Butler, *Gender Trouble* (New York: Routledge [1990] 2006), xxvi–xxvii.

72 Ahmed, *The Cultural Politics of Emotion*, 13.

73 Cited in Glennis Byron, *Dramatic Monologue* (London: Routledge, 2003), 8.

74 Erving Goffman, *Frame Analysis: An Essay on the Organization of Experience* (Cambridge, MA: Harvard University Press, 1974), 231.

75 Erika Fischer-Lichte, *The Transformative Power of Performance: A New Aesthetics*, trans. Saskya Iris Jain (London: Routledge, [2004] 2008), 38–9.
76 Fischer-Lichte describes this as the disciplining of audiences, which resulted in the passing of regulations to forbid disruptive behaviour and prohibit "eating, drinking, latecomers, and talking during the performance." Fischer-Lichte, *The Transformative Power of Performance*, 38–9. Denis Diderot was instrumental in this drive towards an absolute division between stage and audience. It was Diderot who established the notion of the fourth wall, most prominently in his 1758 essay "On Dramatic Poetry" ("Discours sur la poésie dramatique"), in which he famously writes as a guide to actors: "Whether you write or you act, think no more of the audience than if it had never existed. Imagine a huge wall across from the front of the stage, separating you from the audience, and behave exactly as if the curtain has never risen." Cited in Eyal Peretz, *Dramatic Experiments: Life According to Diderot* (Albany, NY: SUNY, 2013), 163.
77 Deborah R. Geis, *Postmodern Theatric(K)s: Monologue in Contemporary American Drama* (Ann Arbor: University of Michigan, 1995), 2.
78 Peter Handke, *Stücke 1* (Frankfurt am Main: Suhrkamp, 1972), 34; Peter Handke, *Kaspar and Other Plays*, trans. Michael Rolloff (New York: Farrar, Straus and Giroux, 1969), 20.
79 Handke, *Stücke 1*, 44; Handke, *Kaspar and Other Plays*, 29.
80 Handke, *Stücke 1*, 44–7; Handke, *Kaspar and Other Plays*, 29–32. It may be noted that I altered one translation: "Nazischweine" is curiously translated as "killer pigs," which clearly does not have the same loaded historical connotation.
81 Handke, *Stücke 1*, 45; Handke, *Kaspar and Other Plays*, 30.
82 Not alive to witness this performance myself in 1966, I was fortunate to find a fantastic recording of the premiere on YouTube. The video frequently and deliberately shows footage of the audience, both in close-up (individually) and in landscape (as a group).
83 Jonas Barish, *The Antitheatrical Prejudice* (Berkeley: University of California Press, 1981), 461.
84 Geis, *Postmodern Theatric(K)s*, 118–19.
85 Elin Diamond, "Brechtian Theory/Feminist Theory: Toward a Gestic Feminist Criticism." *TDR* 32, no. 1 (1988): 84.
86 Without essentializing performance, postmigrant theatre makes space for minoritized performers. At a time when the practice of blackface is still a problem in German theatres, postmigrant theatre and the theatre of anger performatively assert their rightful place on the stage.
87 Geis, *Postmodern Theatric(K)s*, 153.
88 Marvin Carlson, *Performance: A Critical Introduction* (London: Routledge, [1996] 2004), 179.

2 *Get Deutsch or Die Tryin'*

1 Epigraph: This is a quote from Maya Angelou proclaimed during a conversation with Dave Chapelle for the television series "Iconoclast," November 30, 2006. The episode can be viewed on YouTube: https://www.youtube.com/watch?v=okc6COsgzoE.
2 Fatima El-Tayeb, *European Others: Queering Ethnicity in Postnational Europe* (Minneapolis: University of Minnesota Press, 2011), 4.
3 Mark Terkessidis has written extensively on this topic. See for instance his chapter "Zweite Generation" in *Migranten* (Hamburg: Rotbuch, 2000), 50–5.
4 Doris Meierhenrich, "Premieren-Doppel 'Zucken' und 'Mythen der Wirklichkeit,'" *Berliner Zeitung*, March 20, 2017, https://www.berliner-zeitung.de/kultur/gorki-theater-premieren-doppel--zucken--und--mythen-der-wirklichkeit--26228438.
5 Ulrich Seidler, "'Get Deutsch or Die Tryin" am Gorki Theater: Möge die Wut der Anfang der Heilung sein," *Berliner Zeitung*, May 21, 2017. https://www.berliner-zeitung.de/kultur/theater/-get-deutsch-or-die-tryin---am-gorki-theater-moege-die-wut-der-anfang-der-heilung-sein-26939194.
6 My reading of this play focuses on the staged performance. However, I do reference the original text to quote lines from the play. See Necati Öziri, *Get Deutsch or Die Tryin'* (Hamburg: Rowohlt e-book Theater), Track 1. (It bears noting that this edition does not contain page numbers; instead, I will indicate the "Track" in which the citation can be found.)
7 See Kirsten Riesselmann, "Premiere von 'Get Deutsch or Die Tryin'': Grabrede auf dem Vater," *TAZ*, May 27, 2017, http://www.taz.de/!5408187/ and Patrick Wilderman, "'Get Deutsch or Die Tryin" Mutter blau, Vater weg," *Der Tagesspiegel*, May 23, 2017, https://www.tagesspiegel.de/kultur/get-deutsch-or-die-tryin-am-maxim-gorki-theater-mutter-blau-vater-weg/19838820.html.
8 Friedrich Nietzsche, *On the Genealogy of Morals*, trans. Douglas Smith (Oxford: Oxford University Press, 1998), 22.
9 Pankaj Mishra, *Age of Anger: A History of the Present* (New York: Farrar, Straus and Giroux, 2017), 14.
10 Öziri, *Get Deutsch or Die Tryin'*, Track 5.
11 Öziri, *Get Deutsch or Die Tryin'*, Track 5. (This is only mentioned once in the text, but three times during the performance.)
12 This is not in the original text.
13 Öziri, *Get Deutsch or Die Tryin'*, Track 5 (with some variation from the performance).
14 Warsan Shire, *Teaching My Mother How to Give Birth* (London: Mouth Mark Series, 2011), 28.
15 Öziri, *Get Deutsch or Die Tryin'*, Track 16.

16 Lauren Berlant, *Cruel Optimism* (Durham, NC: Duke University Press, 2011), 188.
17 Sara Ahmed, *The Promise of Happiness* (Durham, NC: Duke University Press, 2010), 68.
18 Sue J. Kim, *On Anger: Race, Cognition, Narrative* (Austin: University of Texas Press, 2013), 4.
19 I will try to sketch a brief timeline of these events and their respective urban spaces. Between September 17–30, 1991, there were a series of racist attacks by neo-Nazis and their supporters on Vietnamese and Mozambican workers in Hoyerswerda, a former East German town in Saxony. In particular, this included the arson attack on an apartment complex where many Mozambicans lived, an event in which more than thirty people were injured. From August 22–24, 1992, Germany witnessed its worst postwar pogroms against migrants. Hundreds of right-wing youths attacked a reception centre for asylum seekers (temporary living quarters for mostly Romani people from Romania) and an apartment complex for Vietnamese contract workers in Rostock-Lichtenberg in Mecklenburg-Vorpommern, as thousands of local bystanders watched and applauded. That same year, on November 22, an arson attack in Mölln, Schleswig-Holstein, against two family homes occupied by Turkish migrants resulted in the death of three people. In 1993 came the attack in Solingen. The details of these events have been well documented. See for instance Deniz Göktürk, David Gramling, and Anton Kaes, eds. *Germany in Transit* (Berkeley: University of California Press, 2007). There was even a film made about the Rostock pogroms, *Wir sind jung. Wir sind stark* (*We Are Young. We Are Strong*, 2014). For a fuller chronology of the right-wing wing events between 1989 and 1994, see Hermann Kurthen, Werner Bergmann and Rainer Erb, eds. *Antisemitism and Xenophobia in Germany After Unification* (Oxford: Oxford University Press, 1997), 263–85.
20 It was only with the election of the Social Democratic Party in 1998 that the German naturalization law was finally reformed to allow non-ethnically-German residents to obtain citizenship on January 1, 2000.
21 For further details about the Asylkompromiss, see Wolfgang Bosswick, "Development of Asylum Policy in Germany." *Journal of Refugee Studies* 13, no. 1 (2000): 43–60; Göktürk, Gramling, and Kaes, eds. *Germany in Transit*; Olivia Landry, "'Wir sind alle Oranienplatz!' Space for Refugees and Social Justice in Berlin." *Seminar: A Journal of Germanic Studies* 51, no. 4 (2015): 398–413.
22 May Ayim, *Blues in schwarz weiß: Gedichte* (Berlin: Orlanda Frauenverlag, 1995), 82; May Ayim, *Blues in Black and White*, trans. Anne Adams (Trenton, NJ: Africa World Press, 2003), 4.
23 Étienne Balibar, *We the People of Europe: Reflections on Transnational Citizenship*, trans. James Swenson (Princeton: Princeton University Press, 2004), x.

24 Tom Cheesman, "Talking 'Kanak': Zaimoğlu contra Leitkultur," *New German Critique* 92 (2004): 90.
25 Mark Terkessidis, *Kollaboration* (Berlin: Suhrkamp, 2015), 181.
26 El-Tayeb, *European Others*, 210.
27 José Esteban Muñoz, *Disidentifications: Queers of Color and the Performance of Politics* (Minneapolis: University of Minnesota Press, 1999), 185.
28 See Duygu Gürsel, "Kanak Attak: Discursive Acts of Citizenship in Germany," *Open Democracy*, November 9, 2012, https://www.opendemocracy.net/can-europe-make-it/duygu-g%C3%BCrsel/kanak-attak-discursive-acts-of-citizenship-in-germany.
29 El-Tayeb, *European Others*, 146.
30 During the late 1980s and early 1990s there were gang wars in Kreuzberg, when young Turkish German men (known as the "36 Boys") successfully fought back against neo-Nazi groups, when the police neglected to protect their community. While no literature exists on the group, in 2012 Al Jazeera World produced an informative video about the "36 Boys." For more information, see: http://www.aljazeera.com/programmes/aljazeeraworld/2012/12/2012122411620527434.html.
31 "Kanak Attak Manifesto," http://www.kanak-attak.de/ka/about/manif_eng.html.
32 Sara Ahmed, *The Promise of Happiness* (Durham, NC: Duke University Press, 2010), 68.
33 Ahmed, *Promise of Happiness*, 144.
34 Ahmed, *Promise of Happiness*, 68. See also Audre Lorde, "The Master's Tools Will Never Dismantle the Master's House," in *This Bridge Called My Back: Writings by Radical Women of Color*, ed. Cherríe Moraga and Gloria Anzaldúa (New York: Kitchen Table Press, 1983), 94–101.
35 Ahmed, *Promise of Happiness*, 68.
36 A number of scholars have written on the topic of multiculturalism as an inherently problematic rubric, which homogenizes and simplifies. See Norma Alarcón, "Conjugating Subjects in the Age of Multiculturalism," in *Mapping Multiculturalism*, ed. Avery F. Gordon and Christopher Newfield (Minneapolis: University of Minnesota Press, 1996): 127–48; Slavoj Žižek, "Multiculturalism, or, the Cultural Logic of Multinational Capitalism." *New Left Review* 1, no. 225 (1997): https://newleftreview.org/I/225/slavoj-zizek-multiculturalism-or-the-cultural-logic-of-multinational-capitalism; Eraz Tzfadia, "Abusing Multiculturalism: The Politics of Recognition and Land Allocation in Israel." *Environment and Planning D: Society and Space* 26, no. 6 (2008): 1115–30.
37 Just as Max Czollek refers to his writing more broadly as a form of *Desintegration* (explored in the introduction), for it is both object and method, Öziri considers his writing to be a form of Kanak Attak. See Max Czollek,

"Gegenwärtsbewältigung," in *Eure Heimat ist unser Albtraum*, ed. Fatma Aydemir and Hengameh (Munich: Ullstein, 2019), 180–1.

38 Shermin Langhoff, "Nachwort," in *Postmigrantische Perspektiven: Ordnungssysteme, Repräsentationen, Kritik*, ed. Naika Foroutan, Juliane Karakayali, and Riem Spielhaus (Frankfurt am Main: Campus, 2018), 305.

39 Meropi S. Peponides, "What's Holding Us Back? A Forum on Nationalism, Xenophobia, and American Theater Now," ed. David Bruin and Tom Sellar. *Theater* 48, no.3 (2018): 42.

40 This comment arose from of a discussion during the German Studies Association 2017 Annual Meeting seminar "(Post)Migrant Theater: Then and Now," which I co-organized together with Ela E. Gezen and Damani Partridge.

41 Muñoz, *Disidentifications*, 199.

42 Cited in Onur Suzan Kömürcü Nobrega, "'We bark from the third row': The position of the *Ballhaus Naunynstrasse* in Berlin's cultural landscape and the funding of cultural diversity work." *Türkisch-deutsche Studien Jahrbuch* (Göttingen: Vandenhoeck & Ruprecht, 2011): 92.

43 This is, according to Grossberg, the powerful work of cultural studies. See Lawrence Grossberg, *Cultural Studies in the Future Tense* (Durham, NC: Duke University Press, 2010), 20.

44 Michael Hofmann, "Handicap Islam? Sarrazin-Debatte als Herausforderung des deutsch-türkischen Diskurses," *Türkisch-deutscher Kulturkontakt und Kulturtransfer*, *Jahrbuch Türkisch-deutsche Studien* 1 (2010): 34.

45 This was a comment made by Kenan Kolat, the federal chairman for the Turkish community between 2005–2014, He made this statement in conversation with the journalist Carolin Emcke on the topic of "Rechter Terror und der Inlandsgeheimdienst oder: Wer überwacht eigentlich die Über- wacher?" ("Rightwing Terror and the Internal Secret Service or: Who is monitoring the monitors?"), which took place at the Schaubühne Theatre in Berlin on April 22, 2012. For further information, see http://www.schaubuehne.de/de_DE/program/streitraum/#147513.

46 For an informative study on the NSU, see Daniel Koehler, *Right-Wing Terrorism in the 21st Century: The 'National Socialist Underground' and the History of Terror from the Far-Right in Germany* (London: Routledge, 2017).

47 Langhoff, "Nachwort," 310.

48 The "Reichsbürger" are a group of people in Germany who reject the authority of the modern German state, which includes the borders drawn after the Second World War. This movement has gained a broader profile of late due to the massive increase in membership and support.

49 J.L. Austin, *How to Do Things with Words* (Cambridge, MA: Harvard University Press, [1962] 1975), 22.

50 Bert O. States, "Performance as Metaphor." *Theatre Journal* 48, no. 1 (1996): 9.
51 States, "Performance as Metaphor," 5.
52 Andreas Wassermann, "Wie die AfD das moderne Theater bekämpft," *Der Spiegel*, June 1, 2018. http://www.spiegel.de/plus/wie-die-afd-das-moderne-theater-bekaempft-a-00000000-0002-0001-0000-000157647572.

3 Staging "Muslim Rage"

1 Her Islam-critical book, *The Caged Virgin: An Emancipatory Proclamation for Women and Islam*, trans. Jane Brown (New York: Atria, [2004] 2006), brought her much celebrity both from supporters and detractors.
2 Sara Ahmed, *The Promise of Happiness* (Durham, NC: Duke University Press, 2010), 69.
3 bell hooks, *Killing Rage: Ending Racism* (New York: Henry Holt & Co., 1995), 12.
4 Yasemin Yıldız, "Turkish Girls, Allah's Daughters, and the Contemporary German Subject: Itinerary of a Figure," *German Life and Letters* 64, no. 4 (2009): 466.
5 Fatima El-Tayeb, *European Others: Queering Ethnicity in Postnational Europe* (Minneapolis: University of Minnesota Press, 2011), xxx.
6 I also write this in anticipation of Nora Haakh's forthcoming book, *Muslimisierte Körper auf der Bühne: Die Islamdebatte im postmigrantischen Theater* (2020), in which she takes up these two plays and several others to examine the critical relationship between stage and society vis-à-vis the role of Islam in Germany.
7 Aleks Sierz, *In-Yer-Face Theatre: British Drama Today* (London: Faber and Faber, 2001), 7.
8 Sierz, *In-Yer-Face Theatre*, 7.
9 Elin Diamond, *Unmaking Mimesis: Essays on Feminism and Theatre* (New York Routledge, 1997), 52.
10 Peggy Phelan, *Unmarked: The Politics of Performance* (New York: Routledge, 1993), 12.
11 Feridun Zaimoğlu and Günter Senkel, *Schwarze Jungfrauen* (Hamburg: Rowohlt e-book Theater), Text Seven. (It may be noted that this edition has no page numbers; instead, I will indicate the Text, in which the citation can be found).
12 See Mitchell S. Tepper, "Sexuality and Disability: The Missing Discourse of Pleasure," *Sexuality and Disability* 18, no. 4 (2000): 283–90.
13 Sierz, *In-Yer-Face Theatre*, 9.
14 Zaimoğlu and Senkel, *Schwarze Jungfrauen*, Text Seven.
15 Claudia Breger, *An Aesthetics of Narrative Performance: Transnational Theater, Literature, and Film in Contemporary Germany* (Columbus: Ohio State University Press, 2012), 233.

16 Carol Martin, "Bodies of Evidence," *TDR* 50, no. 3 (2006): 9.
17 See El-Tayeb, *European Others*, 95.
18 Frantz Fanon, "Algeria Unveiled," in *The New Left Reader*, ed. Carl Oglesby (New York: Grove Press, [1959] 1969), 167; Gayatri Chakravorty Spivak, "Can the Subaltern Speak?," in *Colonial Discourse and Post-Colonial Theory: A Reader*, ed. Patricia Williams and Laura Chrisman (New York: Columbia University Press, 1994), 92.
19 Beverly M. Weber, "Freedom from Violence, Freedom to Make the World: Muslim Women's Memoirs, Gendered Violence, and Voices for Change in Germany." *Women in German Yearbook* 25 (2009): 202.
20 Jasbir Puar, *The Right to Maim: Debility, Capacity, Disability* (Durham, NC: Duke University Press, 2017), 99.
21 Zaimolğu and Senkel, *Schwarze Jungfrauen*, Fifth Text.
22 Yıldız, "Turkish Girls, Allah's Daughters," 466.
23 The texts to which I refer here are Seyran Ateş's *Große Reise ins Feuer: Die Geschichte einer deutschen Türkin* (2003) and Necla Kelek's *Die fremde Braut* (2005). For a critical engagement, see Weber, "Freedom from Violence, Freedom to Make the World."
24 Katrin Sieg, "Black Virgins and the Democratic Body in Europe." *New German Critique* 37, no. 1 (2010): 151.
25 In a much-cited interview with the prestigious monthly theatre magazine *Theater heute*, director Neco Çelik expressed his disappointment that the audience in attendance for *Schwarze Jungfrauen* was 95% white German. See "Mal sehen, was Gott sagt." *Theater heute* 47, no. 5 (2006): 44.
26 Cited in Lizzie Stewart, "*Black Virgins*, Close Encounters: Re-examining the 'Semi-Documentary' in Postmigrant Theatre." *Türkisch-deutsche Studien Jahrbuch* (2012): 97.
27 Volkmar Draeger, "Verstörende Abrechnung: 'Schwarze Jungfrauen' entschleiern sich im HAU 3," *Neues Deutschland*, March 23, 2006, https://www.neues-deutschland.de/artikel/87723.verstoerende-abrechnung.html.
28 Sieg, "Black Virgins and the Democratic Body in Europe," 155.
29 Breger, *An Aesthetics of Narrative Performance*, 236.
30 Bertolt Brecht, *Brecht on Theatre*, trans. Jack Davis, Romy Fursland, Steve Giles, Victoria Hill, Kristopher Imbrigotta, Marc Silberman, and John Willett, ed. Marc Silberman, Steven Giles, and Tom Kuhn (London: Bloomsbury, [1957] 2015), 177.
31 Cited in Meyda Yeğenoğlu, *Colonial Fantasies: Toward a Feminist Reading of Orientalism* (Cambridge: Cambridge University Press, 1998), 39.
32 Roland Barthes, *Mythologies*, trans. Annette Lavers (New York: Hill and Wang, [1957] 1972), 84.
33 Adrienne Rich, "The Phenomenology of Anger," in *Diving into the Wreck* (New York: W. W. Norton, 1973), 31.

34 See Sieg, "Black Virgins and the Democratic Body in Europe" and Stewart, "*Black Virgins*, Close Encounters."
35 The opening music is actually taken from Steven Spielberg's 1977 science-fiction film, *Close Encounters of the Third Kind*. See Stewart, "*Black Virgins*, Close Encounters," 87–90.
36 Deborah R. Geis, *Postmodern Theatric(K)s: Monologue in Contemporary American Drama* (Ann Arbor: University of Michigan, 1995), 27.
37 Stanton B. Garner Jr., *Bodies Spaces: Phenomenology and Performance in Contemporary Drama* (Ithaca, NY: Cornell University Press, 1994), 160.
38 Brecht, *Brecht on Theatre*, 212–14.
39 bell hooks, *Talking Back: Thinking Feminist, Thinking Black* (Boston, MA: South End Press, [1989] 2015), 5.
40 hooks, *Talking Back*, 12.
41 During one intimate post-performance discussion, one of the actors responded to the question of an elderly man in the audience with the informal pronoun "du" ("you"). It was visibly evident that the man did not appreciate this. The actor also showed signs of recognition of the man's discomfort but continued to use "du."
42 Geis, *Postmodern Theatric(k)s*, 15.
43 Hans-Thies Lehmann, *Postdramatic Theatre*, trans. Karen Jürs-Munby (London: Routledge, [1999] 2006), 17.
44 Yeğenoğlu, *Colonial Fantasties*, 41.
45 Maha El Hissy, *Getürkte Türken: Karnevaleske Stilmittel im Theater, Kabarett und Film deutsch-türkischer Künstlerinnen und Künstler* (Bielefeld: Transcript, 2012), 111.
46 Zaimoğlu and Senkel, *Schwarze Jungfrauen*, Third Text.
47 Denise Riley, *Impersonal Passion: Language as Affect* (Durham, NC: Duke University Press, 2004), 27.
48 Jean-Paul Sartre, "Preface," in Frantz Fanon, *The Wretched of the Earth*, trans. Richard Philcox (New York: Grove Press, [1961] 2004), lii.
49 J.L. Austin, *How to Do Things with Words* (Cambridge, MA: Harvard University Press, [1962] 1975), 14–15.
50 Jill Dolan, *The Feminist Spectator as Critic* (Ann Arbor: University of Michigan Press, 1991), 63.
51 Geis, *Postmodern Theatric(K)s*, 117.
52 Zaimoğlu and Senkel, *Schwarze Jungfrauen*, Third Text.
53 Cited in William Flanagan, "Edward Albee: The Art of the Theatre," *Paris Review* 39 (1966), 103.
54 Beverly M. Weber, *Violence and Gender in the "New" Europe: Islam in German Culture* (New York: Palgrave, 2013), 58.
55 El-Tayeb, *European Others*, 83.
56 Egbert Tholl cited in Sarah Heppekausen, "Ästhetische Erziehung mit der Knarre," *Nachtkritik*, September 2, 2010, https://nachtkritik.de/index.

php?option=com_content&view=article&id=4634:verruecktes-blut-nurkan-erpulat-erzaehlt-qla-journee-de-la-jupeq-mithilfe-schillers-dramen-als-aesthetische-erziehung&catid=259&Itemid=17.

57 See Thilo Sarrazin, *Deutschland schafft sich ab* (Munich: Deutsche Verlags-Anstalt, 2010).

58 It may be noted that he was the first Turkish German to be trained as a director at the school.

59 Peter Boenisch and Thomas Ostermeier, *The Theatre of Thomas Ostermeier* (London: Routledge, 2016), 4.

60 Bertolt Brecht, "Stage Design for Epic Theatre," *Brecht on Theatre: The Development of an Aesthetic*, trans. John Willett (New York: Farrar, Straus and Giroux [1954] 1992), 233.

61 Cited in [Sasha] Marianna Salzmann, "Sie missüberschätzen uns. Über den Versuch, das Mittelstandsperlenkettchen wie ein Lasso um das Ballhaus Naunynstraβe zu werfen – Eine Komödie." *TRANSIT* 8, no. 1 (2011): 3.

62 José Esteban Muñoz, *Cruising Utopia: The Then and There of Queer Futurity* (New York: New York University Press, 2009), 65.

63 Included in the press booklet for the play are opening remarks by Tunçay Kulaoğlu, the present co-artistic director of the Ballhaus Naunynstraβe, in which he writes that "delikanlı" is a word frequently employed to macho men.

64 Achille Mbembe, *Critique of Black Reason*, trans. Laurent Dubois (Durham, NC: Duke University Press, 2017), 42.

65 According to the Gorki website, *Mad Blood* is the preferred English translation of the title (https://gorki.de/en/company/nurkan-erpulat).

66 Paraphrased from Nurkan Erpulat and Jens Hillje, *Verrücktes Blut* (an unpublished, working draft, version of the play, dated September 9, 2010), 38. I am grateful to Priscilla Layne and Nurkan Erpulat for sharing this material with me For a translation see Nurkan Erpulat and Jens Hillje, *Crazy Blood*, trans. Priscilla Layne-Kopf. *The Mercurian: A Theatrical Translation Review* 5, no. 1 (2016): 45. (Emphasis added.) With minor exception, I exclusively cite the published translation throughout.

67 Erpulat and Hillje, *Verrücktes Blut*, 40; Erpulat and Hillje, *Crazy Blood*, 47.

68 Brecht, *Brecht on Theatre*, 74.

69 In the interest of space, I have only included the English translation of longer quotes. Erpulat and Hillje, *Crazy Blood*, 46.

70 Cited in Priscilla Layne, "Between Play and Mimicry: The Limits of Humanism in 'Verrücktes Blut.'" *Colloquia Germanica* 47, no. 1/2 (2014): 55n11.

71 Friedrich Schiller, *On the Aesthetic Education of Man*, trans. Elizabeth M. Wilkinson and L.A. Willoughby (Oxford: Clarendon Press, 1968), 107.

72 Paul de Man, *Aesthetic Ideology*, trans. Andrzej Warminski (Minneapolis: University of Minnesota Press, 1996), 151.

73 Walter Benjamin, "Critique of Violence," in *Illuminations*, trans. Edmund Jephcott, ed. Peter Demetz (New York: Schocken Books, [1966] 1978), 295.
74 The affinity between "Frau Kelich" in the play and the author "Necla Kelek" is something I also explore in an earlier article. See Olivia Landry, "German Youth Against Sarrazin: Nurkan Erpulat's *Verrücktes Blut* and *Clash* as Political Theatre of Experience." *Jahrbuch Türkisch-deutsche Studien* (2012): 112–13.
75 Erpulat and Hillje, *Crazy Blood*, 52.
76 Erpulat and Hillje, *Crazy Blood*, 63.
77 Erpulat and Hillje, *Crazy Blood*, 67.
78 Cited in Layne, "Between Play and Mimicry," 53.
79 Garner Jr., *Bodies Spaces*, 59.

4 Documentaries of Outrage

1 These are some variations of the questions which open a forum on inter alia the political efficacy of theater and performance in the United States today and are equally relevant to the European context. See David Bruin and Tom Sellar, ed. "What's Holding Us Back? A Forum on Nationalism, Xenophobia, and American Theater Now," *Theater* 48, no. 3 (2018): 39.
2 Stéphane Hessel, *Time for Outrage / Indignez-vous!*, trans. Marion Duvert (New York: Twelve, [2010] 2011), 17.
3 Antonin Artaud, *The Theatre and Its Double*, trans. Mary Caroline Richards (New York: Grove Press, [1938] 1958), 85.
4 Richard Schechner, "Invasions Friendly and Unfriendly: The Dramaturgy of Direct Theater," in *Critical Theory and Performance*, ed. Janelle G. Reinelt and Joseph Roach (Ann Arbor: University of Michigan Press, [1992] 2007), 477.
5 Baz Kershaw, *The Politics of Performance: Radical Theatre as Cultural Intervention* (London: Routledge, 1992), 18.
6 Peter Weiss, "Für *das* Straβentheater gegen *die* Straβentheater" in *Dramen 2* (Frankfurt am Main: Suhrkamp, 1968), 56.
7 Harry J. Elam Jr., *Taking it to the Streets: The Social Protest Theater of Luis Valdez and Amiri Baraka* (Ann Arbor: University of Michigan Press, 1997), 1.
8 Augusto Boal, *Theatre of the Oppressed*, trans. Charles A. McBride and Maria-Odilia Leal McBride (New York: Theatre Communications Group, [1974] 1985), xiiv.
9 Cited in Alison Forsyth and Chris Megson, eds. *Get Real: Documentary Theatre Past and Present* (New York: Palgrave, 2009), 1.
10 Carol Martin, "Bodies of Evidence." *TDR* 50, no. 3 (2006): 14.
11 Consider for instance Rolf Hochmuth's *The Deputy* (1963) (in a production by Erwin Piscator), Heinar Kipphardt's *In the Matter of J. Robert*

Oppenheimer (1964), Peter Weiss's *The Investigation* (1965), Rolf Schneider's *Nuremberg Trial* (1967), and Hans Magnus Enzensberger's *The Havana Inquiry* (1969). All five of these plays dealt with (often) contemporaneous trials and hearings, from the Eichmann trial, to Hiroshima and the hearings of J. Robert Oppenheimer, the Nuremberg Trials, and the interrogation of Cuban exiles taken prisoner during the Bay of Pigs Invasion. For an incisive investigation of documentary theater of the 1960s in West Germany, see Laureen Nussbaum (1981), Thomas Irmer (2006), and Henning Fülle, *Freies Theater* (2016), 55–7.

12 Peter Weiss, "Das Material und die Modelle: Notizen zum dokumentarischen Theater" in *Dramen 2* (Frankfurt am Main: Suhrkamp, 1968), 472.

13 This was officially initiated in 1973 with the theater pedagogy congress hosted by the Academy of Arts in West-Berlin. See Henning Fülle, *Freies Theater* (Berlin: Theater der Zeit, 2016), 126–30.

14 Manfred Brauneck, ed. *Independent Theatre in Contemporary Europe: Structures – Aesthetics – Cultural Policy* (Bielefeld: Transcript, 2017), 16.

15 In an interview with Deutschlandrundfunk in 2013, Shermin Langhoff stated the importance of the political in her theatre. She could not imagine theatre that isn't political. The interview is published online: see Axel Rahmlow, "Ich kann mir gar kein anderes Theater als politisches vorstellen," *Deutschlandfunk Kultur*, November 9, 2013, https://www.deutschlandfunkkultur.de/ich-kann-mir-gar-kein-anderes-theater-als-politisches.990.de.html?dram:article_id=268286.

16 Cited in Azadeh Sharifi, "Theatre and Migration," in *Independent Theatre in Contemporary Europe: Structures – Aesthetics – Cultural Policy*, 225.

17 Arthur Sainer, *The Radical Theatre Notebook* (New York: Avon Books, 1975), 62.

18 Weiss, "Das Material und die Modelle," 466.

19 On a global level, the financial crisis is referred to as the post-2008 crisis (initiated above all in the US with the mortgage crash), and no doubt this broader crisis precipitated the Greek crisis. However, in the literature about the local financial crisis, most scholars refer to it as the post-2010 crisis. It references the Greek government's signing of the "memorandum of agreement" in Athens with its European lenders, which initiated the austerity measures in Greece.

20 Cited in Manolis Pratsinakis et al, "Crisis and the Resurgence of Emigration from Greece: Trends, Representations, and the Multiplicity of Migrant Trajectories," in *European Mobility in Times of Crisis: The New Context of European South-North Migration*, ed. Birgit Glorius and Josefina Domínguez-Mujica (Bielefeld: Transcript, 2017), 83.

21 Martin, "Bodies of Evidence," 9.

22 It may be noted that there were protests throughout Greece during the summer of 2011. As many as fifty-five cities held rallies of various sizes.

23 The Greek debt crisis has been fodder for a number of artistic and performance projects in Greece, but these are rarely explored in the German-Greek context. One example is the 2015 production of the Greek play *The Intrigue of Z.* conceived by director Effi Teodoru and performed in 2015 throughout Europe. This play is, however, more concerned with the rise of the right in Greece in the post-crisis period. Re-investigating the political murder of Grigóris Lambrákis in 1963, this play seeks to draw parallels between this earlier period of political upheaval and corruption to the present, and especially the ramifications of the public murder of the anti-fascist rapper Pavlos Fyssas (Killah P.) by Golden Dawn member Giorgios Roupakias in 2013.
24 Dimitris Dalakoglou, "The Crisis before 'The Crisis': Violence and Urban Neoliberalization in Athens." *Social Justice* 39, no. 1 (2013): 24.
25 Lauren Berlant, "Precarity Talk: A Virtual Roundtable with Lauren Berlant, Judith Butler, Bojana Cvejić, Isabell Lorey, Jasbir Puar, and Ana Vujanović," ed. Jasbir Puar. *TDR: The Drama Review* 56, no. 4 (2012): 166.
26 Ngũgĩ wa Thiong'o, "Enactments of Power: The Politics of Performance Space." *TDR* 41, no. 3 (1997): 13.
27 Dalakoglou, "The Crisis before 'The Crisis,'" 28.
28 Paolo Gerbaudo, "The Indignant Citizen: Anti-Austerity Movements in Southern Europe and the Anti-Oligarchic Reclaiming of Citizenship." *Social Movement Studies* 16, no. 1 (2017): 36–7.
29 Hessel, *Time for Outrage / Indignez-vous!*, 6.
30 It bears noting that the protest movement in Athens also gave rise to the fomenting voices of right-wing groups, such as members and supporters of the extreme right-wing group, Golden Dawn. In Athens and elsewhere, these groups co-opted the protests to rally for their own interests. In some cases, this also led to violent clashes with the protesters.
31 Chantal Mouffe, *The Return of the Political* (London: Verso, [1993] 2005), 95.
32 In 1960, West Germany signed a bilateral recruitment agreement with Greece enabling free labour movement between the countries. As a result, roughly 155,000 Greek citizens migrated to West Germany between 1960 and 1973 (the end of all labour agreements with West Germany); many stayed and settled. There were a number of reasons for Greek emigration during this period, but the decisive factors were high unemployment in Greece, bare subsistence incomes, and the quest for political freedom (especially during the military junta's rule between 1967 and 1974).
33 Martin, "Bodies of Evidence," 9.
34 Anestis Azas, Prodromos Tsinikoris, and Philip Hager, "'Shifting the Gaze': Anestis Azas and Prodromos Tsinikoris in Conversation with Philip Hager." *Journal of Greek Media & Culture* 3, no. 2 (2017): 265.
35 Azas, Tsinikoris, and Hager, "'Shifting the Gaze,'" 260.

36 Martin, "Bodies of Evidence," 9.
37 Janelle G. Reinelt, "The Promise of Documentary," in *Get Real: Documentary Theatre Past and Present*, ed. Alison Forsyth and Chris Megson (New York: Palgrave, 2009), 10.
38 Erika Fischer-Lichte, *The Transformative Power of Performance: A New Aesthetics*, trans. Saskya Iris Jain (London: Routledge, [2004] 2008), 38.
39 Judith Butler, *Precarious Life: The Powers of Mourning and Violence* (London: Verso, 2004), 26.
40 Judith Butler and Athena Athanasiou, *Dispossession: The Performative in the Political* (Cambridge: Polity, 2013), 175.
41 Philip Hager, "Dramaturgies of Crisis and Performances of Citizenship: Syntagma Square, Athens." *Performance Interventions: Performance and the Global City*, ed. D. J. Hopkins and Kim Solga (New York: Palgrave, 2013), 247.
42 Bojana Cvejić and Ana Vujanović, "Precarity Talk: A Virtual Roundtable with Lauren Berlant, Judith Butler, Bojana Cvejić, Isabell Lorey, Jasbir Puar, and Ana Vujanović," ed. Jasbir Puar. *TDR: The Drama Review* 56, no. 4 (2012): 176.
43 Karl A. E. Enenkel and Anita Traninger, eds. *Discourses of Anger in the Early Modern Period* (Leiden: Brill, 2015), 14.
44 For a comprehensive study on this period in Greek history, see Violetta Hionidou, *Famine and Death in Occupied Greece, 1941–1944* (Cambridge: Cambridge University Press, 2006).
45 Carol Martin, *Theatre of the Real* (New York: Palgrave, 2013), 21.
46 Olivia Landry, "Greek Dispossession Staged, or When Street Politics Meets the Theater," *TRANSIT* 10, no. 2 (2016): 12–13.
47 David Harvey, *Rebel Cities: From the Right to the City to the Urban Revolution* (London: Verso, [2012] 2013), 161.
48 Sara Ahmed, *Willful Subjects* (Durham, NC: Duke University Press, 2014), 165.
49 Erdem Yörük, "The Long Summer of Turkey: The Gezi Uprising and Its Historical Roots." *The South Atlantic Quarterly* 113, no. 2 (2014): 421.
50 Leading up to the 2013 protests, the last military coup of significance and duration occurred in 1980.
51 Susan Leigh Foster, "Choreographies of Protest." *Theatre Journal* 55, no. 3 (2003): 395–412.
52 Arzu Öztürkmen, "The Park, the Penguin, and the Gas: Performance in Progress in Gezi Park." *TDR* 58, no. 3 (2014): 41.
53 Öztürkmen, "The Park, the Penguin, and the Gas," 58.
54 Judith Butler, *Notes Toward a Performative Theory of Assembly* (Cambridge, MA: Harvard University Press, 2015), 169.
55 Lyn Gardner, "Staging a Revolution: Can Theatre Be An Effective Form of Activism?," *The Guardian*, March 23, 2016, https://www.theguardian

.com/stage/theatreblog/2016/mar/23/theatre-effective-protest-activism-change-debate.

56 Öztürkmen, "The Park, the Penguin, and the Gas," 61.

57 Lauren Nussbaum, "The German Documentary Theater of the Sixties: A Stereopsis of Contemporary History." *German Studies Review* 4, no. 2 (1981): 239–40.

58 Yörük, "The Long Summer of Turkey," 422.

59 Yörük, "The Long Summer of Turkey," 422.

60 Yörük, "The Long Summer of Turkey," 423.

61 Mely Kiyak, "Auf einmal sind sie alle Kurden," *Die Zeit*, July 12, 2013, https://www.zeit.de/kultur/2013-07/tuerkei-kurden-kuenstler-sener-oezmen.

62 Reinelt, "The Promise of Documentary," 9.

63 Martin, "Bodies of Evidence," 9.

64 Ahmed, *Willful Subjects*, 164.

65 Joseph Roach, *Cities of the Dead: Circum-Atlantic Performance* (New York: Columbia University Press, 1996), 26.

66 Paul Connerton, *How Societies Remember* (Cambridge: Cambridge University Press, 1989), 39; Diana Taylor, *The Archive and the Repertoire: Performing Cultural Memory in the Americas* (Durham, NC: Duke University Press, 2003), 54.

67 Deborah R. Geis, *Postmodern Theatric(K)s: Monologue in Contemporary American Drama* (Ann Arbor: University of Michigan, 1995), 14.

68 Carol Martin, "Reclaiming the Real: Introduction," *TDR* 61, no. 4 (2017): 8.

69 Reinelt, "The Promise of Documentary," 11–12.

70 Lauren Berlant, "The Commons: Infrastructures for Troubling Times." *Society and Space* 34, no. 4 (2016): 393.

71 Boal, *Theatre of the Oppressed*, 155.

5 Salzmann's Angry Youths

1 Epigraph: Sasha Marianna Salzmann, *Die Aristokraten: Drei Stücke* (Frankfurt am Main: Verlag der Autoren, 2017), 90.

2 Sara Ahmed, *The Promise of Happiness* (Durham, NC: Duke University Press, 2010), 68.

3 Ahmed, *The Promise of Happiness*, 68.

4 Aleks Sierz, *In-Yer-Face Theatre: British Drama Today* (London: Faber and Faber, 2001), 108.

5 Sarah Kane, *Complete Plays* (London: Bloomsbury, 2001).

6 In a compelling interview with theater director Milo Rau, author Guy Krneta, and cultural journalist Tobi Müller, Julia Reichert pursues this point. See Reichert, "Einfach machen, was die Zeitung nicht macht?" *Theater der Zeit* 7/8 (2017): 38–42.

7 See Heidi Stephenson and Natasha Langridge, *Rage and Reason: Women Playwrights on Playwrighting* (London: Methuen Drama, 1997), 133.
8 Sierz, *In-Yer-Face Theatre*, 8.
9 Audre Lorde, *Sister Outsider* (New York: Crossing Press [1984] 2007), 124, 127.
10 Sara Ahmed, *The Cultural Politics of Emotion* (London: Routledge, [2004] 2015), 175.
11 Ahmed, *The Cultural Politics of Emotion*, 175.
12 Diana Taylor, *The Archive and the Repertoire: Performing Cultural Memory in the Americas* (Durham, NC: Duke University, 2003).
13 W. B. Worthen, "Antigone's Bones." *TDR* 52, no. 3 (2008): 27.
14 Worthen, "Antigone's Bones," 23.
15 Tom Sellar, "Theater and Violence." *Theater* 35, no. 1 (2005): 8.
16 Fatima El-Tayeb, *European Others: Queering Ethnicity in Postnational Europe* (Minneapolis: University of Minnesota Press, 2011), 99.
17 While Germany's prison population is comparatively low (roughly 63,500, one-tenth of that of the United States) and the conditions in German prisons are overall much more humane than many countries, the percentage of minority prisoners is discernibly higher than that of the overall population. See Nicholas Turner and Jeremy Travis, "What We Learned from German Prisons," *New York Times*, August 6, 2015, https://www.nytimes.com/2015/08/07/opinion/what-we-learned-from-german-prisons.html. For more on the notion of the "Cradle to Prison Pipeline," see Avery F. Gordon, "Globalism and the Prison Industrial Complex: An Interview with Angela Davis," *Race & Class* 40, no. 2/3 (1998/99): 157.
18 Toni Morrison, *Playing in the Dark: Whiteness and the Literary Imagination* (Cambridge, MA: Harvard University Press, 1992), 58.
19 José Esteban Muñoz, "Feeling Brown: Ethnicity and Affect in Ricardo Bracho's 'The Sweetest Hangover (And Other STDs).'" *Theatre Journal* 52, no. 1 (2000): 79.
20 Fatima El-Tayeb offers a succinct description of the events of late October 2005 that resulted in the death of two teenage Muslim boys in Paris and the subsequent protests against institutionalized racism and police violence that erupted in Clichy-sous-Bois on the outskirts of Paris and metastasized as a movement throughout France. See El-Tayeb, *European Others*, 14–19.
21 [Sasha] Marianna Salzmann, *Weißbrotmusik/Satt* (Frankfurt am Main: Verlag der Autoren, [2011] 2015), 12.
22 In Salzmann's text, they identify only a single fourth person, who is "Mom," "Guest," and "Retiree."
23 Richard Schechner, *Environmental Theater* (New York: Applause, [1973] 1994), 40.

24 Schechner, *Environmental Theater*, 1–2.
25 "Mercy" is slang that means something like "definitely."
26 Salzmann, *Weißbrotmusik/Satt*, 26.
27 Salzmann, *Weißbrotmusik/Satt*, 43.
28 For an erudite study on the similarities between the sonic cultures of African American and Turkish German rap, see Alexander G. Weheliye. *Phonographies: Grooves in Sonic Afro-Modernity* (Durham, NC: Duke University Press, 2005).
29 Salzmann, *Weißbrotmusik/Satt*, 49.
30 Salzmann, *Weißbrotmusik/Satt*, 55.
31 Kristina Rath, "Serdat hat die Nase voll, alles Bullenlogik," *TAZ*, March 17, 2012, http://www.taz.de/!608172/.
32 Erika Fischer-Lichte, *The Transformative Power of Performance: A New Aesthetics*, trans. Saskya Iris Jain (London: Routledge, [2004] 2008), 11–13.
33 I am grateful to Salzmann for bringing this to my attention.
34 Of course, Katrin Sieg has importantly problematized the reception of *Nathan the Wise* and its performances throughout German theater history as one which does not simply present a theatrical tale of religious reconciliation. See Sieg, *Ethnic Drag* (Ann Arbor: University of Michigan Press, 2002), 29–72.
35 Salzmann's essay was originally published online on their personal website: http://sashamariannasalzmann.com/mohammed/. I am grateful to Salzmann for providing me with a copy.
36 Rich Noack and Luisa Beck, "Video Shows Belt-Wielding Assailant Screaming 'Jew' as He Attacks Two People on a Berlin Street," *The Washington Post*, April 19, 2018, https://www.washingtonpost.com/news/worldviews/wp/2018/04/19/belt-wielding-assailant-screams-jew-as-he-attacks-two-on-a-berlin-street/?noredirect=on&utm_term=.344da545e03a.
37 Lars Weisbrod, "Kollegah & Farid Bang: Jung, brutal, Antisemit?" *Die Zeit*, April 11, 2018, https://www.zeit.de/2018/16/kollegah-farid-bang-antisemitismus.
38 Already in late 2013 the European Union Agency for Fundamental Rights published the results of a study exploring the experience of Jewish people living in the European Union. In the key findings, it is noted that 66 per cent of respondents claimed that anti-Semitism is a "major problem" in their country and 76 per cent stated that the problem of anti-Semitism has increased in the last five years. See further results of this study on the webpage for the European Union Agency for Fundamental Rights: http://fra.europa.eu/en/press-release/2013/combating-antisemitism-more-targeted-measures-needed. More recently the Jewish World Congress in 2018 revealed astounding statistics with regard to the drastic increase in anti-Semitic acts. In the first half of 2018 alone, over 400 were reported. See

"Weltkongress besorgt über steigende Zahl antisemitischer Straftaten," *Die Zeit*, August 11, 2018, https://www.zeit.de/gesellschaft/zeitgeschehen/2018-08/antisemitismus-deutschland-bundesregierung-juedischer-weltkongress-wjc. One could also add the more recent deadly attack at the Tree of Life Congregation in Pittsburgh, US in October 2018 in which eleven congregants were killed and many more injured. See Campbell Robinson, Christopher Mele, Sabrina Tavernise, "11 Killed in Synagogue Massacre; Suspect Charged with 29 Counts," *New York Times*, October 27, 2018, https://www.nytimes.com/2018/10/27/us/active-shooter-pittsburgh-synagogue-shooting.html.

39 Fatima El-Tayeb, *Undeutsch: Die Konstruktion des Anderen in der postmigrantischen Gesellschaft* (Bielefeld: Transcript, 2016), 187.

40 El-Tayeb, *Undeutsch*, 193.

41 Leslie A. Adelson, "Touching Tales of Turks, Germans, and Jews: Cultural Alterity, Historical Narrative, and Literary Riddles for the 1990s," *New German Critique* 80 (2000): 93–124.

42 Michael Rothberg, *Multidirectional Memory: Remembering the Holocaust* (Stanford, CA: Stanford University, 2009), 3.

43 Ahmed, *The Cultural Politics of Emotion*, 178.

44 Hans-Thies Lehmann, *Postdramatic Theatre*, trans. Karen Jürs-Munby (London: Routledge, [1999] 2006), 104.

45 The balance of this chapter has been drawn from a modified version of a book chapter I published on the play. See Olivia Landry, "Anger as Theatrical Form in Sasha Marianna Salzmann's *Zucken*," in *Postdramatisches Theater als transkulturelles Theater. Eine transdisziplinäre Annäherung*, ed. Teresa Kovacs and Koku G. Nonoa (Forum Modernes Theater, Tübingen: Narr Francke Attempo Verlag, 2018), 335–48.

46 Antonin Artaud, *The Theatre and Its Double*, trans. Mary Caroline Richards (New York: Grove Press, [1938] 1958), 92. One could cite further instances of "Zucken" in literature from Goethe's *Faust* to Mary Shelly's *Frankenstein* as both disruption and failure as well as the force that enlivens.

47 A published translation of *Zucken* does not exist. While "Zucken" translates as "twitching" or "to twitch," throughout I expand on this translation to include "to shudder" and even "to spasm."

48 In conversation, Salzmann has noted that the abbreviation of the title was principally an act of censorship. The play was to be performed with youth and for youth and it was clear that with the longer, provocative title, teachers would not bring their students.

49 Lehmann, *Postdramatic Theatre*, 17.

50 Lehmann, *Postdramatic Theatre*, 163.

51 Doris Meierhenrich, "Premieren-Doppel 'Zucken' und 'Mythen der Wirklichkeit,'" *Berliner Zeitung*, March 20, 2017, https://www.berliner-zeitung

.de/kultur/gorki-theater-premieren-doppel--zucken--und--mythen-der-wirklichkeit--26228438.

52 Sophie Diesselhorst, "Let's talk Dschihad," *Nachtkritik*, March 17, 2017, https://www.nachtkritik.de/index.php?option=com_content&view=article&id=13751:zucken-ein-stueck-ueber-sich-radikalisierende-jugendliche-von-sasha-marianna-salzmann-von-sebastian-nuebling-am-berliner-gorki-theater-uraufgefuehrt&catid=38:die-nachtkritik-k&Itemid=40.

53 Salzmann, *Die Aristokraten*, 25.

54 André Lepecki, *Exhausting Dance: Performance and the Politics of Movement* (New York: Routledge, 2006), 1.

55 Lehmann, *Postdramatic Theatre*, 145.

56 Lehmann, *Postdramatic Theatre*, 37.

57 On anxiety and its lack of attribution, or at least its wooly object, see Søren Kierkegaard, *The Concept of Anxiety: A Simple Psychologically Orienting Deliberation on the Dogmatic Issue of Hereditary Sin*, ed. and trans. Reidar Thomte (Princeton: Princeton University Press, [1844] 1980); Jacques Lacan, *Anxiety: The Seminar of Jacques Lacan, Book X*, trans. Cormac Gallagher, ed. Jacques-Alain Miller (Cambridge: Polity Press, [1973] 2016).

58 It might be noted that this line is not in Salzmann's dramatic text.

59 Lehmann, *Postdramatic Theatre*, 122.

60 Peter Sloterdijk, "Mobilization of the Planet from the Spirit of Self-Intensification," *TDR* 50, no. 4 (2006): 38.

61 Lepecki, *Exhausting Dance*, 14.

62 See Fred Moten, *In the Break: The Aesthetics of the Black Radical Tradition* (Minneapolis: University of Minnesota Press, 2003); Daphne A. Brooks, *Bodies in Dissent: Spectacular Performances of Race and Freedom, 1850–1910* (Durham, NC: Duke University Press, 2006); and C. Riley Snorton, *Black on Both Sides: A Racial History of Trans Identity* (Minneapolis: University of Minnesota Press, 2017).

63 José Esteban Muñoz, *Cruising Utopia: The Then and There of Queer Futurity* (New York: New York University Press, 2009), 74–5.

64 Salzmann, *Die Aristokraten*, 25.

65 Ahmed, *The Cultural Politics of Emotion*, 174.

66 bell hooks, *Talking Back: Thinking Feminist, Thinking Black* (Cambridge, MA: South End Press, 1989), 5.

67 Audre Lorde, *Sister Outsider* (Berkeley: Crossing Press, [1984] 2007), 127.

68 Caitlin Bruce discusses the transnational affective iconicity of the balaclava since Pussy Riot's infamous anti-Putin performance at Moscow's Christ the Savior Cathedral in February 2012. See Caitlin Bruce, "The Balaclava as Affect Generator: Free Pussy Riot Protests and Transnational Iconicity." *Communication and Critical/Cultural Studies* 12, no. 1 (2015): 42–62.

69 Lehmann, *Postdramatic Theatre*, 163.
70 Muñoz, *Cruising Utopia*, 67.
71 Meierhenrich, "Premieren-Doppel 'Zucken' und 'Mythen der Wirklichkeit.'"
72 In my analysis of Salzmann's play *Meteorites*, I begin with the closing words, which are also appropriately in the form of a threat of revenge to the audience. See Olivia Landry, "On the Politics of Love and Post-Migrant Theater in Germany," *TSQ* 5, no. 1 (2018): 30–48.

6 "Theatre of the Twenty-First Century"

1 See [Sasha] Marianna Salzmann, "Sie missüberschätzen uns. Über den Versuch, das Mittelstandsperlenkettchen wie ein Lasso um das Ballhaus Naunynstraβe zu werfen – Eine Komödie." *TRANSIT* 8, 1 (2011): 1–4.
2 Mizrahi Jews are descendants of Jewish communities in the Middle East, in particular from Iraq, Syria, and Yemen.

Conclusion

1 Martha C. Nussbaum, *Anger and Forgiveness: Resentment, Generosity, Justice* (New York: Oxford University Press, 2016), 15.
2 Sara Ahmed, *The Promise of Happiness* (Durham, NC: Duke University Press, 2010), 68.
3 Audre Lorde, *Sister Outsider* (Berkeley: Crossing Press, [1984] 2007), 127.
4 Lorde, *Sister Outsider*, 127.
5 Lorde, *Sister Outsider*, 168.
6 Lorde, *Sister Outsider*, 152.
7 Georg Baselitz and Alexander Kluge, *World-Changing Rage: News of the Antipodeans*, trans. Katy Derbyshire (London: Seagall Books, [2017] 2019), 214.

Bibliography

Adelson, Leslie A. "Touching Tales of Turks, Germans, and Jews: Cultural Alterity, Historical Narrative, and Literary Riddles for the 1990s." *New German Critique* 80 (2000): 93–124.

Ahmed, Sara. *The Promise of Happiness*. Durham, NC: Duke University Press, 2010.

– *Willful Subjects*. Durham, NC: Duke University Press, 2014.

– *The Cultural Politics of Emotion*. 2nd ed. New York: Routledge, [2004] 2015.

– *Living a Feminist Life*. Durham, NC: Duke University, 2017.

Alarcón, Norma. "Conjugating Subjects in the Age of Multiculturalism," in *Mapping Multiculturalism*, edited by Avery F. Gordon and Christopher Newfield, 127–48. Minneapolis: University of Minnesota, 1996.

Aristotle. *Poetics*. Translated by Stephen Halliwell. Cambridge, MA: Harvard University Press, 1995.

– *Nicomachean Ethics*. Translated by Roger Crisp. Cambridge: Cambridge University Press, 2004.

Artaud, Antonin. *The Theater and Its Double*. Translated by Mary Caroline Richards. New York: Grove Press, [1938] 1958.

Austin, J.L. *How to Do Things with Words*. Cambridge, MA: Harvard University Press, [1962] 1975.

Ayim, May. *Blues in schwarz weiß: Gedichte*. Berlin: Orlanda Frauenverlag, 1995.

– *Blues in Black and White*. Translated by Anne Adams. Trenton, NJ: Africa World Press, 2003.

Azas, Anestis, Prodromos Tsinikoris, and Philip Hager. "'Shifting the Gaze': Anestis Azas and Prodromos Tsinikoris in Conversation with Philip Hager." *Journal of Greek Media & Culture* 3, no. 2 (2017): 259–72.

Baldwin, James. *Notes of a Native Son*. Boston: Beacon Press, [1955] 2012.

Balibar, Étienne. *We the People of Europe: Reflections on Transnational Citizenship*. Translated by James Swenson. Princeton: Princeton University Press, 2004.

Barish, Jonas. *The Antitheatrical Prejudice*. Berkeley: University of California, 1981.

Barnett, David. "Toward a Definition of Post-Brechtian Performance: The Example of *In the Jungle of the Cities* at the Berliner Ensemble, 1971." *Modern Drama* 54, no. 3 (2011): 333–56.

Barthes, Roland. *Mythologies*. Translated by Annette Lavers. New York: Hill and Wang, [1957] 1972.

Baselitz, Georg and Alexander Kluge. *World-Changing Rage: News of the Antipodeans*. Translated by Katy Derbyshire. London: Seagall Books, [2017] 2019.

Baydar, Gülsüm and Berfin Ivegen, "Territories, Identities, and Thresholds: The Saturday Mothers Phenomenon in Istanbul." *Signs* 31, no. 3 (2006): 689–715.

Benjamin, Walter. "Critique of Violence." *Illuminations*, edited by Peter Demetz, 277–300. Translated by Edmund Jephcott. New York: Schocken Books, [1966] 1978.

Berlant, Lauren. "The Subject of True Feeling: Pain, Privacy, and Politics." *Transformations: Thinking Through Feminism*, edited by Sara Ahmed, Jane Kilby, Celia Lury, Maureen McNeil, Beverley Skeggs, 33–47. London: Routledge, 2000.

– *Cruel Optimism*. Durham, NC: Duke University Press, 2011.

– "Precarity Talk: A Virtual Roundtable with Lauren Berlant, Judith Butler, Bojana Cvejić, Isabell Lorey, Jasbir Puar, and Ana Vujanović," edited by Jasbir Puar. *TDR: The Drama Review* 56, no. 4 (2012): 163–77.

– "The Commons: Infrastructures for Troubling Times." *Society and Space* 34, no. 4 (2016): 393–419.

Boal, Augusto. *Theatre of the Oppressed*. Translated by Charles A. McBride and Maria-Odilia Leal McBride. New York: Theatre Communications Group, [1974] 1985.

Boenisch, Peter and Thomas Ostermeier. *The Theatre of Thomas Ostermeier*. London: Routledge, 2016.

Boran, Erol. "A History of Turkish-German Theater and Cabaret." PhD diss., Ohio State University, 2004.

Bosswick, Wolfgang. "Development of Asylum Policy in Germany." *Journal of Refugee Studies* 13, no. 1 (2000): 43–60.

Brauneck, Manfred, ed. *Independent Theatre in Contemporary Europe: Structures – Aesthetics – Cultural Policy*. Bielefeld: Transcript, 2017.

Brecht, Bertolt. "Set Design for the Epic Theatre." *Brecht on Theatre: The Development of an Aesthetic*. Translated by John Willett, 230–3. New York: Farrar, Straus and Giroux [1954] 1992.

– *Brecht on Theatre*. Translated by Jack Davis, Romy Fursland, Steve Giles, Victoria Hill, Kristopher Imbrigotta, Marc Silberman, and John Willett, edited by Marc Silberman, Steven Giles, and Tom Kuhn. London: Bloomsbury, [1957] 2015.

Breger, Claudia. *An Aesthetics of Narrative Performance: Transnational Theater, Literature, and Film in Contemporary Germany*. Columbus: Ohio State University Press, 2012.

Brinkema, Eugenie. *The Forms of the Affects*. Durham, NC: Duke University Press, 2014.

Brooks, Daphne A. *Bodies in Dissent: Spectacular Performances of Race and Freedom, 1850–1910*. Durham, NC: Duke University Press, 2006.

Brown, Wendy. *Walled States, Waning Sovereignty*. New York: Zone Books, 2010.

Bruce, Caitlin. "The Balaclava as Affect Generator: Free Pussy Riot Protests and Transnational Iconicity." *Communication and Critical/Cultural Studies* 12, no. 1 (2015): 42–62.

Bruin, David and Tom Sellar, eds. "What's Holding Us Back? A Forum on Nationalism, Xenophobia, and American Theater Now." *Theater* 48, no. 3 (2018): 39–79.

Bulman, Gail A. *Staging Words, Performing Worlds: Intertextuality and Nation in Contemporary Latin American Theater*. Lewisburg, PA: Bucknell University Press, 2007.

Butler, Judith. *Precarious Life: The Powers of Mourning and Violence*. London: Verso, 2004.

– *Gender Trouble: Feminism and the Subversion of Identity*. New York: Routledge, [1990] 2006.

– *Notes toward a Performative Theory of Assembly*. Cambridge, MA: Harvard, 2015.

Butler, Judith and Athena Athanasiou. *Dispossession: The Performative in the Political*. Cambridge: Polity Press, 2013.

Byron, Glennis. *Dramatic Monologue*. London: Routledge, 2003.

Carlson, Marvin. *Performance: A Critical Introduction*. London: Routledge, [1996] 2004.

– "Introduction," in Erika Fischer-Lichte, *The Transformative Power of Performance: A New Aesthetics*, 1–23. London: Routledge, [2004] 2008.

Çelik, Neco. "Mal sehen, was Gott sagt." (Interview mit Neco Çelik). *Theater heute* 47, no. 5 (2006): 43–5.

Cheesman, Tom. "Talking 'Kanak': Zaimoğlu contra Leitkultur." *New German Critique* 92 (2004): 82–99.

Chemaly, Soraya. *Rage Becomes Her: The Power of Women's Anger*. New York: Atria, 2018.

Connerton, Paul. *How Societies Remember*. Cambridge: Cambridge University Press, 1989.

Cooper, Brittney. *Eloquent Rage: A Black Feminist Discovers Her Superpower*. New York: St. Martin's Press, 2018.

Cornish, Matt. *Performing Unification: History and Nation in German Theater after 1989*. Ann Arbor: University of Michigan, 2017.

Czollek, Max. *Desintegriert Euch!* Munich: Hanser, 2018.

– "Gegenwartsbewältigung." *Eure Heimat ist unser Albtraum*, edited by Fatma Aydemir and Hengameh Yaghoobifarah, 167–81. Munich: Ullstein, 2019.

Czollek, Max and Sasha Marianna Salzmann. *Desintegration: A Congress on Contemporary Jewish Positions*. Bielefeld: Kerber, 2017.

Dalakoglou, Dimitris. "The Crisis before the 'Crisis': Violence and Neoliberalization in Athens." *Social Justice* 39, no. 1 (2013): 24–42.

Deleuze, Gilles. *Cinemá 1: The Movement-Image*. Translated by Hugh Tomlinson and Barbara Habberjam. Minneapolis: University of Minnesota Press, [1983] 2006.

de Man, Paul. *Aesthetic Ideology*. Translated by Andrzej Warminski. Minneapolis: University of Minnesota Press, 1996.

Diamond, Elin. "Brechtian Theory/Feminist Theory: Toward a Gestic Feminist Criticism." *TDR* 32, no. 1 (1988): 82–94.

– *Unmaking Mimesis: Essays on Feminism and Theatre*. New York Routledge, 1997.

Diesselhorst, Sophie. "Let's talk Dschihad." *Nachkritik*, March 17, 2017. https://www.nachtkritik.de/index.php?option=com_content&view=article&id=13751:zucken-ein-stueck-ueber-sich-radikalisierende-jugendliche-von-sasha-marianna-salzmann-von-sebastian-nuebling-am-berliner-gorki-theater-uraufgefuehrt&catid=38:die-nachtkritik-k&Itemid=40.

Dolan, Jill. *The Feminist Spectator as Critic*. Ann Arbor: University of Michigan Press, 1991.

Draeger, Volkmar. "Verstörende Abrechnung: 'Schwarze Jungfrauen' entschleiern sich im HAU 3." *Neues Deutschland*, March 23, 2006. https://www.neues-deutschland.de/artikel/87723.verstoerende-abrechnung.html.

Elam, Harry J., Jr. *Taking It to the Streets: The Social Protest Theater of Luis Valdez and Amiri Baraka*. Ann Arbor: University of Michigan Press, 1997.

El Hissy, Maha. Getürkte Türken: Karnevaleske Stilmittel im Theater, Kabarett und Film deutsch-türkischer Künstlerinnen und Künstler. Bielefeld: Transcript, 2012.

El-Tayeb, Fatima. *European Others: Queering Ethnicity in Postnational Europe*. Minneapolis: University of Minnesota Press, 2011.

– *Undeutsch: Die Konstruktion des Anderen in der postmigrantischen Gesellschaft*. Bielefeld: Transcript, 2016.

Emcke, Carolin. *Gegen den Hass*. Frankfurt am Main: Fischer, 2016.

Enenkel, Karl A. E. and Anita Traninger, eds. *Discourses of Anger in the Early Modern Period*. Leiden: Brill, 2015.

Erpulat, Nurkan and Jens Hillje, *Crazy Blood*. Translated by Priscilla Layne-Kopf. *The Mercurian: A Theatrical Translation Review* 5, no. 1 (2016): 8–67.

Fanon, Frantz. "Algeria Unveiled." *The New Left Reader*, edited by Carl Oglesby, 161–85. New York: Grove Press, [1959] 1969.

Fischer-Lichte, Erika. *The Transformative Power of Performance: A New Aesthetics*. Translated by Saskya Iris Jain. London: Routledge, [2004] 2008.

Fischer-Lichte, Erika, Torsten Jost, and Saskya Iris Jain, eds. *The Politics of Interweaving Performance Cultures: Beyond Postcolonialism*. New York: Routledge, 2014.

Fisher, Philip. *The Vehement Passions*. Princeton, NJ: Princeton University Press, 2002.

Flanagan, William. "Edward Albee: The Art of the Theatre." *Paris Review* 39 (1966): 93–121.

Foroutan, Naika, Juliane Karakayali, and Riem Spielhaus, eds. *Postmigrantische Perspektiven: Ordnungssysteme, Repräsentationen, Kritik*. Frankfurt am Main: Campus, 2018.

Forsyth, Alison and Chris Megson, eds. *Get Real: Documentary Theatre Past and Present*. New York: Palgrave, 2009.

Foss, Karen A. and Kathy L. Domenici. "Haunting Argentina: Synecdoche in the Protests of the Mothers of the Plaza de Mayo." *Quarterly Journal of Speech* 87, no. 3 (2001): 237–58.

Foster, Susan Leigh. "Choreographies of Protest." *Theatre Journal* 55, no. 3 (2003): 395–412.

Frijda, Nico H. *The Emotions*. Cambridge: Cambridge University Press, 1986.

Fülle, Henning. *Freies Theater*. Berlin: Theater der Zeit, 2016.

Gardner, Lyn. "Staging a Revolution: Can Theatre Be an Affective Form of Activism?" *The Guardian*, March 23, 2016. https://www.theguardian.com/stage/theatreblog/2016/mar/23/theatre-effective-protest-activism-change-debate.

Garner Jr., Stanton B. *Bodied Spaces: Phenomenology and Performance in Contemporary Drama*. Ithaca, NY: Cornell University Press, 1994.

Geis, Deborah R. *Postmodern Theatric(k)s: Monologue in Contemporary American Drama*. Ann Arbor: University of Michigan Press, 1993.

Gerbaudo, Paolo. "The Indignant Citizen: Anti-Austerity Movements in Southern Europe and the Anti-Oligarchic Reclaiming of Citizenship." *Social Movement Studies* 16, no. 1 (2017): 36–50.

Gezen, Ela E. *Brecht, Turkish Theater, and Turkish-German Literature: Reception, Adaptation, and Innovation After 1960*. Rochester: Camden House, 2018.

Goffman, Erving. *Frame Analysis: An Essay on the Organization of Experience*. Cambridge, MA: Harvard University Press, 1974.

Göktürk, Deniz, David Gramling, and Anton Kaes, eds. *Germany in Transit*. Berkeley: University of California Press, 2007.

Gordon, Avery F. "Globalism and the Prison Industrial Complex: An Interview with Angela Davis." *Race & Class* 40, no. 2/3 (1998/99): 145–57.

Grossberg, Lawrence. *Cultural Studies in the Future Sense*. Durham, NC: Duke University Press, 2010.

Gürsel, Duygu. "Kanak Attak: Discursive Acts of Citizenship in Germany." *Open Democracy*. November 9, 2012. https://www.opendemocracy.net/can-europe-make-it/duygu-g%C3%BCrsel/kanak-attak-discursive-acts-of-citizenship-in-germany.

Hager, Philip. "Dramaturgies of Crisis and Performances of Citizenship: Syntagma Square, Athens." *Performance Interventions: Performance and the Global City*, edited by D. J. Hopkins and Kim Solga, 245–66. New York: Palgrave, 2013.

Hall, Stuart. "Europe's Other Self." *Marxism Today* (1991): 18–19.

Handke, Peter. *Stücke 1*. Frankfurt am Main: Suhrkamp, 1972.

– *Kaspar and Other Plays*. Translated by Michael Rolloff. New York: Farrar, Straus and Giroux, 1969.

Harvey, David. *Rebel Cities: From the Right to the City to the Urban Revolution*. London: Verso, [2012] 2013.

Hemming, Sarah. "Look forward in Anger." *Financial Times*, November 18, 1995.

Heppekausen, Sarah. "Ästhetische Erziehung mit der Knarre." *Nachtkritik*, September 2, 2010. https://nachtkritik.de/index.php?option=com_content&view=article&id=4634:verruecktes-blut-nurkan-erpulat-erzaehlt-qla-journee-de-la-jupeq-mithilfe-schillers-dramen-als-aesthetische-erziehung&catid=259&Itemid=17.

Hessel, Stéphane. *Time for Outrage / Indignez-vous!* Translated by Marion Duvert. New York: Twelve, [2010] 2011.

Hionidou, Violetta. *Famine and Death in Occupied Greece, 1941–1944*. Cambridge: Cambridge University Press, 2006.

Hirsch, Marianne. *The Generation of Postmemory: Writing and Visual Culture After the Holocaust*. New York: Columbia University Press, 2012.

Hirsi Ali, Ayaan. *The Caged Virgin: An Emancipatory Proclamation for Women and Islam*. Translated by Jane Brown. New York: Atria, [2004] 2006.

Hofmann, Michael. "Handicap Islam? Sarrazin-Debatte als Herausforderung des deutsch-türkischen Diskurses," *Türkisch-deutscher Kulturkontakt und Kulturtransfer, Jahrbuch Türkisch-deutsche Studien* 1 (2010): 33–44.

Hoggart, Richard. *Speaking to Each Other*. Vol. II. New York: Oxford University Press, 1970.

hooks, bell. *Killing Rage: Ending Racism*. New York: Henry Holt & Co., 1995.

– *Talking Back: Thinking Feminist, Thinking Black*. Boston, MA: South End Press, [1989] 2015.

Irmer, Thomas. "A Search for New Realities: Documentary Theatre in Germany." *TDR* 50, no. 3 (2006): 16–28.

Kalkan Kocabay, Hasibe. "Searching for Identity." *Glimpse* 13 (2011): 79–83.

Kane, Sarah. *Complete Plays*. London: Bloomsbury, 2001.

Kant, Immanuel. *Anthropology from a Pragmatic Point of View*. Translated by Robert B. Louden. Cambridge: Cambridge University Press, [1798] 2006.

Kershaw, Baz. *The Politics of Performance: Radical Theatre as Cultural Intervention*. London: Routledge, 1992.

Kierkegaard, Søren. *The Concept of Anxiety: A Simple Psychologically Orienting Deliberation on the Dogmatic Issue of Hereditary Sin*. Translated by Reidar Thomte. Princeton: Princeton University Press, [1844] 1980.

Kim, Sue J. *On Anger: Race, Cognition, Narrative*. Austin: University of Texas Press, 2013.

Kiyak, Mely. "Auf einmal sind sie alle Kurden." *Die Zeit*, July 12, 2013. https://www.zeit.de/kultur/2013-07/tuerkei-kurden-kuenstler-sener-oezmen.

Koehler, Daniel. *Right-Wing Terrorism in the 21st Century: The 'National Socialist Underground' and the History of Terror from the Far-Right in Germany*. London: Routledge, 2017.

Kömürcü Nobrega, Onur Suzan. "'We bark from the third row': The position of the *Ballhaus Naunynstrasse* in Berlin's cultural landscape and the funding of cultural diversity work." *Türkisch-deutsch Studien Jahrbuch* (2011): 91–112.

Kurthen, Hermann, Werner Bergmann, and Rainer Erb, eds. *Antisemitism and Xenophobia in Germany After Unification*. Oxford: Oxford University Press, 1997.

Lacan, Jacques. *Anxiety: The Seminar of Jacques Lacan, Book X*. Translated by Cormac Gallagher. Cambridge: Polity Press, [1973] 2016.

Landry, Olivia. "German Youth Against Sarrazin: Nurkan Erpulat's *Verrücktes Blut* and *Clash* as Political Theatre of Experience." *Jahrbuch Türkisch-deutsche Studien* 3 (2012): 105–22.

– "'Wir sind alle Oranienplatz!' Space for Refugees and Social Justice in Berlin." *Seminar: A Journal of Germanic Studies* 51, no. 4 (2015): 398–413.

– "Greek Dispossession Staged, or When Street Politics Meets the Theater." *TRANSIT* 10, no. 2 (2016): 1–15.

– "On the Politics of Love and Post-Migrant Theater in Germany," *TSQ* 5, no. 1 (2018): 30–48.

– "Anger as Theatrical Form in Sasha Marianna Salzmann's *Zucken*." *Postdramatisches Theater als transkulturelles Theater. Eine transdisziplinäre Annäherung*, edited by Teresa Kovacs and Koku G. Nonoa, 335–48. Forum Modernes Theater, Tübingen: Narr Francke Attempo Verlag, 2018.

Langhoff, Shermin. "Die Herkunft spielt keine Rolle: 'Postmigrantisches' Theater im Ballhaus Naunynstraβe." Interviewed by Katharina Donath. *Bundeszentrale für politische Bildung*, March 10, 2011. http://www.bpb.de

/gesellschaft/bildung/kulturelle-bildung/60135/interview-mit-shermin-langhoff?p=all.
– "Nachwort." *Postmigrantische Perspektiven: Ordnungssysteme, Repräsentationen, Kritik*, edited by Naika Foroutan, Juliane Karakayali, and Riem Spielhaus, 301–10. Frankfurt am Main: Campus.

Layne, Priscilla. "Between Play and Mimicry: The Limits of Humanism in 'Verrücktes Blut.'" *Colloquia Germanica* 47, no. 1/2 (2014): 31–57.

Lehmann, Hans-Thies. *Postdramatic Theatre*. Translated by Karen Jürs-Munby. London: Routledge, [1999] 2006.

Lehmann, Johannes F. *Im Abgrund der Wut: Zur Kultur- und Literaturgeschichte des Zorns*. Freiburg: Rombach, 2012.

Lepecki, André. *Exhausting Dance: Performance and the Politics of Movement*. New York: Routledge, 2006.

Lessing, Gotthold Ephraim. *Laocoön: An Essay on the Limits of Painting and Poetry*. Translated by Edward Allen McCormick. Baltimore, MD: Johns Hopkins University Press, [1766] 1984.

Lorde, Audre. "The Master's Tools Will Never Dismantle the Master's House." *This Bridge Called My Back: Writings by Radical Women of Color*, edited by Cherríe Moraga and Gloria Anzaldúa, 94–101. New York: Kitchen Table Press, 1983.
– *Sister Outsider*. Berkeley: Crossing Press, [1984] 2007.

Martin, Carol. "Bodies of Evidence." *TDR: The Drama Review* 50, no. 3 (2006): 8–15.
– *Theatre of the Real*. London: Palgrave Macmillan, 2013.
– "Reclaiming the Real: Introduction." *TDR* 61, no. 4 (2017): 8.

Mbembe, Achille. *Critique of Black Reason*. Translated by Laurent Dubois. Durham, NC: Duke University Press, 2017.

Meierhenrich, Doris. "Premieren-Doppel 'Zucken' und 'Mythen der Wirklichkeit.'" *Berliner Zeitung*, March 20, 2017. https://www.berliner-zeitung.de/kultur/gorki-theater-premieren-doppel--zucken--und--mythen-der-wirklichkeit--26228438.

Miner, Robert. *Thomas Aquinas on the Passions: A Study on Summa Theologiae Iazae*. Cambridge: Cambridge University Press, 2009.

Mishra, Pankaj. *The Age of Anger: A History of the Present*. New York: Farrar, Straus and Giroux, 2017.

Morrison, Toni. *The Bluest Eye*. New York: Alfred A. Knopf, [1970] 2010.
– *Playing in the Dark: Whiteness and the Literary Imagination*. Cambridge, MA: Harvard University Press, 1992.

Moten, Fred. *In the Break: The Aesthetics of the Black Radical Tradition*. Minneapolis: University of Minnesota Press, 2003.

Mouffe, Chantal. *The Return of the Political*. London: Verso, [1993] 2005.

Muñoz, José Esteban. *Disidentifications: Queers of Color and the Performance of Politics*. Minneapolis: University of Minnesota Press, 1999.

– "Feeling Brown: Ethnicity and Affect in Ricardo Bracho's 'The Sweetest Hangover (And Other STDs).'" *Theatre Journal* 52, no. 1 (2000): 67–79.

– *Cruising Utopia: The Then and There of Queer Futurity*. New York: New York University Press, 2009.

Ngai, Sianne. *Ugly Feelings*. Cambridge, MA: Harvard University Press, 2005.

Ngũgĩ wa Thiong'o. "Enactments of Power: The Politics of Performance Space." *TDR* 41, no. 3 (1997): 11–29.

Nietzsche, Friedrich. *On the Genealogy of Morals*. Translated by Douglas Smith. Oxford: Oxford Univeristy Press, 1998.

Noack, Rich and Luisa Beck. "Video Shows Belt-Wielding Assailant Screaming 'Jew' as He Attacks Two People on a Berlin Street." *The Washington Post*, April 19, 2018. https://www.washingtonpost.com/news/worldviews/wp/2018/04/19/belt-wielding-assailant-screams-jew-as-he-attacks-two-on-a-berlin-street/?noredirect=on&utm_term=.344da545e03a.

Nussbaum, Lauren. "The German Documentary Theater of the Sixties: A Stereopsis of Contemporary History." *German Studies Review* 4, no. 2 (1981): 237–55.

Nussbaum, Martha C. *Anger and Forgiveness: Resentment, Generosity, Justice*. New York: Oxford University Press, 2017.

Öziri, Necati. *Get Deutsch or Die Tryin'*. Hamburg: Rowohlt e-book Theater.

Öztürkmen, Arzu. "The Park, the Penguin, and the Gas: Performance in Progress in Gezi Park." *TDR* 58, no. 3 (2014): 39–68.

Peretz, Eyal. *Dramatic Experiments: Life According to Diderot*. Albany, NY: SUNY, 2013.

Phelan, Peggy. *Unmarked: The Politics of Performance*. New York: Routledge, 1993.

Piscator, Erwin. *Political Theatre: A History 1914–1929*. Translated by Hugh Rorrison. New York: Avon, [1963] 1978.

Pratsinakis, Manolis et al. "Crisis and the Resurgence of Emigration from Greece: Trends, Representations, and the Multiplicity of Migrant Trajectories." *European Mobility in Times of Crisis: The New Context of European South-North Migration*, edited by Birgit Glorius and Josefina Domínguez-Mujica, 75–104. Bielefeld: Transcript, 2017.

Puar, Jasbir. *The Right to Maim: Debility, Capacity, Disability*. Durham, NC: Duke University Press, 2017.

Rahmlow, Axel. "Ich kann mir gar kein anderes Theater als politisches vorstellen." *Deutschlandfunk Kultur*, November 9, 2013. https://www.deutschlandfunkkultur.de/ich-kann-mir-gar-kein-anderes-theater-als-politisches.990.de.html?dram:article_id=268286.

Rath, Kristina. "Serdat hat die Nase voll, alles Bullenlogik." *TAZ*, March 17, 2012. http://www.taz.de/!608172/.

Reichert, Julia. "Einfach machen, was die Zeitung nicht macht?" *Theater der Zeit* 7/8 (2017): 38–42.

Reinelt, Janelle G. "The Promise of Documentary." *Get Real: Documentary Theatre Past and Present*, edited by Alison Forsyth and Chris Megson, 16–23. London: Palgrave, 2009.

– *After Brecht: British Epic Theater.* Ann Arbor: University of Michigan, 1996.

Rich, Adrienne. "Phenomenology of Anger." *Diving into the Wreck.* New York: W. W. Norton, 1973.

Richter, Simon. *Laocoon's Body and the Aesthetics of Pain: Winckelmann, Lessing, Herder, Moritz, Goethe.* Detroit, MI: Wayne State University Press, 1992.

Riesselmann, Kirsten. "Premiere von 'Get Deutsch or Die Tryin'': Grabrede auf dem Vater." *TAZ*, May 27, 2017, http://www.taz.de/!5408187/.

Riley, Denise. *Impersonal Passion: Language as Affect.* Durham, NC: Duke University Press, 2004.

Roach, Joseph. *Cities of the Dead: Circum-Atlantic Performance.* New York: Columbia University Press, 1996.

Robinson, Campbell et al. "11 Killed in Synagogue Massacre; Suspect Charged with 29 Counts," *New York Times*, October 27, 2018, https://www.nytimes.com/2018/10/27/us/active-shooter-pittsburgh-synagogue-shooting.html.

Rothberg, Michael. *Multidirectional Memory: Remembering the Holocaust.* Stanford, CA: Stanford University, 2009.

Said, Edward. *The World, the Text and the Critic.* London: Vintage, 1991.

Sainer, Arthur. *The Radical Theatre Notebook.* New York: Avon Books, 1975.

Salzmann, [Sasha] Marianna. "Sie missüberschätzen uns. Über den Versuch, das Mittelstandsperlenkettchen wie ein Lasso um das Ballhaus Naunynstraβe zu werfen – Eine Komödie." *TRANSIT* 8, no. 1 (2011): 1–4.

– *Weiβbrotmusik/Satt.* Frankfurt am Main: Verlag der Autoren, [2011] 2015.

– *Aristokraten: Drei Stücke.* Frankfurt am Main: Verlag der Autoren, 2017.

Sarrazin, Thilo. *Deutschland schafft sich ab.* Munich: Deutsche Verlags-Anstalt, 2010.

Sartre, Jean-Paul. "Preface," in Frantz Fanon, *The Wretched of the Earth*, xliii–lxii. Translated by Richard Philcox. New York: Grove Press, [1961] 2004.

Schaper, Rüdiger. "Nach dem Theatercoup: Wie Langhoff und Hillje das Gorki leiten wollen." *Tagesspiegel*, May 23, 2012. http://www.tagesspiegel.de/kultur/nach-dem-theatercoup-wie-langhoff-und-hillje-das-gorki-leiten-wollen/6661782.html.

Schechner, Richard. *Environmental Theater.* New York: Applause, [1973] 1994.

– "Invasions Friendly and Unfriendly: The Dramaturgy of Direct Theater." *Critical Theory and Performance*, edited by Janelle G. Reinelt and Joseph Roach, 88–106. Ann Arbor: University of Michigan Press, 1992.

Schiller, Friedrich. *On the Aesthetic Education of Man.* Translated by Elizabeth M. Wilkinson and L.A. Willoughby. Oxford: Clarendon Press, 1968.

Seidler, Ulrich. "'Get Deutsch or Die Tryin" am Gorki Theater: Möge die Wut der Anfang der Heilung sein," *Berliner Zeitung*, May 21, 2017. https://www.berliner-zeitung.de/kultur/theater/-get-deutsch-or-die-tryin---am-gorki-theater-moege-die-wut-der-anfang-der-heilung-sein-26939194.

Sellar, Tom. "Theater and Violence." *Theater* 35, no. 1 (2005): 7–15.

Seneca, Lucius Annaeus. *Anger, Mercy, Revenge*. Transated by Robert A. Caster and Martha C. Nussbaum. Chicago, IL: University of Chicago Press, 2010.

Sharifi, Azadeh. *Theater für alle? Partizipation von Postmigranten am Beispiel der Bühnen der Stadt Köln*. Frankfurt am Main: Peter Lang, 2011.

– "Theatre and Migration." *Independent Theatre in Contemporary Europe: Structures, Aesthetics, Cultural Policies*, edited by Manfred Brauneck, 321–407. Bielefeld: Transcript, 2017.

Shire, Warsan. *Teaching My Mother How to Give Birth*. London: Mouth Mark Series, 2011.

Sieg, Katrin. *Ethnic Drag: Performing Race, Nation, Sexuality in West Germany*. Ann Arbor: University of Michigan Press, 2002.

– "Black Virgins and the Democratic Body in Europe." *New German Critique* 37, no. 1 (2010): 147–85.

– "Class of 1989: Who Made Good and Who Dropped Out of German History? Postmigrant Documentary Theater in Berlin." *The German Wall: Fallout in Europe*, edited by Marc Silberman, 165–83. New York: Palgrave, 2011.

Sierz, Aleks. *In-Yer-Face Theatre: British Drama Today*. London: Faber and Faber, 2001.

Sloterdijk, Peter. "Mobilization of the Planet from the Spirit of Self-Intensification." *TDR* 50, no. 4 (2006): 36–43.

– *Rage and Time: A Psychopolitical Investigation*. Translated by Mario Wenning. New York: Columbia University Press, 2012.

Smith, James. "Karagöz and Hacivat: Projections of Subversion and Conformance." *Asian Theatre Journal* 21, no. 2 (Autumn 2004): 187–93.

Snorton, C. Riley. *Black on Both Sides: A Racial History of Trans Identity*. Minneaspolis: University of Minnesota Press, 2017.

Spivak, Gayatri Chakravorty. "Can the Subaltern Speak?" *Colonial Discourse and Post-Colonial Theory: A Reader*, edited by Patricia Williams and Laura Chrisman, 65–111. New York: Columbia University Press, 1994).

States, Bert O. "Performance as Metaphor." *Theatre Journal* 48, no. 1 (1996): 1–26.

Stephenson, Heidi and Natasha Langridge. *Rage and Reason: Women Playwrights on Playwrighting*. London: Methuen Drama, 1997.

Stewart, Lizzie. "*Black Virgins*, Close Encounters: Re-examining the 'Semi-Documentary' in Postmigrant Theatre." *Jahrbuch Türkisch-deutsche Studien* (2012): 81–102.

– "Countermemory and the (Turkish-)German Theatrical Archive: Reading the Documentary Remains of Emine Sevgi Özdamar's *Karagöz in Alamania* (1986)." *TRANSIT* 8, no. 2 (2013): http://transit.berkeley.edu/2013/stewart/.

– "Postmigrant theatre: the Ballhaus Naunynstraβe takes on sexual nationalism," *Journal of Aesthetics & Culture* 9, no. 2 (2017): 56–68.

Taylor, Diana. *The Archive and the Repertoire: Performing Cultural Memory in the Americas.* Durham, NC: Duke University, 2003.

Tepper, Mitchell S. "Sexuality and Disability: The Missing Discourse of Pleasure." *Sexuality and Disability* 18, no. 4 (2000): 283–90.

Terkessidis, Mark. *Migranten.* Hamburg: Rotbuch, 2000.

– *Kollaboration.* Berlin: Suhrkamp, 2015.

Tometi, Opal. "Celebrating MLK Day: Reclaiming Our Movement Legacy," *Huffington Post,* March 20, 2015, http://www.huffingtonpost.com/opal-tometi/reclaiming-our-movement-l_b_6498400.html.

Tomkins, Silvan S. *Affect Imagery Consciousness: Vol. 2: The Negative Affects.* New York: Springer, 1963.

Traister, Rebecca. *Good and Mad: The Revolutionary Power of Women's Anger.* New York: Simon & Schuster, 2018.

Turner Nicholas and Jeremy Travis. "What We Learned from German Prisons," *New York Times,* August 6, 2015, https://www.nytimes.com/2015/08/07/opinion/what-we-learned-from-german-prisons.html.

Tzfadia, Eraz. "Abusing Multiculturalism: The Politics of Recognition and Land Allocation in Israel." *Environment and Planning D: Society and Space* 26, no. 6 (2008): 1115–30.

Wassermann, Andreas. "Wie die AfD das moderne Theater bekämpft." *Der Spiegel,* June 1, 2018. http://www.spiegel.de/plus/wie-die-afd-das-moderne-theater-bekaempft-a-00000000-0002-0001-0000-000157647572.

Weber, Beverly M. "Freedom from Violence, Freedom to Make the World: Muslim Women's Memoirs, Gendered Violence, and Voices for Change in Germany." *Women in German Yearbook* 25 (2009): 199–222.

– Violence and Gender in the "New" Europe: Islam in German Culture. London: Palgrave, 2013.

Weisbrod, Lars. "Kollegah & Farid Bang: Jung, brutal, Antisemit?" *Die Zeit,* April 11, 2018. https://www.zeit.de/2018/16/kollegah-farid-bang-antisemitismus.

Weiss, Peter. "Das Material und die Modelle: Notizen zum dokumentarischen Theater," 464–72. *Dramen* 2. Frankfurt am Main: Suhrkamp, 1968.

– "Für *das* Straβentheater gegen *die* Straβentheater," 51–62. *Dramen* 2. Frankfurt am Main: Suhrkamp, 1968.

Wellbery, David. *Lessing's Laocoon: Semiotics and Aesthetics in the Age of Reason*. Cambridge: University of Cambridge Press, [1984] 2009.

Weheliye, Alexander G. *Phonographies: Grooves in Sonic Afro-Modernity*. Durham, NC: Duke University Press, 2005.

Wilderman, Patrick. "'Get Deutsch or Die Tryin" Mutter blau, Vater weg," *Der Tagesspiegel*, May 23, 2017, https://www.tagesspiegel.de/kultur/get-deutsch-or-die-tryin-am-maxim-gorki-theater-mutter-blau-vater-weg/19838820.html.

Williams, Raymond. *Marxism and Literature*. Oxford: Oxford University Press, 1977.

Workneh, Lilly. "Nina Turner quotes James Baldwin to sum up the Anger among Black Protestors." *The Huffington Post*, August 23, 2016. http://www.huffingtonpost.com/entry/nina-turner-quotes-james-baldwin-to-sum-up-the-anger-among-black-protesters_us_57e420d1e4b0e28b2b52cf14.

Worthen, W. B. "Antigone's Bones." *TDR* 52, no. 3 (2008): 10–33.

Yeğenoğlu, Meyda. *Colonial Fantasies: Toward a Feminist Reading of Orientalism*. Cambridge: Cambridge University Press, 1998.

Yıldız, Yasemin. "Turkish Girls, Allah's Daughters, and the Contemporary German Subject: Itinerary of a Figure." *German Life and Letters* 64, no. 4 (2009): 465–81.

Yörük, Erdem. "The Long Summer of Turkey: The Gezi Uprising and Its Historical Roots." *The South Atlantic Quarterly* 113, no. 2 (2014): 419–26.

Zaimoğlu, Feridun and Günter Senkel. *Schwarze Jungfrauen*. Hamburg: Rowohlt e-book Theater.

Žižek, Slavoj. "Multiculturalism, or, the Cultural Logic of Multinational Capitalism." *New Left Review* 1, no. 225 (1997). https://newleftreview.org/I/225/slavoj-zizek-multiculturalism-or-the-cultural-logic-of-multinational-capitalism.

Index

Italicized page numbers refer to illustrations.

Achilles, 28
"acts of transfer," 130
Adelson, Leslie A., 146
aesthetics, 12, 16, 37, 40, 75, 166, 179; aesthetic forms of resistance, 103, 179; aesthetic ideology (de Man), 96; aesthetics of anger, 40, 48, 62, 66; aesthetics of performance, 16, 82; Brechtian aesthetics, 85; relational aesthetics of theatre, 132; *Über die ästhetische Erziehung des Menschen* (Schiller), 91, 96. *See also* Laocoön
affect, 6, 23, 24, 76, 132, 134, 148, 160, 179; *Affect Imagery Consciousness* (Tomkins), 17, 25; affect theory, 17, 25; affective force, 40, 86, 115, 116, 148; affective iconicity, 213n68; affective-political, 6, 13, 19, 48, 50, 63, 105, 125, 135, 137; affective politics, 178, 181, 182; affective presence, 42, 76; affective speech act, 43; "affective virtuosity," 116; angry affectivity, 4, 34; embodied affect, 116, 117; as form, 13, 136, 158, 160; "forms of the affects," 35; history of, 28–9; of Laocoön, 34–8, as negative, 17, 21, 25, 172; in postdramatic theatre, 153. *See also* anger
Aganaktismenoi movement, 112, 114, 177
Age of Anger, The (Mishra), 17, 24, 54–5, 74
agitprop, 104, 105
Ahmed, Sara, 17, 19, 25, 26, 29, 34, 171, 180; on anger as futurity, 137, 156–7; on anger as speech act, 32, 43, 147; on attributed anger, 25, 59, 134; on the feminist killjoy, 63, 64; on protest and rebellion, 121–2, 129; on sticky feelings, 73, 178
Akın, Fatih, 7, 8
Alpa Gun, 143
Alternative for Germany (AfD), 6, 70, 71, 170, 176, 177
Angelou, Maya, 49, 54, 197n1
anger: Adrienne Rich on, 84; as affect, 25, 160; angry politics, 29, 58, 65; angry youths, 145, 147, 157; as antitheatrical, 38; as attributed, 17, 25, 58–9, 88, 157, 178; Black feminist anger, 17, 25–6, 32, 136, 147, 179–80; as care, 27–8; as *Desintegration*, 4–5; as experience, 23, 160, 171; as form,

36–8, 75–6, 115–17, 148, 152, 154–6; as future, 9, 40, 137, 179; history of, 17, 27–30, 180; linked to hate and violence, 17, 22, 24, 74, 172, 178; philosophy of, 19, 27–9; as protest, 6, 32–4, 112, 122, 132, 182, 183–5; as *ressentiment*, 54–5, 136; as speech act, 16, 32, 43, 46, 54, 147, 179; vs. rage, 193n36. *See also* theatre of anger
Angry Young Men, 40, 41
"antiassimilationism," 11
anti-austerity protests, 122
Antigone, 38
anti-Semitism, 4, 23, 26, 69, 87, 146, 168, 170, 179, 211n38
antitheatrical, 46; *Antitheatrical Prejudice, The* (Barish), 193n83; antitheatricality, 39, 99
anxiety, 152, 213n57
apatheia, 20, 28, 29
Aquinas, Thomas, 192n17
Arab Spring, 21, 104, 124
archive and the repertoire, 137. *See also* Taylor, Diana
Aristokraten, Die (*The Aristocrats*), 135, 140
Aristotle, 19, 29, 30, 31–2, 38, 88, 157, 180; *Nicomachean Ethics*, 17, 27–8; *Poetics*, 35
Artaud, Antonin, 21, 22, 38, 41, 104, 148, 180, 182
Asylkompromiss, 60, 198n21
Athens, 21, 103–4, 107–14, 117, 182, 206n19, 207n30
Aufstand: Monolog eines wütenden Künstlers (*Rebellion: Monologue of an Angry Artist*, 2014), 6, 21, 52, 103, 107, 108, 119–32, 182; image of (MAIFOTO), *127*
August: Osage County, 174
Austin, J.L., 43, 71, 76
Ayim, May, 60–1
Azas, Anestis, 21, 103, 107, 109, 110, 112, 114

Bademsoy, Aysun, 7
Baldwin, James, 19, 29, 30, 31–2, 168, 176, 193n29, 194n41
Balibar, Étienne, 61
Ballhaus Naunynstraße, 82, 90–1, 102, 107, 109, 110, 161, 162, 163, 165; history of, 8, 10, 18, 66–7
barking dog, 67; image of (Landry), *67*
Barthes, Roland, 83
Ben Yishai, Sivan, 136, 173
Benjamin, Walter, 96
Berlant, Lauren, xii, 58, 73, 111, 131
Berlin, 3, 6, 8, 10–13, 66, 67, 161, 164, 175, 185; calling Athens, 108–10, 113–19; calling Istanbul, 119–21, 129–31
Beyond Belonging – Migration2, 8, 66
black box, 3, 119, 120, 194n41
Black Lives Matter, 19, 31, 33, 104, 193n30
Blasted, 40, 135
Boal, Augusto, 15, 98, 105, 132
Boran, Erol, 11
boxing, 23, 152, 158, 171; ring, 92
Brecht, Bertolt, 11, 12, 14–15, 51, 76, 91, 92, 105, 138; against pathos, 34; on alienation, 82, 93; on epic theatre, 38, 95; on *Gestus*, 15, 46, 85, 158; on monologue, 85; plays of, 101, 180; political theatre, 147, 180. *See also* post-Brechtian
Breger, Claudia, 12, 79, 82
Brooks, Daphne A., 155
Brown, Wendy, 9, 189n16
Büchner, Georg, 44, 180
Butler, Judith, 43, 115–16, 124

care, 28, 122, 179
Carlson, Marvin, 47
Carvalho, Wagner, 10
catharsis, 35, 37, 38
Çelik, Neco, 66, 77, 78, 81, 82, 84, 87, 202n25
Charlie Hebdo, 159
Cheesman, Tom, 61, 188n14
citizenship, 49, 50, 51, 55, 59, 94, 112, 181, 198n20; *jus sanguinis*, 49, 59, 94; *jus soli*, 49
civil rights movement (United States), 31, 32, 180, 193n29
Clash, 13, 68
Cleansed, 135
Common Ground, 118
Connerton, Paul, 130
Cooper, Brittney, 17, 25
Cornish, Matt, 12, 15
coup (Turkey), 42, 56, 57, 122, 208n50
coup de théâtre, 119, 154
cultural performance, 20, 47
Cultural Politics of Emotion, The (Ahmed), 17

debt crisis (Greece), 107, 110, 112, 207n23
Deleuze, Gilles, 194n54
Desintegration, 11, 18, 70, 161, 167–68, 175; definition and derivation of, 3–6, 187n6; *Desintegration: A Congress on Jewish Contemporary Positions*, 3, 4, 136, 170; Third Herbstsalon, 5, 70, 169. *See also* "theatre of disintegration"
Deutsches Theater, 68
Deutschland schafft sich ab (Sarrazin), 68, 91
Diamond, Elin, 15, 46, 76
Diderot, Denis, 196n76
"direct theatre," 16, 20, 41, 104, 111, 123, 182
Discourses of Anger in the Early Modern Period (Enenkel and Traninger), 116
disidentification, 16, 62, 94, 100
Diyarbakır, 107, 119, 120, 121, 125, 126, 128
documentary theatre, 102, 103, 119, 121, 124–6, 131–32, 182, 205n11; definition of, 79, 114; history of, 21, 105–7
Dolan, Jill, 88–9
Dömötör, András, 51, 120

Elam Jr., Harry J., 105
El Hissy, Maha, 86, 188n11
El-Tayeb, Fatima, 30, 50, 61, 62, 75, 90, 139, 146, 189n18, 210n20
Emcke, Carolin, 17, 24, 200n45
"environmental theatre," 16, 141
Ernst Busch Academy of Dramatic Arts Berlin, 91, 109, 140
Erpulat, Nurkan, 10, 13, 20, 66, 68, 69, 72, 90, 91, 97, 159, 181; on *Telemachos*, 110; on theatre and method, 93, 96, 101, 163
Ethnic Drag, 11. *See also* Sieg, Katrin

Fanon, Frantz, 62, 175
feedback loop, 16, 40, 44, 46, 63, 144, 171
Fischer-Lichte, Erika, 9, 16, 18, 39, 44, 115, 144, 196n76
forbearance, 28, 29
fourth wall, 16, 39, 44, 94, 119, 126, 144, 154; history of, 196n76
"freies Theater," 6, 10, 21, 106
FREITEXT, 136
fringe theatre, 10, 106
futurity, 112, 137, 147, 179, 183

Garner Jr., Stanton B., 15, 85, 101, 138
Geis, Deborah R., 44, 47, 86, 89, 130

Gesluierde Monologen, De, 79
Gestus, 15, 85, 158
Get Deutsch or Die Tryin', 20, 48–58, 67, 71, 72, 76, 87, 142, 150, 160, 181; promotional poster (Rotthoff), *52*
"Get Rich or Die Tryin'," 51
Gezen, Ela E., 12, 200n40
Gezi Park (protests), 21, 104, 107, 108, 120–31, 176
Goffman, Erving, 44
Gorki – Alternative für Deutschland? (Gorki – Alternative for Germany?), 18
Grossberg, Lawrence, 68, 200n43

Hager, Philip, 116
Hall, Stuart, 30
Hartnagel, Nick, 140, 144, 171
hate speech, 21, 68, 87, 88
Hebbel am Ufer (HAU), 6, 8, 66, 77
Hemming, Sarah, 40
Hessel, Stéphane, 21, 103, 104, 112
Hillje, Jens, 6, 20, 66, 72, 90, 91–2, 180, 181
Hirsch, Marianne, 9
Hirsi Ali, Ayaan, 73, 81
homophobia, 4, 23, 26, 87, 149
hooks, bell, 17, 19, 25, 26, 29, 34, 157, 168, 171, 180; on rage, 33, 75, 193n36; on talking back, 21, 86

Ibsen, Henrik, 44, 76, 166
Idle No More, 104
Im Abgrund der Wut (Lehmann), 17, 24
"in-yer-face theatre," 14, 20, 22, 40–1, 76, 134, 135, 160, 168, 174–5
intercultural theatre, 9
"irascible man," 27, 32
Islam, 72, 73–5, 80–1, 87, 89, 90–1, 97
Islamkonferenz, 81
Islamophobia, 21, 73–5, 90–1, 97, 102, 146, 181–2

Istanbul, 21, 42, 43, 119–24, 126–7, 129, 131, 182. *See also* Saturday Mothers of Istanbul

Jenseits, bist Du Schwul oder bist Du Türke (Beyond – Are You Gay or Are You Turkish), 53, 66
Journée de la Jupe (Skirt Day), 91
Judeo-Christian tradition, 29

Kabale und Liebe (Love and Intrigue), 94, 96
Kahn, Daniel, 3
"Kampfbegriff," 66, 92
Kanak Attak, 13, 20, 48, 50, 58–65, 68, 72, 79, 181; *Der Spiegel* cover reproduction (Willenbücher), *65*
Kane, Sarah, 22, 40, 134–5, 137, 174–5
Kant, Immanuel, 29
Karagöz in Alamania (Black Eye in Germany), 11, 39
Kelek, Necla, 81, 97, 202n23, 205n74
Keloğlan in Alamania, 11
Killing Rage (hooks), 17, 33
King, Jr., Martin Luther, 33, 128
Kiyak, Mely, 6, 21, 103, 107, 119–20, 124–5, 134
Kohl, Helmut, 59, 106
"Kopftuchstreit" (headscarf debate), 90
Koppstoff (Zaimoğlu), 79
Kulaoğlu, Tunçay, 10, 66, 78, 79, 204n63
Kurdistan Workers' Party (PKK), 42, 125
Kushner, Tony, 174

labour migration, 8, 39, 61–2, 69, 109, 113, 117, 118, 207n32
Langhoff, Shermin, 6–10, 65–7, 69–70, 164, 175, 180, 206n15; on documentary theatre, 106–7; on

postmigrant theatre, 66–7, 92, 162, 188n14. *See also* postmigrant theatre
Laocoön, 14, 20, 26, 35–8, 40, 76, 102, 116, 180
Layne, Priscilla, 12, 204n66, 204n70
Lehmann, Hans-Thies, 15, 39, 86, 147, 149, 152, 157–8. *See also* postdramatic theatre
Lepecki, André, 16, 152, 154–5
Lessing, Gotthold Ephraim, 14, 20, 26, 35–8, 145. *See also* Laocoön
Letts, Tracy, 174
"Liste, Die" (Cennetoğlu), 70
Living a Feminist Life (Ahmed), 17, 64, 187n2
Lö bal Almanya, 10, 69, 97
Lö Grand Bal Almanya: 57 Jahre Scheinehe (57 Years of Fictitious Marriage), 69
Look Back in Anger, 40
Lorde, Audre, 17, 19, 26, 29, 30, 86, 157, 171, 180; on anger, 25, 32–4, 137, 179, 183, 193n36; on listening, 181; on the master's tools, 18

Madres de la Plaza de Mayo, Las, 41–2, 104. *See also* Taylor, Diana
Malcolm X, 33, 62, 168, 193n29, 194n41
Man, Paul de, 96
Martin, Carol, 79, 105, 107, 109, 114, 119, 126, 130
Marx, Karl, 59, 82; Marxian, 62
Maxim Gorki Theatre, 3, 10, 51–3, 66, 103, 136, 150, 164, 175; AfD, 18, 176; funding structure, 18; Herbstsalon *Desintegriert Euch!*, 4–5, 70–2, 169; repertoire, 180; "Theatre of the Year," 11, 163
Medea, 38
Mein Kampf, 3
memory, 4, 5, 109, 129, 130, 146
menis, 28
Meteoriten (*Meteorites*), 51, 136, 172, 214n72
migrant, 49, 58, 60, 61, 70, 75, 82, 108, 130, 139, 142, 145, 162, 183; as concept, 8–9, 50, 56, 188n11; Greek crisis migrants, 109, 110, 113, 114; "melancholic migrant," 63; "migrant shame," 165. *See also* postmigrant theatre
monologue, 16, 20, 21, 27, 84–6, 102, 120, 130; history of, 43–7. *See also* raging monologue
"moralischer Anstalt," 35
Morrison, Toni, 19, 24, 29, 32
Moten, Fred, 155
Mouffe, Chantal, 112
multiculturalism, 64, 188n11, 199n36
Muñoz, José Esteban, 16, 62, 67, 93, 94, 139, 155, 158. *See also* disidentification
#muslimrage, 74
Muttermale Fenster blau, 173
Muttersprache Mameloschn (*Mameloschn Mother Tongue*), 135, 140, 174

Nach Uns das All – Das Innere Team kennt keine Pause (*The Universe after Us – The Inner Team Knows No Break*), 71, 150, 177
Nathan the Wise, 145, 211n34
National Socialist Underground (NSU), 6, 69, 70, 200n46
naturalist theatre, 16, 21, 22, 40, 41, 44, 76, 94, 95, 182
New Institute for Dramatic Writing (NIDS), 57, 136
Newsweek, 73, 74
Ngai, Sianne, 30
Ngũgĩ wa Thiong'o, 111
Nicomachean Ethics, 17, 27–8. *See also* Aristotle

Nietzsche, Friedrich, 38, 54
Nübling, Sebastian, 50, 53, 71, 148, 150–3, 158, 159, 174
Nussbaum, Martha C., 17, 24, 178

Occupy (movement), 21, 104, 122
Odyssey, 108, 109, 133
Ören, Aras, 7
Osborne, John, 40
outrage, 18, 73, 75, 81, 147, 171, 193n30; documentaries of, 21, 103–5, 107, 110, 112, 125, 129, 132
Özdamar, Emine Sevgi, 7, 11, 12, 13, 39, 66
Öziri, Necati, 49–51, 53, 56–7, 72, 142, 181; in-yer-face theatre, 40; on Kanak Attak, 72, 199–200n37
Özmen, Şener, 125

pedagogy, 27, 29, 35, 68, 95, 99, 206n13
PEGIDA, 6, 70
Peponides, Meropi S., 66
performative theatre, 16, 44, 144. *See also* Fischer-Lichte, Erika
performativity, 86
Phelan, Peggy, 76–7
Piscator, Erwin, 79, 105
play (Schiller), 96
Polat, Ayşe, 7
post-Brechtian, 82, 85, 134, 138, 147, 165, 180; definition of, 14–15
postcolonial, 15, 16, 30, 62, 155
postdramatic, 12, 22, 39, 86, 147–9, 152, 154, 157–8; definition of, 15–16
postmigrant theatre, 19, 39, 58, 78, 118, 158, 161–7, 172–5; definition and derivation of, 5, 8–9, 188n14; discourse on, 10–13, 15; documentary theatre, 106; history of, 7–8, 18, 65–8; as theatre of anger, 6, 58
Promise of Happiness, The (Ahmed), 17, 64
proscenium, 44, 110, 141
Publikumsbeschimpfung (*Offending the Public*), 20, 45–7, 130, 165

racism, 4, 6, 23, 30, 31, 68, 90, 146, 164, 189n18; anger as response to, 25, 32, 33, 59, 137; in postunified Germany, 50, 61, 63; in theatre, 101
Radikale jüdische Kulturtage (*Radical Jewish Culture Days*), 136
rage, 16, 20, 21, 23, 26–9, 31, 33, 40; of Laocoön, 26, 36, 37, 102; "Muslim Rage," 73–4, 85, 86
raging monologue, 16, 27, 46, 48, 54, 76, 85, 86, 100, 120, 126, 157, 181
rap, 51, 139, 143, 146, 207n23, 211n28
Räuber, Die (Schiller), 94–7, 100
refugee, 56, 61, 70, 133, 146, 162; Refugee Tent Action, 104
"Reichsbürger" (Reich Citizens), 70, 200n48
Reinelt, Janelle G., 15, 114–15, 125–6, 131
Riley, Denise, 88
Rimini Protokoll, 110
Roach, Joseph, 129
Rothberg, Michael, 146

Said, Edward, 30
Sainer, Arthur, 107
Salzmann, Sasha Marianna, 4, 19, 22, 133–60; on anger, 171–3; on contemporary German politics, 18, 132; on *Desintegration*, 167–9, 170; on influence and methods, 23, 40, 165–6, 173–6; on postmigrant theatre, 161–5, 166
Sartre, Jean-Paul, 71, 88
Saturday Mothers of Istanbul, 20, 42, 104

#SayHerName, 193n27
Schaad, Dimitrij, 51, 53, 66
Schauspielhaus Bochum, 12, 66
Schechner, Richard, 16, 41, 104, 123, 141, 182
Schiller, Friedrich, 35, 91, 94–6, 99, 100, 101
Schwarze Jungfrauen (*Black Virgins*), 21, 47, 72, 75–90, 99, 102, 160, 181–2, 202n25; emergence of postmigrant theatre, 8, 13, 66; image of (MAIFOTO), *84*
Schwimmen lernen, 136, 140, 173
Sellar, Tom, 138
Seneca, Lucius Annaeus, 28
Senkel, Günter, 72, 77, 78, 79, 181
shadow puppet theatre, 20, 38, 39
Sharifi, Azadeh, 12, 190n33
"Short Organum for Theatre, A," 3, 38
Sieg, Katrin, 11, 12, 81, 82, 84, 211n34
Sierz, Aleks, 14, 18, 41, 76, 78, 135. *See also* "in-yer-face theatre"
Sister Outsider (Lorde), 17
Sloterdijk, Peter, 24, 28, 154
Snorton, C. Riley, 155
Solingen (Arson Attack), 59–60, 198n19; image of (Henkel), *60*
Spiegel, Der, 63–5
Stanislavski, Konstantin, 91; Stanislavskian, 44, 92, 94, 95
state theatre, 10, 163, 164
States, Bert O., 71
Stewart, Lizzie, 8, 12, 81, 84, 188n14
Stoics, 28–9
street theatre, 104, 106
Studio Я, 6, 10, 22, 57, 108, 120, 136, 164, 165, 169; image of (Landry), *169*

Talking Back (hooks), 17
Taylor, Diana, 42, 130, 137
Telemachos – Should I Stay or Should I Go?, 21, 103, 107, 108–19, 121, 125, 132, 182
temperance, 35
Terkessidis, Mark, 61, 197n3
terrorism, 17, 22, 41, 74, 136, 148, 156, 157
"Theater der Unruhigen," 105
Theater Strahl, 6, 140, 144
Theatertreffen, 10, 23, 57, 90, 166, 169
theatre of anger: definition and derivation of, 5–7, 9, 12–13, 16, 23, 38, 39, 40
"theatre of cruelty," 195n64. *See also* Artaud, Antonin
"theatre of disintegration," 187n6
"theatre of the oppressed," 105, 124. *See also* Augusto Boal
36 Boys, 63, 199n30
thrust stage, 141
Tiyatrom, 7, 12
Tometi, Opal, 31, 193n27
Tomkins, Silvan S., 17, 25
"travelling theory," 30
Tsinikoris, Prodromos, 21, 103, 107, 108, 109, 110, 112, 113, 114
Turner, Nina, 193n30

Über die ästhetische Erziehung des Menschen (*On the Aesthetic Education of Man*) (Schiller), 91. *See also* Schiller, Friedrich
unification, 12, 50, 59; postunification, 20, 48, 61, 62; "postunification theatre," 15. *See also* Cornish, Matt
"Uses of Anger" (Lorde), 183

Vagina Monologues, The, 47, 79
Verrücktes Blut (*Mad Blood*), 10, 13, 21, 75, 76, 90–102, 159, 160, 163, 181–2
violence, 21, 28, 40, 51, 172, 179, 181, 182, 183; Benjamin on, 96; pedagogy of, 95–102; police, 31, 33, 117, 121, 145, 193n27, 193n30,

195n69, 210n20; "on the rebound," 88; in theatre, 138, 140

Weber, Beverly, 80, 81, 90
Weiss, Peter, 21, 104, 105–6, 107, 125, 182, 205n11
Weißbrotmusik (*White Bread Music*), 22, 136, 138–48, 151, 160, 164, 171–4, 182
Willi, Magda, 52, 92, 151
Williams, Raymond, 34
World-Changing Rage (Baselitz and Kluge), 184
Worthen, W.B., 137
wrath, 28, 29
"Wutbürger," 177–8

X Wohnungen Migration, 66

Yeğenoğlu, Meyda, 83, 86
Yıldız, Yasemin, 75, 81

Zaimoğlu, Feridun, 62, 66, 72, 77–9, 181
Zucken (*Twitching*), 22, 47, 52, 133, 136, 148–160, 173, 182, 184; image of (Heinrich), *156*; title of, 212n46, 212n47, 212n48

German and European Studies

General Editor: Jennifer L. Jenkins

1 Emanuel Adler, Beverly Crawford, Federica Bicchi, and Rafaella Del Sarto, *The Convergence of Civilizations: Constructing a Mediterranean Region*
2 James Retallack, *The German Right, 1860–1920: Political Limits of the Authoritarian Imagination*
3 Silvija Jestrovic, *Theatre of Estrangement: Theory, Practice, Ideology*
4 Susan Gross Solomon, ed., *Doing Medicine Together: Germany and Russia between the Wars*
5 Laurence McFalls, ed., *Max Weber's 'Objectivity' Reconsidered*
6 Robin Ostow, ed., *(Re)Visualizing National History: Museums and National Identities in Europe in the New Millennium*
7 David Blackbourn and James Retallack, eds., *Localism, Landscape, and the Ambiguities of Place: German-Speaking Central Europe, 1860–1930*
8 John Zilcosky, ed., *Writing Travel: The Poetics and Politics of the Modern Journey*
9 Angelica Fenner, *Race under Reconstruction in German Cinema: Robert Stemmle's Toxi*
10 Martina Kessel and Patrick Merziger, eds., *The Politics of Humour: Laughter, Inclusion, and Exclusion in the Twentieth Century*
11 Jeffrey K. Wilson, *The German Forest: Nature, Identity, and the Contestation of a National Symbol, 1871–1914*
12 David G. John, *Bennewitz, Goethe, "Faust": German and Intercultural Stagings*
13 Jennifer Ruth Hosek, *Sun, Sex, and Socialism: Cuba in the German Imaginary*
14 Steven M. Schroeder, *To Forget It All and Begin Anew: Reconciliation in Occupied Germany, 1944–1954*

15 Kenneth S. Calhoon, *Affecting Grace: Theatre, Subject, and the Shakespearean Paradox in German Literature from Lessing to Kleist*
16 Martina Kolb, *Nietzsche, Freud, Benn, and the Azure Spell of Liguria*
17 Hoi-eun Kim, *Doctors of Empire: Medical and Cultural Encounters between Imperial Germany and Meiji Japan*
18 J. Laurence Hare, *Excavating Nations: Archeology, Museums, and the German-Danish Borderlands*
19 Jacques Kornberg, *The Pope's Dilemma: Pius XII Faces Atrocities and Genocide in the Second World War*
20 Patrick O'Neill, *Transforming Kafka: Translation Effects*
21 John K. Noyes, *Herder: Aesthetics against Imperialism*
22 James Retallack, *Germany's Second Reich: Portraits and Pathways*
23 Laurie Marhoefer, *Sex and the Weimar Republic: German Homosexual Emancipation and the Rise of the Nazis*
24 Bettina Brandt and Daniel Leonhard Purdy, eds., *China in the German Enlightenment*
25 Michael Hau, *Performance Anxiety: Sport and Work in Germany from the Empire to Nazism*
26 Celia Applegate, *The Necessity of Music: Variations on a German Theme*
27 Richard J. Golsan and Sarah M. Misemer, eds., *The Trial That Never Ends: Hannah Arendt's "Eichmann in Jerusalem" in Retrospect*
28 Lynne Taylor, *In the Children's Best Interests: Unaccompanied Children in American-Occupied Germany, 1945–1952*
29 Jennifer A. Miller, *Turkish Guest Workers in Germany: Hidden Lives and Contested Borders, 1960s to 1980s*
30 Amy Carney, *Marriage and Fatherhood in the Nazi SS*
31 Michael E. O'Sullivan, *Disruptive Power: Catholic Women, Miracles, and Politics in Modern Germany, 1918–1965*
32 Gabriel N. Finder and Alexander V. Prusin, *Justice behind the Iron Curtain: Nazis on Trial in Communist Poland*
33 Parker Daly Everett, *Urban Transformations: From Liberalism to Corporatism in Greater Berlin, 1871–1933*
34 Melissa Kravetz, *Women Doctors in Weimar and Nazi Germany: Maternalism, Eugenics, and Professional Identity*
35 Javier Samper Vendrell, *The Seduction of Youth: Print Culture and Homosexual Rights in the Weimar Republic*
36 Sebastian Voigt, ed., *Since the Boom: Continuity and Change in the Western Industrialized World after 1970*
37 Olivia Landry, *Theatre of Anger: Radical Transnational Performance in Contemporary Berlin*